P9-CER-878

© 1991

0001156413K

LOS ALAMOS COUNTY LIBRARY

WE HEARD

THE ANGELS
of
MADNESS

WE HEARD

THE ANGELS

of

MADNESS

One Family's Struggle with Manic Depression

DIANE AND LISA BERGER

Foreword by Alexander Vuckovic, M.D.,
Harvard Medical School

MESA PUBLIC LIBRARY
1742 Central Ave.
Los Alamos, New Mexico 87544

William Morrow and Company, Inc.
NEW YORK

616.89
B453w
VPLC '94
ØPLC 05

Copyright © 1991 by Diane Berger and Lisa Berger

The line from "A Storm of Angels" from *Selected Poems of May Sarton,* edited by Serena Sue Hilsinger and Lois Brynes, is reprinted with the permission of W. W. Norton & Company, Inc. Copyright © 1978 by May Sarton.

All rights reserved. No part of this book may be reproduced or utilized in any form or by any means, electronic or mechanical, including photocopying, recording or by any information storage and retrieval system, without permission in writing from the Publisher. Inquiries should be addressed to Permissions Department, William Morrow and Company, Inc., 105 Madison Avenue, New York, N.Y. 10016.

Recognizing the importance of preserving what has been written, it is the policy of William Morrow and Company, Inc., and its imprints andf affiliates to have the books it publishes printed on acid-free paper, and we exert our best efforts to that end.

Library of Congress Cataloging-in-Publication Data

Berger, Diane, 1942-
    We heard the angels of madness : one family's struggle with manic depression / Diane and Lisa Berger.
        p.   cm.
    ISBN 0-688-09178-4
    1. Manic-depressive psychoses—Patients—United States—Biography.
2. Manic-depressive psychoses—Patients—United States—Family
relationships.   I. Berger, Lisa.   II. Title.
RC516.B44   1991
616.89'5'0092—dc20   90-48215
                                                                   CIP

Printed in the United States of America

First Edition

1 2 3 4 5 6 7 8 9 10

BOOK DESIGN BY PATRICE FODERO

"To those in Hell who can imagine Heaven"

For Mark,
and other sufferers and their families

Brodart (19.95) 4/9/91

All the events in this book happened as we describe them. The people and the institutions are real, not composites or fictional re-creations. However, for the sake of privacy, we have changed the names of Mark's doctors, and the hospitals and centers where he has been treated. For the same reason, Diane Berger is using her maiden name, and Mark, his brother, his father, our friends, and other family members also have pseudonyms.

FOREWORD

*T*he patient usually comes with a companion. The patient looks relaxed, but the companion's eyes betray fear, uncertainty, endless questions. I remember meeting Mark, accompanied by his mother. I remember the inadequacy of the hour spent with them and feeling that ten or one hundred hours would not quench the fire of their pain.

Every week, one or two families reenact this scenario in my office. Throughout the country, in hospitals, clinics, and emergency rooms, hundreds more join them. Because the major mental illnesses are what psychiatrists dryly call "familial disorders," many people have gone through the experience before with a parent, sibling, or child. For these family members, the pain is duller but more certain, and may kindle tribal memories of curses, of uncleanliness. For other families, there are no memories, no signposts. There are only hurried, hushed professionals, who seem to distance and blame in equal measure. And there is time, passing so much more slowly than in surgical waiting rooms, coronary-care units, or even cancer wards.

Major psychiatric illness feels like forever. Hospitalizations are measured in weeks and months, patients return home unwell, anger and frustration rise.

And yet, compared with the amount of professional time given to education and support in such diverse fields as oncology and cardiology, psychiatric efforts are uneven at best. Too often, our interventions are uninformative and patronizing. Simple, important pieces of information become unexpected gifts: The great majority of psychotic episodes resolve without a trace; preventive medication exists and does not turn a person into a zombie; Mom, Dad, or that hit of grass didn't cause it; children, brothers, or parents are not likely to become ill; and on and on.

Clinicians know all this—why don't the families? Well, many seem not to want to know, at least at first. The reasons are fairly self-evident: Psychosis takes a patient away from those who love him, much more surely than a tumor or a clogged artery. A stranger arrives and smirches the intimate space between mother and son, husband and wife. The stranger is often angry and unresponsive to expressions of love or acceptance. Withdrawal and denial by uncomprehending and frightened relatives follow.

My profession has historically responded to this state of affairs by unconsciously duplicating this unhealthy, if understandable, behavior: We distance ourselves from the family and the patients. Partially, this stems from dealing with disorders that, until the past couple of decades, have been almost impossible to treat. Partially, we sensed the guilt of families who believed that they did this to their children, and we concurred. Partially, we shared the hubris of the medieval barber-surgeons, relying on anecdote more than scientific method in developing arcane treatments whose failures were proof of patients' inadequacies.

These are explanations, not excuses. All medical specialties grow more sophisticated with time, over the bodies of wretches bled to death by leeches, impervious to the repetitive wails of the lobotomized. Clinicians are wise to keep their eyes and ears open, their memories fresh to history, and their hearts available to shared pain.

While some aspects of psychiatry have changed for the better in the last generation, educational efforts have lagged. Of late, the National Institute of Mental Health has begun to take a leadership role in spreading useful information to the public. Larger hospitals, including the one I am affiliated with, have followed suit.

But the resources available to patients and families are limited to scientific-journal publications, useful but dated general-interest books written by psychiatrists twenty years ago, and first-person, self-help tomes of no depth, offering few practical suggestions. Swamping all of these moderately helpful works is a barrage of talk-show propaganda, pseudoscientific revelation, narratives devoted to discrediting those who did the author wrong, and similar narrow-agenda flotsam of a media-mad age.

Which brings me to this book. This book is different. In simple English and from a nonprofessional perspective, it details one family's experience with mental illness over two years. The pain is there, as is the hope, in the words of Mark and his mother. Entwined around this backbone is a rich lode of refreshing, demystifying, solidly researched and referenced information about psychiatric illness: The professionals, the treatments, and the research, up to date and unencumbered by an ideological agenda.

Note the word "hope," used for the first time here. Progress has come slowly in this field. Research funding pales when compared with big-ticket agendas such as the optimistically titled War on Cancer, War on Heart Disease, or War on AIDS. Nevertheless, two to three million Americans of all ages, races, socioeconomic backgrounds, both sexes, all sexual preferences, all religions and party affiliations, are permanently disabled by the most severe psychiatric illness, schizophrenia.

Unlike the majority of victims of other illnesses, the victims of major mental illness remain with us year after year, decade after decade. They're our sons and daughters, brothers and sisters, wives and husbands. We need to do more for them, and for the even larger pool of recurrently and moderately ill patients with manic depression, depression, and anxiety disorders.

This larger group has benefited the most from recent research into antidepressants and mood-stabilizing treatments, light therapies, and psychotherapies. But they suffer silently. They see and hear the casual, demeaning references to mental illnesses in coworkers and friends, and realize the prudence of tending their own gardens, educating their own families, and leaving the larger task of education to us, the professionals.

I believe we are still failing them, and their sicker counterparts in the state hospitals and on park benches. But Diane and Lisa Berger are doing right by them, and by you and me.

I am honored to have been able to be of assistance in editing the technical portions of this book. I am pleased to have Mark as a patient, and I hope I am serving him well.

Alexander Vuckovic, M.D.
Harvard Medical School
McLean Hospital
Belmont, Massachusetts

ACKNOWLEDGMENTS

Many people helped us with this book, sharing their knowledge and personal experiences.

While we take complete responsibility for its contents, its value was enhanced many times by the insightful professional advice of Alexander Vuckovic, M.D., instructor in psychiatry, Harvard Medical School. Dr. Vuckovic shared with us not only his sharp medical and editorial eye, but also his extensive knowledge of clinical psychopharmacology. We are very grateful to him.

We talked to hundreds of people in researching this book, and some gave us extraordinary amounts of time and information. Special thanks to Lynn Baglia, R.N., emergency-room staff nurse; Lloyd I. Sederer, M.D., assistant general director, McLean Hospital, and president, Massachusetts Psychiatric Society; Kay R. Jamison, Ph.D., associate professor, Johns Hopkins University School of Medicine; Donald F. Klein, M.D., science adviser, National Institute of Mental Health; Donald G. Langsley, M.D., executive vice president, American Board of Medical Specialties; Joseph Lipinski, M.D., McLean Hospital; Benjamin Liptzin, M.D., assistant general director of Quality Assurance and Managed Care, McLean Hospital; Sally Mink, R.N., DRADA coordinator; Jean Murphy, R.N., M.S.W., National Institute of Mental Health; Robert Phillips, M.D., director of the Whiting Forensic Institute, Middletown, CT.; Lynne Saunders, National Alliance for the Mentally Ill; Robert Shallett, American Psychiatric Association; Kathleen D. Thayer, R.N., M.S.C.S., psychiatric nurse clinician; and Mauricio Tohen, M.D., McLean Hospital.

We couldn't have written this without the inspiration, cheerleading, and wise counsel of friends and family. More special thanks to our agent, Gail Ross, and Rosemary Beer, Tina Michaud Bernacki, Dr. Robert Britten, Janet Eiden, John B. Fahey, Jr., Priscilla Gallagher, Dr. Hrair Garabedian, Catharine Gilson, Isobel and Price Glover, Nina Graybill, Joanne Greenberg, Daniel C. Hale, Sally Kleaveland, Dr. Richard Kleaveland, Barbara Kraut, John Lavery, Susan Lehmann, Bill and Jenny Mead, Stephen W. Player, George and Sheila Raines, Katherine and Roy Reynolds, Dr. Bob Seltzer, Jim and Jane Travis, and Nick and Karen Valvano.

CONTENTS

Foreword by Alexander Vuckovic, M.D.   9

Acknowledgments   13

Introduction   17

Chapter 1   Thanksgiving   23

Chapter 2   What Is Manic Depression?   43

Chapter 3   Magical Thinking   67

Chapter 4   Drugs and Other Antidotes   91

Chapter 5   Satanic Winter   119

Chapter 6   Finding Professional Help   141

Chapter 7   Musical Summer   161

Chapter 8   Hospitals to Halfway Houses and Beyond   185

Chapter 9   Autumn Revelations   205

Chapter 10 Twists and Turns   229

Chapter 11 Hope   251

            Appendix A: Studies   257

            Appendix B: Support Groups   261

            Appendix C: State Organizations   267

Notes   271

Index   293

INTRODUCTION

November

None of the other Colorado students paid any attention to Mark as he trudged across campus lugging a microwave oven. He occasionally shifted the boxy weight from side to side, but he didn't tire or slow. He picked his way around the icy patches that laced the sidewalks and dead grass, emerged from the flagstone and evergreen quadrangle, and headed for the Hill, a small commercial area that catered to the university. It was a cold November evening, and small cliques of students roamed the Hill, looking for friends or the loudest tavern.

Scowling and intense, his eyes red from crying, Mark proceeded toward Stella's delicatessen. He had chosen Stella's because it seemed to invite trouble by posting descriptions of known shoplifters. With both arms wrapped around the microwave, he caught his breath for a few moments outside the deli, then heaved the appliance through the plate-glass window.

The sounds of breaking glass and the jangling alarm startled the half-dozen students inside, who wheeled around to stare at Mark. He belligerently glared back. The store manager slammed shut the cash register and exploded outside.

"What the hell did you do that for? Son of a bitch, you broke my window. Don't you go anywhere. You're in big trouble. Goddamn punk. You high on something? Don't run away. Somebody call the police." The manager couldn't stop yelling.

"Yeah, yeah. Don't worry, I'm not going anywhere," Mark's voice was heavy with sarcasm and disdain. The manager kept his distance, inching around Mark's side to herd him into the deli. Mark sauntered into the brightly lit shop, slid down a wall to sit on the floor, and pulled out a bag of Jolly Rancher candies.

The two police officers were mystified. As they led him to the cruiser, one asked, "Why a microwave through a window?" Mark shrugged, as if the answer was beyond them. It probably was. They never would have understood if Mark had told them about the voices commanding him to commit an act in order to redeem all the sinners of the world.

With his one phone call, Mark located a girlfriend to raise three hundred dollars' bail. But she could not get the money together until the next morning. So eighteen-year-old Mark, who had never seen the inside of a jail, spent the night. A freshman at the University of Colorado from an affluent Connecticut family, Mark's only previous contact with the justice system had been a speeding ticket when he was a senior in high school. And this brush with the law was mild compared with what was to come.

The next day, Mark returned to his room in Baker Hall. The dorm was quiet, with students either at late classes or in the dining hall. Carefully avoiding any possession that belonged to his roommate, Mark ripped books, smashed a mirror and lamp, and shredded cassette tapes. Oblivious to exclamations from a kid watching from the doorway, he burst from his room and headed for the dining hall in nearby Libby Hall.

The hall was half-full, students trickling in for their evening meal. Mark's friend Hank waved to him, but Mark saw no one. He rushed up to the salad bar, dumped toppings and dressings to the floor, and ran back to his room.

Unable to sit still, he paced between the twin beds, tonelessly humming notes from Michael Jackson's *Bad* album. Fifteen minutes later, two police officers appeared. Dormitory officials had summoned them about a vandalized room. When they began to question Mark about what had happened, he spit at them and called them fascists.

Experienced at subduing students high on LSD, PCP, crack, and all sorts of laboratory concoctions, they closed in on Mark, grabbing his arms for a hammerlock. Handcuffs squeezed his wrists. He kicked and yelled as they pushed him from the room toward the side door and the waiting squad car. Mark continued to struggle, trying to land a kick and squirm away from the clawlike fingers clenched to the back of his neck. He screamed that they were pigs, devil worshipers, and murderers, then began to cry.

They shoved him into the backseat of the car. One of the officers climbed in beside him, grabbed his chin, squeezed his cheeks, and shoved a pistol into Mark's mouth.

"Look, you little fucker. One more word and this is going to be a very unpleasant trip. You understand?" Mark's teary, cross-eyed pupils were riveted on the gun. He nodded.

Mark was locked in maximum security, and for the first few hours he was suspended across the corner of the cell with his hands cuffed to one set of bars and his ankles to another. Still, he banged and yelled most of the night. The police kept him there until he calmed down almost twenty-four hours later.

I first heard about Mark's troubles late that afternoon when I answered the telephone and a strange female voice identified herself as Detective Sergeant Callahan of the Boulder Police. She enumerated the charges against Mark and matter-of-factly described his presumably drug-induced behavior and his refusal to cooperate with the public defender.

"It isn't customary to call parents on these sorts of cases," she added, her voice softening. "But he seemed so lost, and no one was coming to help him. It took some doing to find you." She explained the bail procedure.

"What about an attorney? He'll need one, and we don't know anybody in Boulder." My hands were shaking, and I was sitting on the floor next to the kitchen telephone.

"Call Bob King . . . I'll give you his number. Don't tell anyone I did, though. We're not supposed to do this, but I've seen him in court with students and he does right by them. He really seems to care."

I gratefully thanked her for calling, and booked the next flight to Denver.

I almost didn't recognize the thin blond youth the officer escorted from the back of the jailhouse. Mark wouldn't look at me, answer my questions, or offer any explanations. No apologies, no sheepish "Thanks for coming, Mom." Simply, harshly, "Get me out of here."

I told myself he was in shock, that once we were away from the police, the old Mark would resurface. I suggested a hamburger at Wendy's, thinking a milkshake and fries would do the trick. Food for comfort. I was wrong. As we ate, he stared at my face as if looking for a sign.

"What is it?" I asked helplessly.

"You don't know, do you?" He smiled secretively.

"What? Tell me." His silence hung over the Formica table like a bad odor. What was I supposed to say? He volunteered nothing. His face was blank, his composure icy.

The only subject that triggered a response was mention of his father. "He doesn't want to chew you out," I explained in a soft voice. "He just wants to talk to you. He cares so much for you, and he doesn't understand what has happened. Just talk to him."

"No." That was it. A flat refusal. My son, this stranger, finished his hamburger in silence.

That experience was the beginning for our family's passage through insanity. At the time, I didn't know the details of Mark's attack on the deli, what happened with the police, or why he was so angry and mysterious. And I never could have imagined that he was hearing voices. I had assumed Mark was simply being rebellious—flexing his independence and settling imagined scores with me and his dad within the safe boundaries of his first semester away from home. My worst fear was that he, like millions of other middle-class college kids, had acquired a drug problem.

The terrifying truth came later: Mark wasn't being rebellious, he was in the throes of a life-threatening mental illness—manic depression. This was very hard for me to accept not only because mothers have selective vision with their children and glorious dreams for them, but also because there had been no warning, no hint of illness. Through his childhood and teen years, he was a B student who got along with teachers, played soccer, had an after-school job, fretted about acne, and palled around with a gang of boys just like him. I think his biggest transgression was slipping through his bedroom window one night to join his friends for pizza. He wasn't a model child of saintly obedience—he was just a normal kid.

I tried to put the Boulder incident into the "collegiate rebellion" category, but it didn't fit for long. Two months later, when the family gathered in California for Thanksgiving, we collided with manic depression.

This book is about that collision. While the story begins at Thanksgiving, the idea to write it emerged months later from my sister Lisa, a professional writer. I had been sharing with her everything that was happening with Mark and me. My daily phone calls to her prompted her suggestion that we write a book about it.

I grabbed at the idea. Part of my reason was to vent my anger. I was angry at psychiatrists, hospitals, insurance companies, Mark, the disease, everything. It seemed so unfair, so irrational. I wanted to scream at the world. My anger subsided as I began to write, and then the process offered a release, a catharsis. In the chapters about me and Mark, I could explain and understand the emotions and pain, and maybe make them a little less hurtful.

Mark collaborated on the book, and this was one of his reasons too. He and Lisa talked for months, reliving his time in Boulder, the months in Connecticut, the summer, and his hospital experiences. He revealed the hidden side of his illness, he said, so that it would never come back to haunt him. "I don't want it to be this dirty, dark secret that pops out of the closet twenty years from now. If it's hidden and secret, it has too much power over me. I want to rob it of its power, make it ordinary. It happened. I'm a little embarrassed, but so what?" Lisa's talks with Mark are the basis for the "Mark" nuggets in the story chapters.

This book is really two in one: my personal story about what manic depression did to my family, and information about the illness itself. During Mark's very sick months, when I was desperate to learn about this disease, I discovered few books on it. If it was mentioned in a book about mental illness, it rated only a couple of paragraphs. While clinical depression has dozens of titles to its name, only Ronald Fieve's informative *Moodswings* deals with manic depression.

Lisa suggested filling this vacuum and alternating the chapters about me and Mark with information about the illness. She suggested that informational chapters parallel and explain things in more or less the same order that I learned about them. Lisa did the research and writing of the informational chapters, positioning them to give the reader information in the same order I would have needed it.

In the end, we wove together *Angels of Madness*. A word about this title: We chose it because it speaks to the overwhelming emotions and experiences Mark and we went through. Mark saw and heard angels. They came to him in his manic episodes, singing songs and voicing commands. And he responded, and tried to re-create their likeness in clay and paint. We too heard these angels—through the chaos of Mark's illness. There are many names for Mark's experience, from antiquated terms like "lunacy" to scientific labels like "psychosis." But for us, "madness" best describes the mystery and power of mental illness.

This book is for the person I was that day in Boulder. We hope its combination of facts and feelings will give comfort and hope to other families and patients.

Chapter 1

THANKSGIVING

*T*he Wednesday evening before Thanksgiving is the worst travel day of the year, so it was no surprise when the flight from Denver to San Jose was three hours late. Those three hours just gave me more time to think about Mark.

I last saw him three weeks ago in Boulder, when I had dropped him off at the library on my way to the airport. Other than a brief telephone conversation about airline tickets, neither Chris nor I had talked with him. Maybe I had been dramatizing his behavior in Colorado.

Usually, only one person made the airport run on holidays but this year both Chris and I were at the gate. Mark still refused to talk to his father; fearful of starting our Thanksgiving family reunion with a confrontation at the airport, I suggested Chris melt into the background at first. He slouched his six-foot-four-inch frame as inconspicuously as possible against a pillar.

I was relieved Mark was coming at all. In our one telephone call, he first claimed he was too busy to leave Colorado, then declared he'd like to see the ocean. He got very angry when I tried to put Chris on the line. Finally, he said he would meet us for Thanksgiving because everyone—all eighteen members of the family—was gathering at the beach for the first complete family reunion in years.

I finally spotted the top of his head in the swarm that surged through the gate. He was thin, his dark blond hair uncombed, and he had dark smudges under his eyes. He seemed frail and small inside his oversized Banana Republic overcoat with ragged hem and missing buttons. From the epaulets and buttonholes hung narrow strips of fabric in various colors. With a start, I recognized the tatters were the remains of a polo shirt I had sent him. Poking from a book bag was a tennis-racquet handle wrapped in orange Day-Glo tape. Mark hated tennis. His Reeboks were covered in unintelligible writing in thick Magic Marker ink. He looked as if he had been living in the park, sleeping on grates and scavenging food. He smelled like a panhandler.

"I'm going to play some tennis . . . it's good to be back in the Bay Area." His sentences were punctuated with the mirthless smile and dry laugh I had seen in Colorado. I made tentative conversational forays, with comments about airline food, crowds, and the weather, as we waited by the carousel for his duffel. Mark shuffled his feet and kept twisting side to side as if looking for someone. He avoided looking at me.

Chris shot me a hard glance behind Mark's head, a what-is-going-on-here? glare. I looked away. I was just grateful Mark had arrived, and wasn't going to probe any deeper just now. I suspended judgment on Mark's appearance, but not one detail escaped his father.

"I smoke now," Mark declared, rolling down the car window and fumbling for cigarettes and matches. No one commented about the smoke that would have been fodder for an argument a few months ago. Chris scowled, and I pretended not to notice.

"My classes are so easy, I'm going to knock off straight A's. I don't even know why I bother with college. It's such a waste of time. My mind can learn everything so fast I shouldn't even have to go to classes. I could teach those classes if I wanted." Mark's monologue tumbled out in rapid bursts.

I sank into my seat in silence. Mark's rambling brought back my sense of dread. I concentrated on not listening too carefully.

"This thing with the police . . . I broke the window, but the police beat me up. Police brutality. I'm going to talk to Bob about that." Bob King was the attorney the police sergeant had recommended. I winced when I remembered the $3,500 retainer I gave him. He said that it could cost up to $10,000 to get Mark off the felony charge.

The sharp, briny smell of the ocean and the distant roar of surf greeted us as we walked down the wooden path across the sand dunes by my parents' beach house. Walking in from the starry night to the brightly lit front room, I saw Mark as my family must have seen him—bizarre and outlandish in his strange clothes. My embarrassment quickly shifted to a surge of protectiveness for my younger child.

My parents had reared five children, and noticed how kids dressed. They would recognize that Mark's appearance was more than freshman grubbiness. His gaunt face, thin laugh, and nonstop monologues would also raise their eyebrows.

I couldn't ignore the telltale signs. As they say, if it looks like a duck and quacks like a duck . . . This duck was hard drugs. The police had no doubt his assault had been triggered by drugs. I would be foolish to ignore both my instincts and the police.

"Too much partying and drinking," Chris concluded as we walked across the sand to our rented condo. He had no doubts about Mark's behavior. In college, he could down a pitcher in seventeen seconds. He knew Mark's problem, he had been there. His analytical engineer's mind examined the evidence and drew a conclusion.

"Maybe so." I eagerly accepted his interpretation. Mine was too frightening.

I slept fitfully, waking up every few hours to the sound of Mark rummaging through his duffel. A couple of times I heard someone leave or come through the front door. Maybe it was Mark, maybe I dreamed it.

MARK

She's coming, Yesyesyes, I feel it, yes, any second she'll appear on the beach, over there by the shimmering tide, drifting-sifting-lifting, coming to me. We'll meet, embrace, no words. Our thoughts swirl between us like a warm wind. From Boulder she's found me. The stars will light her eyes and give us sight. Mine-eyes-have-seen-the-light. Throw away your glasses, Mark, you don't need them, you have the sight. She'll help you see everything. Fling 'em, zing 'em. Ringringring, no artificial eyes for you.

Maybe it's too dark out here. I don't mind the cold or wet sand. I'll wait forever if I have to, but maybe she can't see me. Another cig. Let the soft red glow bring her to you. Light a cig, pop a caffeine pill, be ready. Any moment now.

Looooooooooooooooook. Lightinthesky. Shescomingshescoming shescoming. Ohmygod, they're coming closer. It's not her. Two, floating through the black-

ness. Jesuschrist, they're angels. Blurred, but I know they're angels. Dancing swirling twirling. Ohgod, my eyes can't take it any more, my brrrraaaain can't take it. I want to cry, sleep, kill this numbness. Oh please hurry.

The sun rising over the artichoke and brussels-sprout fields that border Monterey Bay woke me up. Chris was still sound asleep, motionless. He had been on a marathon business trip the week before, and countless in-flight meals, Ramada Inns, and late-night-customer dinners had flattened him.

Chris worked for a small computer-software company, and in the way of start-ups, he did everything from sales to marketing to management. It was a rough-and-scramble business, and he loved it, but his days often lasted eighteen hours and his frequent-flyer miles bulged into six figures. "We'll take a great trip for free when I have more time," he would tantalize me.

Married twenty-three years and having lived in eight states and fifteen houses, Chris and I often have had no other best friends but each other even though we're very different. I'm the oldest of five children, and like many firstborn am self-confident, love solving complicated problems, and can be abrasive and argumentative when I don't get my way.

Chris, on the other hand, is an only child, and loves solitude and independence. As a father, he was never a roll-on-the-carpet-with-the-babies type. Instead, he'd show them the wonders of his stamp collection or endlessly practice throwing balls with them. I think many of his parenting qualities were a reaction to his father, Evan. Evan was a back-slapping man known for relentless philandering and nightly visits to the local tavern. Chris had always felt betrayed by Evan's disinterest in his son. He hadn't seen or talked to his father for ten years.

Chris was the consummate engineer—from meticulously tended vegetable garden with name tags above every row to his color-coded closet to his love of computer programming. He was a perfectionist with himself and his sons. His best and worst feature is his brutal honesty, his inability to tell the comforting white lie. He has no use for subtlety. Thoughtful, methodical, and direct, he describes himself as if he were a kind of machine: "Wysi-Wyg," or "What-you-see-is-What-you-get."

We're the odd couple. While he picks up my used coffee cups and unseen lint off carpets, I hoard nests of magazines and am oblivious to dropping cookie crumbs as I putter around the house. Nevertheless, we are both nesters, and happiness is Friday night at home with a bottle of Cabernet, a movie from the video shop, and Jake, our retriever, by the fire.

I slipped out of bed, pulled on a warm-up, and padded down the hall to check on Mark. He was sprawled on his bed, in the same clothes as the day before, dead asleep. I headed over the dunes to my parents' house.

My father, Frank, was practicing the piano. "Where's Chris?" he asked, pausing.

"Asleep. He did five cities in five days last week. Here's the paper, it was on the doorstep." I busied myself with juice and coffee.

"How's Mom feel about a catered Thanksgiving dinner? I'm glad you talked her into it. Fixing a bird for eighteen would be too much," I said.

"She feels it's cheating, but she'll like not worrying about the clean-up," he said, fishing out the sports section. My father, like my husband, was a nester. Dad loved the confusion of a large family around him. This weekend, all five children, plus assorted spouses and children, promised a nonstop medley of old jokes, ancient stories, and lots of laughter. Dad often said that caring for a family was like tending a circle of campfires. You get one burning brightly and another dims. It was a constant job tossing logs in the needed places and the right times. He tossed a log in my direction.

"How's Mark doing?" he ventured casually.

"I know, Dad. Mark." I sighed, and busied myself looking for eggs in the refrigerator. I didn't want him to know how worried I was. He returned to his paper.

Slowly, the family wandered in for breakfast. People grabbed sections of the paper, coffee, and croissants. My sister Kate's kids whined for Frosted Flakes, and everyone raised his voice to talk over their noise. Chris and our other son, Robert, were plotting the day's football schedule.

Robert was the family optimist. Born with a sunny disposition, he took people at their word. He was voted "most gullible" by his high school class. A senior at the University of Washington in Seattle studying engineering, he was a typical college kid. He joined a fraternity, rowed Husky crew, pulled down B's and C's, and worked weekends at Nordstrom's selling ladies' shoes. His aunts loved to tease him about being a shoe peddler; they'd wave their bare feet in the air and ask for an immediate assessment of their size, then erupt into giggles. He enjoyed the attention.

His current aspiration, he announced with mock determination, was "to be a yuppie." He hoped that yuppiedom would wait for him. He was worried that being a yuppie might pass out of fashion before he acquired a Saab.

Mark slipped wordlessly into the kitchen for a glass of orange juice. His hair was rumpled with sleep, and he hadn't changed his clothes from the day before. He perched on the edge of his chair, tapping his fingers on the tabletop. The finger tapping increased, and he began to bob his head and hum tonelessly.

"Mark, you're bothering people. Tone it down," Chris said sternly from behind his newspaper. Mark ignored him, focusing his eyes on the ceiling.

Chris got up and stood over Mark. "Stop that noise. Go outside if you must. You're bothering everyone." Mark defiantly stared away.

"All right, out you go." Chris grabbed him by his arms to escort him outside. His voice was angry with the frustration of Mark's mysterious behavior. Mark yanked away.

"Get your hands off me!" Mark snarled, and twisted from his father's grasp. The table rocked, chairs toppled, and spilled orange juice flowed onto the beige carpet as father and son punched and twisted each other. Finally, Mark broke free and ran outside to the beach.

The family watched in frozen silence. No one moved or spoke for a long count, then everyone erupted simultaneously. Lisa dashed for a rag to wipe up the juice while Kate and Dad righted the furniture. I watched them bustle around, pretending this was an everyday occurrence. Chris mumbled apologies and followed Mark out the door.

My family's private problem was not in the public domain. By being witnesses, everyone had earned a right to an opinion.

"Cocaine," declared my youngest brother, Sam. "He shouldn't go back to Boulder." Everyone nodded. There it was: the gorilla at the dinner party. He couldn't be ignored anymore.

Other suggestions followed:

"Someone should take his airplane ticket so he can't leave."

"He'll need money to buy drugs. We should watch our wallets."

"Someone should check his room for drugs."

I didn't argue or try to defend Mark. Maybe for once, I thought helplessly, they know more than I do. Unable to think or move, I sat while everyone else tried to patch up my family's problem.

"How could he ruin our reunion like this?" Robert was very angry. "How could he be that stupid?" he asked with the certainty of a jock who wouldn't date girls who even smoked.

"Come on, grab your racquet. Let's go." Lisa stood in front of me, a can of tennis balls in hand. Might as well, I thought, nothing else I can do. We walked to the courts along a path lined with aromatic eucalyptus trees.

"It'll be okay," Lisa said after we had walked in silence for a few minutes. "You know the family—Mom, Dad, me—everyone will help. We'll solve this, believe me." I nodded, unable to speak over the lump in my throat.

Tennis was our passion, and ordinarily I would have relished a game. Our styles were fast and fierce. No patient baseline rallies but lots of slices, midcourt volleys, and going for winners. Lisa was hot, spinning serves elusively away from me. All her volleys caught the lines. My feet wouldn't move, and the sets were over quickly.

We put on our warm-ups and walked back to the house. The doors to the deck were open, and the chaise longues occupied by oiled bodies. Kate's children were playing in the sand, and Mother was setting out lunch. Mark was still gone.

The afternoon floated by with sunbathing, book reading, and walks on the beach. No one mentioned the morning fight, but I couldn't think of anything else.

I wasn't used to worrying about my children. Mothering had come easily. Mother had come to stay right after Robert was born, and I learned from her how to be caring yet relaxed with my children. No fussing over crying, no worrying about picky eating, and no panicking at sudden tears. The boys grew up without any traumas, and I never questioned whether I had done a good job rearing my children. Until now.

When they were infants, Chris joined the Air Force to avoid being drafted. He ended up flying fighter planes over Southeast Asia. While our friends were sitting in classes in graduate school, Chris was dropping napalm.

At Stanford reunions, Chris was often odd man out, considered not shrewd enough to avoid the draft, or worse yet, a man who relished the art of warfare. Mark was born in January 1969, while Chris was in Vietnam. It was the height of the war, and he was flying nightly missions over Laos. It was a hard, brutal time for us. Thank God we were too young to know just how hard.

*   *   *

I wandered upstairs to find Chris and Robert in front of the first football game of the day, with curtains drawn against the bright November sunshine.

"I called Paul Marshall about Mark," Chris said flatly, not moving his eyes from the screen. Paul was an old college friend and lawyer.

"What'd he say?" I asked, wondering how Chris, who was always so private, approached Paul.

"He'll get back to us with the names of some good local drug-treatment programs. Mark won't be going back to school," he stated categorically.

"We don't know that for sure," I replied. "Maybe he can join a program in Boulder." Mark had to finish—finals were in two weeks. If he got behind, he wouldn't graduate with his class. He had to graduate. Everyone did. Even my grandparents, all four, went to college. Months later, I would have loved to have such a simple concern.

Chris spun around and glared at me. "Where have you been the past twenty-four hours? Can't you see he's off on some drug high? We don't know how to deal with this." I felt tears, swallowed hard, and left the room without saying anything. I couldn't think of anything to say.

MARK

Hahahahahahahaha. My father doesn't know anything, so stupid, so ignorant no one talks to him, tells him anything, he doesn't hear the singing or the Truths I hear he'll never know. Hahahahahaha. So stupid I don't think he's really my father. Monterey's straight ahead through the fields across the highway and we're there, I'll find her there. Oh shit, no shoes, how far with no shoes.

Iiiiimaannuuuel, iiiimaannuuuelll, Immanuel, the voice said. Our child will be Immanuuuel. I must make a birthing place for her, she'll be here soon to have Immanuuuel. These brussels sprouts, their bushes, tear them out, dig a hole, spread them down, build a birthing place. Quick, Hurry, Now. Before she's here. A gift they're like a gift. A rift, a tift, a gift. Sift through the sand. Small, round layers of green life, mud of the earth. They're a symbol of our abundance.

Immanuel is coming. Candles, I must have candles at the birthing place. Mustmustmust. Trust the must. Candles, cigarettes, samesame. Yes, bury seven cigarettes, to be candles. She's coming, and Immanuel our child is coming. Soon.

Mark reappeared in the late afternoon, like a shadow, saying nothing and slipping into the kitchen to put something in the refrigerator. We were all scattered all over the house—watching TV, sunbathing on the deck, napping—but everyone knew he was back.

Lisa broke the brittle silence and invited him outside to a game of volleyball. Mark wanly smiled. Then, without a word, he pressed something into each person's hand and left the room. Each of us held a muddy brussels sprout.

Thanksgiving dinner looked like family night at the Elk Lodge. Card tables covered with cloths were clustered in the living room so everyone could sit together. Hours earlier, caterers arrived with two fifteen-pound gold-brown birds. The rest of the meal was spread out for a buffet. Dad presided at the head of the table, scanning glasses and plates, making sure enough wine was open, everyone had their fill of stuffing, and we were sitting up straight, one of his pet peeves.

"Mark not here?" he asked, as if the thought had just occurred to him.

"No, Dad, not yet. I'm sure he'll come soon. He was really looking forward to Thanksgiving," I said without conviction. He nodded, but I knew he wasn't fooled.

Our family meals were legendary for their noise. TVs, radios, or telephones were no match for us as we swapped stories, teased, and shouted down the table for more wine. Kate's children pushed their food around, then wiggled out of their chairs and scurried away to cartoons upstairs. Leo, Dad's Rhodesian Ridgeback, was ensconced under the table, happily cleaning up. Even Mark's elusive behavior couldn't rob us of a raucous gathering.

"Diane, maybe this isn't a drug problem," said my sister-in-law Leslie who was once a nurse. "This could be a medical problem—a psychiatric one, not drugs."

"Impossible," I shot back. "Why would such a problem turn up now? He's always been normal, healthy. No one in the family has *ever* had mental problems." I dismissed her remarks.

Mark materialized midway through the meal, looking like a beach bum. I flushed with embarrassment as I compared him with Kate's well-scrubbed children. He took a plate, heaped it with mashed potatoes, drained the gravy boat over the white mound, and scooped it in. He spoke to no one, and everyone, obeying the unwritten rules of the weekend, left him alone. When he finished, he deposited his plate in the sink and disappeared to the beach.

"I'm going to wait for him to come back," Robert declared after dinner. "Maybe talking to someone who knows the drug thing will help." Chris and I were too tired to do more than shrug and go to bed.

Robert found me after breakfast the next day.

"He came back about three o'clock, and I tried to talk to him. First he says he's using heroin, then he says it's just caffeine pills. It's hard to talk to him. He didn't make sense. He may try to buy some stuff here. I'm going to watch him, Mom. Don't worry, he'll be all right." My twenty-year-old sounded so sensible, so mature. Maybe I had done something right.

Paul Marshall called back Saturday with the names of two drug-treatment programs in the San Francisco area. Chris made appointments for Monday. All we had to do now was keep Mark close at hand. We all agreed to hide our cash, airline tickets, car keys, credit cards—anything that could be turned into drug or escape money. The burden of believing Mark was a potential thief blunted the festivities, bringing a deep sadness particularly to Dad, who had reared us with an abundance of trust and responsibility.

Mark had a special place in my father's affections. Like my father, my son was an iconoclast, a sharp freethinker who rarely followed the crowd. He was quick-witted, irreverent, clever with verbal puns, and full of opinions. He loved to stir up dinner-table conversation by quoting Rolling Stone and David Letterman.

Mark was just like Dad, who was the consummate commodities trader working the angles, turning penny margins into hefty profits, and always taking the contrarian route. Dad dismissed the opinions of others, but managed to maintain a strict consistency with his own ethics. He would never do anything illegal or immoral, but he would push it to the edge.

Mark faded and reappeared over the rest of the weekend. He mostly showed up at mealtime, then disappeared to the beach.

The reunion was over by late Sunday afternoon. Everyone except Chris, Mark, me, my parents, and Lisa were headed their separate ways home. We packed up, closed the house, and drove over the mountain pass to the Bay Area for Sunday night at my parents' house. Mark's appointments with the drug centers were for the next day, and Lisa had a Monday flight.

An eerie calm settled over the family after unpacking the beach things at my parents' house. We ate carry-out enchiladas in front of 60 Minutes. Mark sat on the floor, barely inches from the screen, riveted to the story of a 1968 murder in Santa Monica. By ten o'clock, he announced he was going to bed. Lisa, Dad, and I gravitated into the living room to dissect the weekend's events and brood over Mark's future. The postmortem was interrupted by loud voices from Mark's room.

"*Fine!* If you want to leave, *leave.* Just remember, if you go out that door, there's no coming back. I've had it. If you don't want to help yourself, then we can't. So leave." Chris was furious.

I held my breath. Mark can't leave—no one but us would help him. He would disappear into the streets, one of thousands of young drug addicts panhandling for change. I closed my eyes. How could Chris cast out his own son?

Chris stormed into the living room. He was struggling with his rage to form coherent sentences. "If he wants to go, let him. He probably was going to look for drugs. I don't care. I've had it with him." His hard-edged fury was contained, his voice firm, almost detached. This was tough love at its toughest. Mark stood at the doorway behind him.

Chris explained with disgust, "He was trying to sneak out. He shoved pillows under the blanket, and the screen was out of the window."

"I just wanted to walk around. I can't sleep," Mark insisted.

"At eleven o'clock at night? In the middle of nowhere?" Chris challenged. The house sat at the end of a cul-de-sac in a new development miles from anything but other subdivisions, pastures, and orchards.

"Yeah, but what do you care, you murderer," Mark spit out.

Chris lashed back, "All right! Let's have it out. What are you talking about? Nothing you have said or done this weekend makes any sense." He calmed himself as he slumped into a chair. Lisa and Dad, trapped in the middle of another family's private fight, stared into their laps. Although they shared our agonies, they had no desire to know our personal secrets. I was deeply embarrassed for their discomfort and the spectacle of my family disintegrating in front of me. I sat watching my son and husband, as if they were two characters on a stage and I had no control over their words. I couldn't leave either. This was my mess too.

"Okay, I'll tell you. I know about you," Mark began in a modulated, lecturing voice. His tone was coherent and rational, but the words were senseless or oddly old-fashioned. His eyes narrowed, and his face was set in a mask of deep and intense hatred.

"I *know* these things because of the voices. They're in the laser helmet, and they've told me about you. How you have women to your room when you're traveling, and what they do to you. And how you humiliate my mother. They know all about you, and they have told me *everything*. You're a whoremonger, an Antichrist, and a murderer." Mark's voice had risen to an evangelical frenzy. He could have been Cotton Mather on a Puritan pulpit.

"I know, I know you're a murderer. I know what you did and how you did it. You can't hide it from me. Voices have told me. And that's not all. I know more than I'm telling," he said conspiratorially, his face assuming a sly, almost superior expression. "I know *secrets*, secrets no one else knows. Very important secrets."

Chris stared at Mark, speechless, his anger evaporating. Although the accusations were clearly irrational ramblings, I could see Mark hurt Chris terribly. His son had attacked him like a vicious pit bull.

"I swear to God," Chris spoke in a solemn tone, as if on a witness stand, "I have never done those things. I have never cheated on your mother." He left it at that, perhaps knowing that any protest was probably meaningless to his son.

Chris and Mark retreated to their separate rooms. I sat rigid, my mind escaping into the floral print on the sofa and picking out the repeating pattern. All weekend, I had secretly hoped we were all wrong, that we had been overreacting to Mark's behavior. Until now, nothing he had said or done was overly bizarre. He hadn't arrived naked at dinner, eaten the dog's food or painted his face red. Who was Mark? The face and body before me, or the vague instincts and hunches? Mark's rage and non sequiturs compelled me to face a new truth. He was completely out of control, and none of us understood it. Everyone was terrified. For the first time, I shivered at the thought that he could be violent.

I am not usually a crier. I have a hopelessly sentimental streak that waters up at the slightest provocation—from news stories of whale slaughters to music by Ravel—so I keep myself in check. This squishy sentimentality is not the way I want to be. Conversely, when real tragedies occur, life-and-death events such as friends killed in car accidents, I can't find ready tears. In a crisis, I freeze, my face turns to stone, and I try to function and be practical, and not reveal my feelings.

Now, the inner resolve crumbled. The tears I had suppressed all weekend spilled out. Lisa and Dad surrounded me in their arms, each of us choking with sobs. I felt so tired, so drained of strength. Chris had staked out his position with brutal finality, and I felt I was Mark's only defender. From here on, my husband and I would occupy different ground. My biggest fear was that compromise was impossible, and I would have to choose between Chris and Mark.

Dad and Lisa, looking shell-shocked, mumbled goodnights and left. Mother, who obviously heard everything from the bedroom, came into the living room with two snifters of B&B. We sat on the sofa, our feet curled under robes.

"This is hard for Chris," she said. "He is so used to being in control, and here is something in his own family over which he has no control. He's just like your father. Give him time."

My parents had been married forty-six years, and my calm, collected mother was really the only one who understood and managed my volatile, sometimes combative father. She never fought the unnecessary fight, and shrugged off the small firefights or nasty outbreaks. "He skipped lunch today," she would say in response to his ill temper, and sure enough, after a good dinner he would be cheerful again. At other times, she practiced the fine art of lying low without being caught. When his temper flared over inconsequential things, she slid out the door on an errand or to take a shower. She chose her battles with great care, and almost always won. I always took her advice seriously. The evidence of almost fifty years of happy marriage was too overwhelming not to.

"Mark's going to be all right. You have to believe that. So will Chris. Hold tight and do what you feel is the right thing. It will be the best for all of you. I just know it," she continued. I basked in the balm of her reassuring words flowing over me. There is nothing in this world like a mother's comfort.

MARK

"Waaaait," they whispered, "find the dark spot at the end of the driveway." Goddamned murderer almost ruined it, I showed him, now he knows I know. That'll teach him. Bastard. The nose knows. No matter, I'm leaving, I'm going, they're going to pick me up, take me away. "Wait," they commanded.

Lights flicker, disappear. Good night. The houses, the hills twinkle good night. Crickets, fucking dogs, angry cats, we're all out here together. Hear that? Rumble, stumble, tumble in the distance. Something's nearing, from that ridge, awesome noise, sound waves before light waves. Holy shit!

Wedges, pyramids, no, triangles. Three flat triangles. Look how they blot out the stars! Like Close Encounters! *These are real, hear the engines, the thrusters, running lights, in formation. How do they move, so big yet so quiet? Those three fireballs at the back? This is fucking amazing! So slow, so low. Swinglowsweetchariot. So majestic, like a floating fantasy, like underwater.*

This isn't what the voices meant, this is more. A demonstration, a sign. Oh Mark, are you ready, can you see this read this know this?

Monday morning I awoke around 5:00 A.M., while sleepwalking in the hallway. I couldn't remember where I was. Not since finals week at Stanford had I sleepwalked like that. Chris would be up soon, and I decided to get dressed. He had announced as I came to bed the night before that he was going back East to work. Always practical and sensible, he acknowledged that his presence around Mark only made things worse. I sadly agreed, although I was also somewhat relieved that, like Mother slipping out for an errand, I could avoid a confrontation with him over the solution to Mark's problem.

After an early breakfast, I walked Chris out to the rental car in the predawn chill.

"You do what you have to." He stood beside the door. "I'll support whatever you decide. I'm just not the one now to make any sort of decisions for Mark."

I wanted Chris to tell me everything was going to be fine, that Mark would get help, get well, and resume his life—a happy ending. He couldn't do it. It was not in Chris to utter easy lies or less than the unvarnished truth. But he was as firm and committed as he was honest. His promise to me was absolute. He would support *whatever* I decided. I always knew that he would be there for me, that nothing in this world would tear apart our bond. He was the rare animal that mates once and for life.

"This is only the beginning with Mark. You have to accept that he may strike out on his own to solve this thing. He's over eighteen, he's legally an adult. You may lose him." His voice was so unemotional he might have been talking about repair options for a fender bender. I nodded silently, looking at my feet, not wanting to see the truth in his eyes. He gave me a long, engulfing hug, and disappeared down the driveway into the fog.

By eight o'clock, Dad, Mark, and I were headed for our first appointment at Fremont Hospital. Mark silently chain-smoked in the front seat. His silence sat in the car like a deformed passenger. It was not going to be an easy day, and I worried about Dad. I wanted to contain the pain Mark inflicted. But supporting your family was a religious credo with my father, and I couldn't have kept him home if I wanted to. In truth, I was thankful.

The drug-treatment center was at the back of the hospital, at the end of a warren of corridors. We waited in a softly lit, plant-filled room. Dad and I stood, hesitant to sit down for fear Mark would run. We weren't going to get caught flat-footed. An earnest young man called us into a back office and introduced himself as a counselor. Mark waited outside as I described his behavior. The counselor asked us to wait while he interviewed Mark.

I finally began to let some of the tension inside me uncoil. Mark was with a professional, someone who would recognize the pattern and know what to do. He probably talked to kids like Mark every day. All the behavior that so mystified us would be commonplace for him. I relaxed a bit more.

Dad and I waited in an empty office across the hall. We talked quietly about his business, Robert's knee, Chris's new job. We gazed out the window and wondered if the gray sky would produce the much-needed rain. While we talked, he held my hand, gently patting it. But all the while we strained to hear what was happening behind the counselor's door.

Suddenly a door slammed, and someone shouted. It was Mark. The force of the slam shook the office partitions rattling the diplomas on the wall.

A flustered drug counselor hurried in and hastily informed us that this probably was not a drug problem. How could he tell so quickly? Mark had only been with him fifteen minutes. He offered no information other than volunteering to find a staff psychiatrist and to look into putting Mark in the hospital for a three-day evaluation.

In the meantime, Mark was gone. He had burst out of the office and tore down the corridor to the elevators. He had no money or car, but he was angry and not acting rationally. I closed my mind to the possibilities. We had to find him.

Apparently, the counselor triggered his outburst by listing an array of street drugs and pressuring Mark to tell him which he was using. Mark insisted more and more vehemently that he was on nothing. "Test me. Test me. Then you'll know," he repeated. When no test was forthcoming, he bolted.

Mark was sitting calmly in the main lobby, flipping through *Time*.

We almost missed him in our headlong rush through the double doors. He wants help, I thought, or why else would he stay? You don't act crazy in a hospital unless you're asking for help the only way you know how. I clung to that thought.

Dad and the staff psychiatrist each approached Mark from our huddle around the corner out of his line of sight. We wanted him to voluntarily admit himself into the hospital. It was like nearing a deer in the forest, afraid that any quick motion or loud noise would scare it off.

He refused to go into the hospital. Why should he? he asked. He rambled on about the laser helmet that he couldn't turn off that was sending rapid thoughts flying through his head.

I slowly crossed the lobby, soundlessly sat beside him, and reached for his hand. He angrily pulled it away and twisted around so I couldn't see his face.

"Why can't you understand, Diane, I want to be left alone." He spit out the words as one would a rotten shrimp. He had never called me by my name before. Wheeling around, he shoved his face inches from mine and menacingly locked his eyes in mine.

"Don't you see, bitch, this is my life, not yours. Go away." He casually resumed reading the *Time* in his lap. For the first time, I was physically afraid. The only words that came to me were "demonic possession."

The scene was beginning to feel like a surreal nightmare. Mark, my son, was dying, and I felt the wild panic every mother knows when she can't find her child. When Mark was three, he wandered from the beach house when we thought he was napping. We found him wet, frightened, and cold hours later about a mile down the beach. The moment I recognized his blond head, the pain, the secret prayers, the torment of his vanishing, were forgotten. But now, those feelings came back. Mark was lost again. This time, perhaps forever.

I slid away from him and found the doctor in the hallway. Ordinary hospital business eddied around us, and I was aware of covert glances in our direction. I was crying, sobbing really. I couldn't stop.

"In order to commit Mark involuntarily for a three-day observation, you need to sign the commitment papers." The doctor held out a pen and form. How could I not sign? I replayed the scene with Mark's face in mine and him calling me Diane. That person was not my son. I had to do anything and everything to get him back. I wiped away my tears, breathed deeply to steady my hand, and scrawled my name on the line with the X.

Dad and I were shown to a small, private room from where we could watch the hastily summoned police encircle Mark, deftly slip on handcuffs, and guide him to a waiting gurney. He lay down, and a nurse locked leather straps around his wrist and ankles, then walked alongside him as the stretcher moved to the emergency room.

"We don't have a locked bed here, but they do at Foothills Hospital in San Jose," the doctor told me. What did he mean, "locked bed"?

Dad and I followed Mark to the empty emergency room, afraid to let him out of our sight. Strapped down, he was completely helpless, and I wanted to watch over him, protect him. He was vulnerable. I was grateful he didn't resist. The Boulder police must have made an impression. He looked like Gulliver tied down by Lilliputians. But he was alert, and I could sense that he was calming down. For a few minutes, no one said anything. Then Dad noticed his socks, one green, one blue.

"I do that sometimes," he said tenderly. "When it's dark in the bedroom, and I'm not paying attention . . . some days I don't notice until I take them off at night." I smiled despite the pain and dried tears. My father's penchant for odd color combinations was one of his endearing quirks.

Mark chuckled. "Yeah. That happens."

I ventured tentatively, "Hungry? There's got to be food here somewhere."

Mark replied as if just to humor me, "Yeah, sure. I haven't eaten in a while." I returned ten minutes later with a plastic tray of brown meat and creamed vegetables, and a nurse to unlock his wrist strap. I pulled off the metal cover.

"Sorry, it's all I could find."

"That's lunch?" Mark asked with mock disappointment. A flash of the person we knew. "I'm not that crazy," he quipped.

The ambulance arrived by late afternoon. Enveloped by gloomy fog and rain, we followed the flashing red light through the rush-hour traffic.

The adult psychiatric ward of Foothills Hospital in San Jose was hidden at the end of another maze of corridors. We waited outside the wire-reinforced glass doors for someone to let us in. My reflection was drawn, pale and hollow. Finally, a muscular man in white pants and shirt spotted us and opened the door.

"You must be Mark's family. He's in his room and being sedated. I have to ask you some questions to complete the admission. First, check your handbag and any sharp objects in your pockets." He gestured to an officious-looking woman in a small office beside the door.

The ward had a shabby, institutional look, with vinyl-covered chairs, sofa, and a large central table. The walls were decorated with what looked like paintings by patients. It felt like the waiting room in my internist's clinic, except for the people.

A woman in a blue chenille robe sat at a table, slowly turning the pages of the morning paper. She carefully smoothed every page after she turned it, as if folding laundry. Her lank gray hair hid her face. Beside the paper was an orange ceramic ashtray with a smoldering, forgotten cigarette. As we approached, she stared at me. I refused to make eye contact, and said something to Dad. I didn't want anything to do with these people. Other patients shuffled past us or meandered around the room, muttering and arguing with themselves. From somewhere I could hear a television game show, and the canned laughter jangled through the corridors. The sound of a woman crying added another layer of noises.

The nurse gave me an information form to fill out about Mark's medical history and health insurance. I wished I had a pencil, because I kept crossing out answers. Finally, I simply printed slowly. The nurse reappeared and sat beside me to ask about family mental history. No, I told him, no history of depression, mania, or mental illness in the immediate family. I paused. Was Great Aunt Helen, my grandmother's younger sister, "immediate"?

Grandmother kept a framed photograph of Aunt Helen on her dresser. I remembered a petite blond girl in a twenties dress with a shy smile. No one openly talked about Aunt Helen. All I knew was that around her thirtieth birthday, something happened, she was diagnosed as hopelessly schizophrenic, and was sent to an institution where she died fifty years later. Grandmother used to visit her regularly, and afterward she stopped by our house for a glass of sherry and she and Mother whispered. I later learned about those visits, especially the hard days when Helen acted completely normal and wanted out. Less terrible were the times when she recognized no one, not even her sister. Until now, I had completely forgotten about Aunt Helen.

"What about alcoholism?" asked the nurse.

"Absolutely not. No one in our family has a problem with alcohol." I paused again in the middle of my knee-jerk reaction. Not true, I thought. Maybe Evan.

Evan, Chris's estranged father, had never lost a job or been arrested for DWI, but it was no secret that he drank constantly. One of my first memories of him was his insisting on saving overnight for me a scotch and water I hadn't finished. Married twice, his infidelities and nightly visits to the corner bar had besmirched Chris's childhood.

I wavered in my certainty that I didn't belong here.

"The involuntary commitment can be based on one of three criteria under California law," the nurse explained. "Danger to self, danger to others, inability to function. What do you feel applies here? Is Mark suicidal? Violent?"

I hesitated. Should I tell him about the assault charge in Colorado? I decided not to mention it. It might prejudice them against his treatment. I opted for the least damning explanation: "inability to function."

As I finished the rest of the questions, I was acutely aware that I was creating for Mark a record as a mental patient. The expression "former mental patient" kept running through my mind. Bizarre crime stories always contained that person. Was I shutting out his future with this form? Labeling him for life? Would this follow him through schools and jobs? I couldn't answer these questions, but I had to get him help now.

Mark arrived with only the clothes on his back, so I sought out the gift shop downstairs. I stood in the aisle lined with personal-care items, wondering if a large or small bottle of shampoo would depress him. I picked up and put back item after item. A large bottle could mean he would be here a while; a small bottle a sign of stinginess. I couldn't remember what kind of toothpaste he used. All my thoughts and actions seemed riddled with sad meanings and hidden consequences.

I left the things at the desk in the ward to be checked before being delivered to Mark. Driving back to Los Altos Hills, Dad and I rode in silence, our faces illuminated by the glow from the dash, lost in our painful memories of the day.

The next day, drawn and exhausted, I returned to the hospital. My eyes were gritty from the night's tears, and my head pounded with a monster headache that aspirin didn't touch. I was going to a meeting with the staff psychiatrist.

Dr. Lee was brief and to the point, as if dictating lab results into a tape recorder. The drug screen was completely negative, and free of any "offending substances." In his opinion, based on Mark's behavior and the family history, he was probably manic-depressive, possibly schizophrenic. They couldn't be positive so early, but manic depression was the tentative diagnosis. Manic depression, he continued, was a mood disorder, and Mark should immediately start on lithium.

I was speechless. I understood very little of what Dr. Lee said, except that a "mood disorder" smacked of something an overindulged socialite or pampered movie star might suffer from. It sounded like a vague phrase given to undisciplined behavior. A mood was a whim—controllable and trivial. Mood rings, "Mood Indigo," moody Monday, flashed through my mind. A bad mood was what you woke up with after the dog barked all night, and a good mood was how you felt when your tennis game was on. Moods were the stuff of advertising copy, not medical jargon. A mood surely could not lead to what happened to Mark.

Dr. Lee's conclusion confused me even more. "Compared to this, a drug problem would be a blessing."

Chapter 2

WHAT IS
MANIC DEPRESSION?

Naming the Disease

*T*he term *manic depression* answers a few questions about the disease but raises many more. It certainly says more than the nineteenth-century label *melancholia,* which encompassed dramatic mood changes, or the brand *madness,* also used to describe irrational shifts in behavior and temperament. Some medical professionals consider even manic depression to be imprecise and outdated.

The names for this disease have been in flux for decades, and the descriptions and diagnoses are riddled with permutations, exceptions, and atypical twists. Even doctors have different notions of what they mean, and the terms continue to be modified as more is learned about the disease. Today, the manic-depression umbrella is shared by "mood disorder," "affective disorder," "bipolar illness," and "bipolar affective disorder."

The language used to describe symptoms of manic depression is also inexact and often confusing, so we have tried here to clarify and simplify the jargon as much as possible. While we may not stick to a strict medical vocabulary, the information and concepts are as accurate as the subject will allow.

One reason the labels keep changing is that the disease is akin to a Hydra, the multiheaded monster from Greek mythology. Doctors have struggled since ancient times to define and more precisely identify the various forms of mania and depression, and it keeps revealing its multiple shapes. Like the Hydra that could not be slain because it could grow a new head and take on deviant forms, manic depression is a virulent disorder with many faces.

Just as the disease has many faces, so too do its victims. Diagnosticians constantly confront the complicated task of separating the disease from the so-called baseline personality, that is, distinguishing between symptoms of the illness and an individual's personal traits and quirks. Manic depression is not like measles, which looks more or less the same on everyone. Identifying each symptom has to take into account a person's normal personality and usual way of behaving. For instance, one of the characteristics of mania—excess activity—can be very different in an eighteen-year-old from someone in his forties.

The lives of many historical figures demonstrate how difficult it is to distinguish personality from illness. Anyone observing Isaac Newton, Vincent Van Gogh, Leo Tolstoy, John Keats, Ernest Hemingway, or Friedrich Nietzsche would have strained to differentiate their creative fervor from rampant mania or depression. (Chapter 10 has more on insanity and creativity.)

Another twist in the complicated process of separating personality from illness is that many psychiatrists first meet their patients after the illness has surfaced. They don't know the healthy individual and what he or she was like before the mental illness attacked. While doctors treating physical ailments are likely to know their patient before the fever, swelling, or whatever appears, doctors treating mental illness must rely on anecdotal information from family and friends to learn what someone was like before mania or depression grabbed hold.

Watch and Listen

Complicating diagnosis is the absence of exact diagnostic methods. No blood test or X ray can unequivocally demonstrate that someone is manic-depressive. Manic depression is diagnosed through observation by trained medical personnel and interviews with patients and families. Despite the numerous rating scales and interview protocols professionals use, diagnosis is ultimately a subjective process. What one doctor concludes is a primary bipolar disorder another may believe is a schizoaffective illness. ("Primary" means that the disorder predates any other illness a patient has, such as alcoholism.)

We could ignore these medical debates if they took place only in professional journals, medical schools, or the halls of the National

Institute of Mental Health. But they spread much further. Patients and families frequently encounter doctors and hospitals with different opinions or diagnoses, and widespread uncertainty about how the disease might progress. Every manic-depressive patient has unique qualities that complicate and cloud conclusions and predictions.

All this leads to a caveat: Few absolutes exist in the diagnosis and treatment of manic depression. Much of the information here is taken from research reported in medical journals and papers. Researchers are the first to acknowledge the limitations of their studies, and often are reluctant to draw conclusions. Frequently, their samplings are remarkably small, and their studies may be based on fewer than fifty patients. However, a number of large studies following hundreds of patients have been done, enabling doctors to get a flavor of the natural history of the disorder.

Manic depression is, at times, an amorphous disease, lacking solid boundaries and a clear shape. Not surprisingly, hard facts and convictions about it can be equally elusive. What follows is a survey of facts and findings as well as an amalgam of theories, ideas, and simply hunches.

So, what is manic depression?

What It Looks Like

To understand manic depression, we need to see where it fits in the larger realm of major mental illness. As the name indicates, manic depression comprises two markedly opposite behaviors. "Behavior" is only a half-right word, for manic depression is frequently described as a mood disorder. In professional nomenclature, doctors distinguish among disorders of thought, character, and mood (or affect). Schizophrenia is regarded as a thought disorder and characterized by persistent, bizarre thought patterns, such as delusions, hallucinations, and irrationality.

Manic depression has often been misdiagnosed as schizophrenia (especially in the United States) because these diseases share some symptoms, at least at first glance. Over time, however, the schizophrenic's disordered thoughts, hallucinations, and delusions are much more incapacitating and persistent than those in manic depression. Another form of mood disorder is "unipolar depression," which does not alternate with agitated manic states. The anxiety disorders, including agoraphobia and panic disorder, appear to be close relatives of mood disorders or may occur as a symptom of a mood disorder. The third category, character or personality disorders, refers to long-standing patterns of self-destructive behavior, which, in effect, become normal for a patient. Habitual criminals are thought to have a personality disorder.

Changes in Daily Patterns

A very noticeable characteristic of manic depression is a changed sleeping pattern. A person may sleep very little, not sleep for days, or sleep for ten or fifteen hours a day. Altered sleeping habits are so typical of the disorder that professionals often point to it as a cardinal sign of the beginning of a manic-depressive episode.

Eating habits are sometimes skewed too, with gorging, binges, a sudden commitment to vegetarianism, or near-starvation. In the same vein, a manic-depressive may drink excessively or suddenly begin to abuse drugs. Excessive activity is another feature of mania, and the typical examples are spending sprees, reckless driving, and foolish business investments. Sex drive is often heightened dramatically, and someone who has been faithful or chaste may exhaust his or her partner or become wildly promiscuous.

Telltale Moods

The label "mood or affective disorder" describes a disruption of a person's normal emotional states, such as happiness or sadness. The moods of manic depression include, at one end, sadness, passivity, lethargy, fatigue, and, as the extreme, delusions, hallucinations, and thoughts of suicide. The other extreme reveals elation, expansiveness, agitation, restlessness, excitement, irritability, grandiosity, hyperactivity, and again, when severe, delusions and hallucinations. These symptoms repeatedly sweep over the manic-depressive and dramatically alter his or her normal personality.

These moods can become all-consuming and produce bizarre behavior. Feelings of elation, exaggerated overconfidence, and grandiosity are often translated into boasting, unrealistically ambitious work plans, or lavish spending. A manic-depressive's racing thoughts are called "flight of ideas" and revealed through rapid, hard-to-understand speech (called "pressured speech"). The person may talk nonstop for hours, with words and sentences holding no order or logic. Ideas just tumble out. Puns and rhymes may dominate a person's speech.

Bizarre Behavior

The hyperactive manic-depressive may hit the telephone, calling old friends and relatives at all times of day or night, oblivious to expense or consideration for anyone on the other end. The manic moods may compel a person to dress differently, or more eccentrically, or be completely indifferent about clothing and personal care. Manics may turn into collectors, hoarding books, pictures, bottle caps—all sorts of items. The first couple of times, this erratic behavior may look like whim or even an endearing spontaneity, but over time it may become indistinguishable from a patient's personality.

It is not unusual for a manic-depressive to be fascinated by a certain piece of music or a particular musical instrument. Another strange symptom is hypergraphia, or an obsession with writing, with the person producing pages and pages of scribbling.

Delusions or hallucinations may emerge, although the manic-depressive might not tell anyone she is hearing voices or seeing religious figures, UFOs, or other sights. Delusions are thoughts or feelings sincerely felt that are simply untrue. These may be paranoid thoughts—a person may believe someone is trying to poison her or insist it is really another family member who is sick and needs hospitalization. Delusions can include grandiose beliefs; a person may think she has special skills or talents, or is related to a famous person. Mania may also encompass "ideas of reference." A manic might believe that she is the object of attention and whispers by friends and strangers, or that Dan Rather is sending her special messages during his newscast.

Although hallucinations may affect all senses, they usually are imagined sights or sounds. Auditory hallucinations are more common and may have a religious overtone, such as the voice of God or angels, and may sound like commands.

Recent research suggests that hallucinations can be considered almost a behavioral disorder as opposed to a thought disorder. Researchers studying schizophrenics who heard constant voices discovered the voices stopped when patients held their mouths open. After further tests, the doctors concluded that the voices, were, in fact, unconscious, subvocal speech by the patients. Patients were voicing their disordered thoughts. Yet even after doctors showed patients how to stop the voices by keeping their mouths open, the patients still believed the voices to be persons outside themselves.

Hallucinations and delusions appear to be more common features of mania when the first episode comes early in life, in the teens. As a result, adolescent manic-depressives are sometimes misdiagnosed as schizophrenic. This can have tragic consequences because mood-stabilizing treatment is delayed or not given at all.

Signs of Depression

Depressive symptoms include feelings of worthlessness, low self-esteem, and great sadness. A person's life may seem empty and point-less, and suicide attempts among manic-depressives are common. One study indicates that more than half of manic-depressive patients at-tempt suicide, although the "success" rate is closer to 15 percent.

Other symptoms include loss of interest in people, activities, and subjects that once were important. The person may also be physically slowed down—unable to get out of bed in the morning, go to work or school—or may simply sit and stare much of the day. In severe cases, delusions and hallucinations can also be a feature, but the content of the depressive episode is frightening, punitive, and self-destructive. Command hallucinations directing the patient to kill herself may occur. This so-called psychotic depression may be the most dangerous syn-drome in psychiatry.

While these symptoms are considered typical and almost universal, they and all others must be viewed in light of the individual and his pre-illness personality. For instance, what do these symptoms look like in someone who always seems to be racing around, or conversely, in a shy, quiet adolescent?

This was a critical issue for researchers who investigated affective disorders among the Old Order Amish in Lancaster, Pennsylvania. This remarkable study took six years and probed thousands of Amish med-ical and family histories to gather information about the causes, diag-noses, symptoms, and distribution of the illness. The Amish, a closed, agrarian society dedicated to a simple, nontechnological lifestyle cen-tered around religion, are an especially fertile source of such data because their records are very complete, drugs and alcohol are forbid-den, and any abnormal or antisocial behavior is likely to be recognized immediately.

In diagnosing manic depression among the Amish, researchers had to redefine symptoms to account for the group's unique culture and lifestyle. Thus, the usual examples of hyperactivity were adapted to the circumstances and the individual people, and were defined as racing one's horse and carriage too hard, buying or using forbidden worldly items, treating livestock too roughly, excessive use of the public telephone, or planning vacations during the planting season.

The whole question of what manic depression looks like suggests that it can be frozen in time, pinned down, and examined. But it can't. Like the Hydra, it has many heads and forms, and develops and changes through the course of a person's lifetime.

Whom It Strikes

Estimates of how many people are or will become manic-depressive fall somewhere around one percent of the general population, or two-and-one-half million people. If we take into account mild forms of bipolar illness, the number may near 10 percent. Add to these figures family and friends of people with manic depression, and you have many millions of people encountering some form of the disorder.

Manic depression usually strikes early in life. According to one doctor, one in three manic-depressives is hospitalized before age twenty-five, and at least one in five experiences an episode during adolescence. This doctor points to "a significant number of cases in the late teens," while acknowledging that other researchers fix the median age of onset at twenty-four years.

Professionals disagree about the gender split. One school of thought maintains that, unlike major depression, men and women suffer equally from manic depression (for depression, the split is 2:1, women to men). However, others have found that more women than men are being treated for it, raising the issue of whether they truly suffer more or are simply more apt to seek help.

Another quirk of the disease is that it seems to strike more frequently among educated, professional, and upper-middle-class groups than do other major mental disorders. However, this may be due to a "downward drift" of patients incapacitated by illnesses such as schizophrenia toward lower achievement levels. That is, manic-depressives, who have remissions and can work and study and earn, naturally seem to outachieve schizophrenics. So it's not a certainty that manic depression is an illness of overachievers.

The First Episode

Manic depression can begin gradually or dramatically. If the first episode is manic, it may develop over days, weeks, or months. A person's normal mood and behavior become erratic. The person may become hyperactive and irritable, with disjointed, rambling speech. In short, a person gets hyper—everything about him begins to race. Mania can last for days or weeks, and decreased sleep is a compounding feature. Once manic depression has started, an acute manic episode lasts on average two to nine months, although researchers point out that for some people this may stretch into years.

The behavior at onset obviously is different if the illness is weighted toward depression. This, too, may creep up on a person or be abrupt. A person may be depressed for weeks, even months, but not until he has also gone through a manic episode is the full disorder evident. To be considered "bipolar," a person must go through a manic episode. A number of people thought to have "simple" or unipolar depression become bipolar with a subsequent manic episode. Manic and depressive episodes that start suddenly also tend to end abruptly.

Triggering the Illness: Stress and Drugs

No one knows what exactly triggers the first episode, yet we can point to possible culprits. Bear in mind that what *triggers* an episode is not necessarily what *causes* the disease.

Personal stress connected with school, job, marriage, relationships, or money may play a role, although not as a single event or incident. An accumulation of life stresses, especially if they interfere with sleep, may be to blame. Stressful situations could include the birth of a child, moving or changing jobs, or coping with the long-term illness of a loved one.

The role of stress may vary depending on a person's age at his first episode. Researchers at Syracuse University studied forty-six bipolar patients and found that almost two thirds of the over-twenty patients had gone through serious stress, while less than one quarter of the under-twenty group had experienced stressful events.

Besides acting as a direct trigger, stress may also play a role in the onset of the disease by disrupting a person's normal sleep pattern. Researchers have discovered in experiments that depriving a person of sleep can induce a manic episode. As a result, they think that the psychological, interpersonal, and environmental pressures that seem to trigger mania do so because a person sleeps less when faced with these kinds of events. Once a pattern of insomnia has been created, the resulting mania becomes self-perpetuating. A cycle begins. While these conclusions are from a single study and not definitive, they point to a strong connection between stress, sleep, and mania.

Certain drugs are another suspected trigger. Doctors Harrison Pope and David Katz studied forty-one athletes who had used anabolic steroids and reported that clear affective or psychotic symptoms developed in about one third of these athletes. While pointing out that most of these athletes took doses ten to one hundred times higher than reported in other medical studies, and "stacked" or ingested different kinds of drugs on top of each other, the researchers concluded that "major psychiatric symptoms may be a common adverse effect" from steroids. Almost a quarter of the subjects developed either a full manic or full depressive syndrome. However, the doctors also noted that the psychotic symptoms disappeared when an athlete stopped taking steroids.

Researchers have also been making connections between cocaine and manic episodes. Doctors have known for years, certainly long before the crack epidemic of the 1980s, that cocaine can create symptoms and moods that resemble mania. Biologically, cocaine stimulates the "activating" brain neurotransmitters dopamine and norepinephrine, making a person hyperactive, restless, and euphoric, with racing thoughts. (Addicts may also unwittingly use the drug to self-medicate and reduce depression. More on this in Chapter 4.)

Recently, doctors at the National Institute of Mental Health have hypothesized that repeated use of cocaine may trigger or "kindle" a reaction in the brain and produce a seizure that leads to manic depression. They suggest that just as constant stress wears down a person's resistance and somehow trips a manic episode, so too could cocaine sensitize the brain to the point where an episode is ignited. The mania then becomes spontaneous. While the principles of the kindling theory are well-established and widely accepted, their application to cocaine use and manic depression is still hypothetical.

The Path of the Illness

Once the mania or depression begins, some patterns may come to light. For instance, there is often a seasonal ebb and flow, with mania predominantly in spring and fall and depression in winter. Just as likely, the pattern can be unpredictable. Most people experience many more episodes of depression than mania. Some experts put the ratio at nine to one. Unfortunately, it is impossible to predict the exact course of someone's episodes of depression or mania.

One of the first hopes of patients and families is that their particular case is the rare single episode. Single episodes of the bipolar disorder do occur, with some patients experiencing one go-round of mania and depression, then never again. A single episode happens in only about 10 percent of patients, although some experts believe that all patients experience a recurrence at various points during their lifetime and that the apparent single-episode patients are just not watched long enough. Since patients who stay well may be lost to medical follow-up, their number may be underestimated.

For most people, manic depression is a chronic, lifelong disease that can become more pronounced as they age. This seems to be especially true for people who experience the first episode after age forty. A manic-depressive typically goes through long cycles of remission and relapse. A person may be relatively symptom-free, with only mild mood swings for years, then for any number of reasons (say, the person goes off her medication), the cycle returns. Researchers have found that almost half of bipolar patients treated with lithium stop taking their medication at least once during their lives.

Regardless of a patient's drug regime, doctors believe the illness tends to accelerate over the years. As someone gets older, the ups and downs of mania and depression, especially if they were severe at the outset, come more often.

Although the path of the illness through a person's life is impossible to predict, doctors believe that its features at onset—severe, mild, more manic than depressive, more depressive than manic, regular, intermittent—will characterize it through the years.

But any simple declarative sentence about this disorder is almost impossible without exceptions and limitations. And so, there are some people who go through dramatic mood swings in the early years, then over time the illness quiets down, and no one knows why.

The *median* interval from the beginning of a first cycle of illness to the beginning of a second cycle is about four years. In practical terms, this means that the symptoms of each episode may persist for months or longer.

For people on both sides of the midpoint, their first episode may not be a steady succession of extreme moods. This illness cannot be charted with a symmetrical wavy line that predictably dips into depression and rises into mania. Even in the course of a day, a person may appear lucid for minutes to hours and then abruptly break into psychosis.

Researchers have found that there is often a long lull between first and second episodes, a time that may last for years and is called the "latency period." However, as the disease progresses or develops, episodes may arise more frequently and last longer.

Varieties of the Illness

The moods and behavior can be so bizarre that they are far removed from the moods of healthy people. Even today, with flamboyant cultures and peculiar lifetyles stretching our ideas of what's acceptable, manic depression is conspicuous and, to a trained professional, glaring. While the manic-depressive may blend into a college dormitory during finals or the floor of a trading exchange, the camouflage will be only temporary. The disease is obvious before long.

Yet diagnosing and understanding manic depression becomes tricky, especially for family and friends close to it, because moods often overlap, and periods of bizarre behavior may vanish.

The term "bipolar disorder" deceives, because the mania and depression do not occur in even opposition. It is not like the North Pole and the South Pole; instead, it more closely resembles two points on the equator. They're side by side, sharing a border and overlapping. Some people are both manic and depressed at the same time.

Mixed Mania

Overlapping moods are called "mixed mania" or "mixed states." In this condition, a person may be hyperactive, talkative, and sleepless, while feeling deeply depressed and unhappy with himself. Some medical experts believe that most manic episodes have a flavor of underlying depression. Nevertheless, a nonprofessional trying to decide whether someone is manic-depressive can be thrown off by the apparent absence of distinct bipolar behavior. It may be there but not clearly visible.

Mixed mania strikes about half the people diagnosed as manic-depressive. Thus, mixed mania can be an inherent part of the disorder.

Mixed mania not only perplexes doctors and hospitals because of a patient's abnormal behavior, but also can confuse family or friends seeing it for the first time. Trying to understand someone in the throes of mixed mania is like trying to pick up a drop of mercury. It defies containment. To the nonprofessional, mixed mania may elude identification—a person's moods can be so jumbled that the sickness is hard to identify.

Rapid Cycling

For some, the disease moves quickly back and forth between mania and depression. Doctors call this condition "rapid cycling." Rapid cyclers go through four or more episodes a year, with mania and depression following on the heels of each other and no relief between episodes. This cycle can be as regular as clockwork.

Doctors have learned that rapid cycling is often aggravated by antidepressant drugs. Thus, attempts to relieve the suffering of a depressed patient may worsen the illness. Very rapidly cycling bipolar disorder is also more likely to resist lithium treatment.

Bipolar I & Bipolar II

The disorder we have been discussing is called "bipolar I," the classic form of manic depression. Another version of the disorder is "bipolar II," which encompasses people who feel similar mood swings but with a less pronounced mania called "hypomania." Experts consider bipolar II the stepchild of affective disorders, because it is not quite manic depression and not quite major depression. This milder form is otherwise very similar to classic manic depression in terms of course, treatment regime, and family patterns.

From an observer's viewpoint, someone caught in bipolar II may go through deep, debilitating depression, but the mania is muted, and none of the manic symptoms last long or prevent a person from functioning in daily life. In fact, the hypomanic episodes may energize a person's work or social life. Nevertheless, while some of the symptoms may be short-lived or less pronounced, bipolar II can be a very serious disorder. According to researchers, people with the bipolar II disorder are more likely to attempt suicide, more likely to have multiple episodes, and more likely to be hospitalized than people suffering from major depression.

Unipolar Depression

Manic depression—bipolar illness—is sometimes confused with major depression, clinically known as "unipolar depression." Though everyone at some time feels depressed, sad, or helpless, a person diagnosed with clinical major depression may be hospitalized, have great difficulty functioning at work or socially, and can be suicidal. It's a serious, life-threatening illness.

While depression and manic depression are both affective illnesses, their names announce the difference between them. Yet names are deceptive because unipolar depression isn't simply one half of manic depression. It's a whole different animal. Differences include when the disorders first appear in a person, the symptoms, treatment, family incidence, and lifetime course. Depression in someone who is manic-depressive may not be so identifiable.

One reason for the confusion between bipolar and unipolar may be because the latter is much more prevalent. Major depression, experts estimate, affects ten times more people than manic depression. Major depression tends to strike twice as many women as men.

Depression generally invades a person slowly and over months, even years. Its onset usually isn't sudden or abrupt. Children have been diagnosed with major depression and it appears in people of all ages. Unlike manic depression, it doesn't tend to cluster in late adolescence.

Another striking feature distinguishing depression from manic depression is that in its milder forms, it's much more treatable. To treat depression, doctors prescribe antidepressant medication, sometimes use electroconvulsive therapy, and usually recommend psychotherapy. Drugs like lithium and neuroleptics that are given to manic-depressives are not normally applied to depression as primary treatment.

Cyclothymia

Another, less grievous form of manic depression is cyclothymia. In terms of severity, this disorder is one notch down from bipolar II. Some experts argue that cyclothymia has more in common with personality disorders than with mood disorders. Basically, the cyclothymic patient goes through repeated episodes of depression and hyperactivity, and while these hurt social functioning, they do not usually lead to hospitalization.

A person suffering from cyclothymia can be thought of as the walking wounded. While the exaggerated moods may not be intense or long, the illness can bring about a string of unhappy and painful crises although a person may continue to function (albeit marginally) at work and home. Someone with this disorder may be moody, irritable, antisocial, unstable, impulsive, and volatile. The cyclothymic sometimes abuses drugs or alcohol. He may have marital problems or be promiscuous; start projects or jobs that he never finishes; change jobs or homes constantly; argue loudly, then feel very contrite; swing between feeling inferior and feeling grandiose and superior; or go on spending sprees.

To be diagnosed as cyclothymic, a person must have gone through episodes of mildly manic and depressed moods for at least two years. Another feature is that it often appears in a person's childhood or teen years.

The underlying mood in cyclothymia seems to be depression, and many of its victims progress to more marked depression and a bipolar II diagnosis. Others may live their entire lives without medical attention or treatment, and are simply known as very moody people who can't hold down a job, drink excessively, and go through many marriages or romances. In short, they barely cope or cope miserably.

The Catchall Category: Schizoaffective

Imagine a line—thin at one end and thick at the other—representing major mental illness with affective disorders at the thin end and schizophrenia at the thick end, where the symptoms are most powerful, more incapacitating. In the middle is bipolar I, primary manic depression. On the thin half are bipolar II and cyclothymia. On the other side, the thicker, more pronounced half, is another form of the illness, "schizoaffective." As its name implies, schizoaffective has something in common with both affective disorders and schizophrenia. It is a controversial category because doctors disagree over where it fits on the spectrum and argue that it may not be a genuine, distinct disorder but simply a catchall for people who do not fit into the other two categories.

Schizoaffective symptoms are a motley collection of the bipolar symptoms of depression and mania plus the schizophrenic signs of disordered thinking. The psychiatrist's handbook, *Diagnostic and Statistical Manual of Mental Disorders—III-R*, defines it as a ". . . category for conditions that do not meet the criteria for either schizophrenia or a mood disorder, but that at one time have presented with both a schizophrenic and a mood disturbance and, at another time, with psychotic symptoms but without mood symptoms."

The disordered thoughts usually entail hallucinations (sights or sounds), delusions, and paranoia. While a manic-depressive also may have hallucinations or delusions, the content of these sights, sounds, and thoughts in the schizoaffective may be at odds with his prevailing mood. The person may feel euphoric and hyperactive, but the hallucinations may consist of taunting, frightening voices or disturbing visions, such as ominous spaceships. When the hallucinations and delusions do not match a person's underlying mood, they are called "mood incongruent" and, some doctors believe, more a symptom of schizophrenia than an affective disorder. If a manic-depressive's symptoms are "mood congruent," the mood matches the nature of the hallucinations. For example, a person will feel euphoric and see Jesus walking behind him. Most ominously, the schizoaffective patient's disturbed thinking may persist beyond an episode of altered mood, and so ravage daily living.

It is not uncommon for a doctor to diagnose someone as schizoaffective, especially if the person is hearing voices, feeling paranoid, and showing signs of mania or depression, then alter the finding after studying the patient. Certain telltale signs—responsiveness to lithium treatment, family history of affective disorder or schizophrenia, how long symptoms last, the presence or absence of a full remission of symptoms—often push a diagnosis toward bipolar or schizophrenia.

For a patient or family, a diagnosis of schizoaffective disorder is useful in describing someone's symptoms, but only time reveals the true nature of the illness and the best way to treat it.

Making a Diagnosis

One of the first steps in diagnosing someone behaving strangely is to identify and exclude possible physiological explanations. It is essential that doctors interview the patient and family about previous injuries and run tests that may reveal unknown causes. For instance, doctors have found links between strokes and subsequent depression and between head trauma and mania.

Numerous physical conditions or diseases may produce symptoms similar to phases of manic depression. These include some hormonal or metabolic disorders, epilepsy, other neurologic illness, infectious diseases, syphilis, tumors, systemic lupus erythematosus, blood diseases, and metal intoxications. Drugs can set off mania or depression, especially corticosteroids, antidepressants, and bronchodilators, as well as drugs of abuse, such as amphetamines and cocaine. Doctors use computerized tomography and magnetic-resonance scans, electroencephalograms, blood and urine screens, and thyroid-function tests to pinpoint organic causes.

The Psychiatrists' Bible
Since the early 1950s, psychiatrists have relied on the *Diagnostic and Statistical Manual of Mental Disorders* (DSM) as the handbook for identifying various forms of mental illnesses. Over the years, this volume has been updated to include new findings. Nevertheless, its system of

categorization and diagnosis had always been dependent on subjective judgments and personal interpretations. That was until 1980, when the American Psychiatric Association published *Diagnostic and Statistical Manual of Mental Disorders—III* (*DSM-III*).

The *DSM-III* set forth for the first time relatively precise definitions and diagnostic criteria for all the major mental disorders, including manic depression. Diagnosis and nomenclature became even clearer in 1987, when the APA revised *DSM-III*. Today, *DSM-III-R* is truly the bible of the psychiatric profession and is likely to grace the bookshelves of most mental-health professionals.

This book outlines specific, identifiable criteria or symptoms for dozens of classes of psychiatric disorders. Perhaps most important is that it has helped to establish consistent diagnoses among psychiatrists across the country and eliminated much of the subjectivity in the diagnostic process.

In *DSM-III-R*, manic depression falls under the mood-disorders section. To make a diagnosis of manic depression or bipolar disorder, readers are instructed that one or more manic episodes must be apparent. What follows here are the diagnostic criteria from *DSM-III-R* for each of these features and the codes or scale used to denote severity.[*]

Manic Episode

A. A distinct period of abnormally and persistently elevated, expansive, or irritable mood.
B. During the period of mood disturbance, at least three of the following symptoms have persisted (four if the mood is only irritable) and have been present to a significant degree.

1. inflated self-esteem or grandiosity.
2. decreased need for sleep, e.g., feels rested after only three hours of sleep.
3. more talkative than usual or pressure to keep talking.
4. flight of ideas or subjective experience that thoughts are racing.
5. distractibility, i.e., attention too easily drawn to unimportant or irrelevant external stimuli.

[*] By permission, *Diagnostic and Statistical Manual of Mental Disorders Third Edition-Revised*, Washington, D.C.: American Psychiatric Association, 1987.

6. increase in goal-directed activity (either socially, at work or school, or sexually) or psychomotor agitation.

7. excessive involvement in pleasurable activities which have a high potential for painful consequences, e.g., the person engages in unrestrained buying sprees, sexual indiscretions, or foolish business investments.

C. Mood disturbance sufficiently severe to cause marked impairment in occupational functioning or in usual social activities or in relationships with others, or to necessitate hospitalization to prevent harm to self or others.

D. At no time during the disturbance have there been delusions or hallucinations for as long as two weeks in the absence of prominent mood symptoms (i.e., before the mood symptoms developed or after they have remitted).

E. Not superimposed on schizophrenia, schizophreniform disorder, delusional disorder or psychotic disorder (not otherwise specified).

F. It cannot be established that an organic factor initiated and maintained the disturbance. Note: somatic antidepressant treatment (e.g., drugs, electroconvulsive therapy) that apparently precipitates a mood disturbance should not be considered an etiologic organic factor.

Manic Episode Codes

1. Mild: meets minimum symptom criteria for manic episode (or almost meets symptom criteria if there has been a previous manic episode).

2. Moderate: extreme increase in activity or impairment in judgment.

3. Severe without Psychotic Features: almost continual supervision required in order to prevent physical harm to self or others.

4. With Psychotic Features: delusions, hallucinations or catatonic symptoms. If possible, specify whether the psychotic features are "mood congruent" or "mood incongruent."

5. In Partial Remission: full criteria were previously, but are not currently met; some signs or symptoms of the disturbance have persisted.

6. In Full Remission: full criteria were previously met, but there have been no significant signs or symptoms of the disturbance for at least six months.

Major Depressive Episode

A. At least five of the following symptoms have been present during the same two-week period and represent a change from previous functioning; at least one of the symptoms is either (1) depressed mood, or (2) loss of interest or pleasure. (Do not include symptoms that are clearly due to a physical condition, mood-incongruent delusions or hallucinations, incoherence, or marked loosening of associations.)

1. depressed mood (or can be irritable mood in children and adolescents) most of the day, nearly every day, as indicated either by subjective account or observation by others.

2. markedly diminished interest or pleasure in all, or almost all, activities most of the day, nearly every day (as indicated either by subjective account or observation by others of apathy most of the time).

3. significant weight loss or weight gain when not dieting (e.g., more than 5 percent of body weight in a month), or decrease or increase in appetite nearly every day (in children, consider failure to make expected weight gains).

4. insomnia or hypersomnia nearly every day.

5. psychomotor agitation or retardation nearly every day (observable by others, not merely subjective feelings of restlessness or being slowed down).

6. fatigue or loss of energy nearly every day.

7. feelings of worthlessness or excessive or inappropriate guilt (which may be delusional) nearly every day (not merely self-reproach or guilt about being sick).

8. diminished ability to think or concentrate or indecisiveness, nearly every day (either by subjective account or as observed by others).

9. recurrent thoughts of death (not just fear of dying), recurrent

suicidal ideation without a specific plan, or a suicide attempt or a specific plan for committing suicide.

B. It cannot be established that an organic factor initiated and maintained the disturbance. The disturbance is not a normal reaction to the death of a loved one.
C. At no time during the disturbances have there been delusions or hallucinations for as long as two weeks in the absence of prominent mood symptoms (i.e., before the mood symptoms developed or after they have remitted).
D. Not superimposed on schizophrenia, schizophreniform disorder, delusional disorder or psychotic order (not otherwise specified).

Major Depressive Episode Codes

1. Mild: few, if any symptoms in excess of those required to make the diagnosis, and symptoms result in only minor impairment in occupational functioning or in usual social activities or relationships with others.

2. Moderate: symptoms or functional impairment between "mild" and "severe."

3. Severe without Psychotic Features: several symptoms in excess of those required to make the diagnosis and symptoms markedly interfere with occupational functioning or with usual social activities or relationships with others.

4. With Psychotic Features: delusions or hallucinations. If possible specify whether the psychotic features are mood-congruent or mood-incongruent.

5. In Partial Remission: intermediate between "In Full Remission" and "Mild" and no previous dysthymia (low-grade depression).

6. In Full Remission: during the past six months no significant signs or symptoms of the disturbance.

Scales and Interviews
While doctors may consult *DSM-III-R* first, they also use other scales or criteria for evaluating symptoms, making a diagnosis, or mapping out a course of treatment. Over the years, individual doctors or teams of

doctors have developed sets of criteria to help them assess and diagnose patient behavior. A diagnostic scale generally rates the severity of a patient's illness and is often named after the researcher or physician most prominent in its creation. There are dozens of these scales and interview criteria, and they vary according to who does the assessing (doctors, trained personnel, nurses, patients, or families), what exactly they measure, and whether they are for diagnosis or other purposes, namely research or treatment.

The big drawback with these scales and criteria is the subjective nature of the information-gathering process, the conclusions and the judgments. In short, their real-world reliability. So, doctors and researchers are constantly tinkering with them, adding nuances of detail while trying to keep them relatively simple and convenient to administer.

The Family History

An essential part of a diagnosis is interviewing family members not only about the patient's moods and behavior but also about the illnesses of immediate relatives. A standard interview tool is the Family History Research Diagnostic Criteria.

Spouses or parents are often a better source of facts than the patient, who may be in a manic or depressed state, or in remission and denying the illness. Manic-depressive patients are also notorious for their lack of insight into their own behavior, at least while they're ill. Despite intellect, education, or tangible evidence, they may not perceive their behavior as unusual.

Affective disorders run in families and through generations, and while some relatives may have been diagnosed and treated, others may seem relatively healthy but show subtle signs of illnesses. The family interview goes far beyond normal family medical records, and looks into the lives of grandparents, aunts and uncles, siblings, and the family milieu, including noteworthy events, socioeconomic status, and emotional atmosphere.

Questions for the Family. Family members should expect to answer a range of questions about themselves and the patient. Here are the kinds of questions they may encounter:

- Describe the patient's life and habits over the past six months, especially any possibly stressful events.

- Are there any special problem areas in a patient's life—for instance, repeated trouble at school, at work, or in a marriage? What is the nature of these problems (e.g., argumentative, overly aggressive, inability to concentrate or inattentiveness, infidelity)?
- When and how did you first notice a change in behavior or actions?
- Has the patient been involved in an accident or been sick recently? Is the patient on any medication? Any combinations of medications?
- Did the patient complain of any side effects to medications?
- Any history of drug or alcohol abuse?
- Any suicide attempts by the patient or suspicious accidents?
- Any relatives (grandparents, parents, children, siblings, aunts, uncles) with a history of psychiatric difficulties?
- Any relatives who are alcoholics or suspected alcoholics?
- Any history of suicide in the family?

Charting Home Life

Interviews with family members provide clues to how a person will respond to treatment and adjust to home life after hospitalization. One such interview is the Camberwell Family Interview, which measures the emotional atmosphere between a patient and key relatives just prior to a manic-depressive episode. It consists of a one-and-one-half-hour meeting with a patient's parent or spouse, and details the beginning and course of the current psychotic episode, and explores its impact on the family in the months prior to hospitalization.

The interview is taped, and responses to questions about a patient are assessed by doctors and researchers in terms of their level of emotional involvement and attitudes, and the number of critical and supportive statements made about a patient. Researchers believe that the emotional atmosphere in a family influence a patient's response to treatment and the course of the illness.

Researchers at the National Institute of Mental Health suggest that manic-depressive patients and their families help doctors prepare a chronological chart of key events and episodes. This chart indicates when manic and depressive episodes occur, the length of the episodes, and surrounding noteworthy experiences, such as changing jobs, moving, marital separation, or a painful anniversary. The result is a timeline that helps doctors gauge the progress of treatment and highlights connections between manic-depressive episodes and critical life events. The chart may also signal the onset of coming episodes so that doctors can intervene and prescribe medication appropriately.

These scales and interviews all suggest that identifying manic depression can be reduced to neat pigeonholing: Match the symptoms to an item in the scales, and up pops a diagnosis and treatment regime. But in dealing with someone who has a serious mental illness, especially in a crisis admission or medical confrontation, the diagnosis at first may well be muddy and messy.

A Collection of Causes

The causes of manic depression are a tangle of heredity, biology, and environment. Complicating the search is the belief that manic depression has more than one cause and that there are varieties of manic depression, each with a separate set of causes—in medical jargon, the disorder is "heterogeneous."

Researchers have been focusing on defective genes, brain-wave activity, and brain chemistry as the main culprits. Scientists have not yet positively identified specific biological actions or sites, but they have strong suspicions. While their findings don't offer complete answers, they do suggest certain insights that make sense. The information here is not conclusive, but it does represent the current thinking of active researchers.

For certain, we know that manic depression runs in families and through generations, and so probably has genetic origins. While suffering families have been telling doctors this for years, this fact has just recently been substantiated scientifically in a number of studies.

Another certainty is that relatives of manic-depressives have a much greater chance of also having an affective illness. For a relative of an affectively ill patient, the risk of being manic or depressive ranges, studies conclude, from 15 percent to 35 percent. The risk of manic depression alone, not counting unipolar depression, is 5 to 10 percent. (Remember, the risk or incidence in the general population is around 1 percent). Other researchers think the risk is even higher for female relatives. Scientists continue to explore exactly which genetic material contains the codes or mechanisms that may cause or affect the course of affective disorders.

Brain chemistry is another realm for researchers. It's an exciting area because discoveries can lead directly to effective drug treatments. Among the brain chemicals (called neurotransmitters), the primary suspects are norepinephrine (also called noradrenaline), dopamine, serotonin, and acetylcholine.

Hormones, which circulate through the blood to various glands and organs, are also suspects. Yet individual hormones don't circulate alone but in a system of closed loops, with levels being adjusted and regulated by other hormones and ultimately, brain chemicals. So, theories about one hormone must include other hormones. Also, some hormones share cells with certain neurotransmitters, and both send signals over the same fibers; their actions may be closely intertwined. It is an intricate, complicated process, and science is just beginning to understand it.

A person's emotional life is another field in the search for causes of manic depression. A person's chemistry and biology interact with his life course; nature and nurture are tangled up, distinguishable but probably inseparable.

Declares the eminent researcher and psychiatrist Nancy Andreasen, in *The Broken Brain*: "Some people appear to have more natural resilience to recovering from personal disappointment than others do. An inherited lack of emotional resilience may be the predisposing factor— the necessary but not sufficient cause—in the development of affective disorders. This resilience could be programmed in the brain in its neurotransmitter systems, such as the norepinephrine and serotonin systems."

Despite all the medical, chemical, and statistical research, the causes of manic depression remain a mystery. Until someone comes up with a neat blood test, patients, families, and their healers are at the mercy of interpreting what they see.

However, as you will read in Chapter 4, treating manic depression is not a mystery. Doctors have discovered a pharmacopoeia of medication and an array of talking therapies to quell the main symptoms as well as the psychological reverberations of the illness.

Chapter 3

MAGICAL THINKING

December

"Could you tell me where Mark Wakefield's room is?" I asked the nurse bending over charts at the desk.

"Room Two-twenty-two down the hall. He's still asleep. They used restraints on him last night and sedated him," she replied offhandedly, without looking up from her papers.

The ward had the lingering bacon scent of breakfast. I knocked timidly, then pushed the heavy door. Mark was curled under a sheet, his clothes scattered around the room. He was breathing slowly and still as death. I sat and quietly watched his face. Tears ran unchecked down my cheeks.

Where from here? Was I crying for myself or Mark? His precipitous fall from Normal College Kid to Mental Patient in four days left me adrift with confusion and doubt as to what was real and what wasn't. Was all my confidence about myself as accomplished wife and mother just illusion? Dr. Lee had been very clinical in his diagnosis, and had offered nothing about what my problems were to be. Maybe they were too gruesome, I speculated, maybe he didn't want to give me both barrels until I had adjusted to the idea of mental illness.

I felt a perverse vindication at the negative drug tests. The stigma of being the parent of a child with a drug problem was substantial. It was tangible evidence of parental failure, discipline not carried out, care not given, diligence not exercised. But any relief I felt at being acquitted of the drug charge was quickly replaced by fears for what I had before me now. I had to know more.

I left Mark sleeping and headed for the Stanford Bookstore for a medical text. Bookstores always soothed me, with their shelves of pristine volumes waiting for the first reader. I found the psychiatry section. Although I had majored in social sciences in college, I had assiduously avoided psychology and sociology, dismissing them as organized common sense. I wasn't going to waste my time on something I could figure out on my own.

I considered myself fortunate that I never needed to consult a psychiatrist. I had lots of stereotypes—goateed doctors smoking pipes, listening to patients stretched out on black leather couches in dimly lit offices—and little respect for the profession. I chose the fattest book with the most recent publication date and a long glossary. The jargon at the hospital had been so confusing. The doctors crammed a person's entire psyche into catchphrases and psychiatric shorthand. Know the language, know the land, I told myself. The hefty text was comforting. I was doing something besides crying, regaining some degree of control, imposing order on chaos.

"You had a call from Connecticut while you were out," announced my mother. "Phyllis something. She was returning your call."

I had called Phyllis last night to cancel our Wednesday tennis game. But I wanted to talk to her too. I had remembered a casual conversation one summer afternoon over a year ago. We had just finished a couple sets of tennis and were lingering over a soda before running out to finish dull errands. I had known her for some time, but knew nothing about her troubles with her youngest son.

"He's manic-depressive," she divulged. I didn't know exactly what that meant, but didn't want to make her explain. Sharing her family troubles was difficult, but something made her open up that day. "We have been through three suicide attempts with him. I have mentally planned his funeral many times to prepare myself." I was horrified and surprised. The deep wounds didn't appear on her calm exterior except for a lingering sadness in her eyes. I could think of nothing to say, feeling as one does when an intimate detail of someone else is revealed. I mentally looked away.

She was silent on the other end of the telephone after I briefly recounted the weekend. "You are in for a real roller coaster, and the worst is still to come," she declared softly but bluntly. "You are not going to be able to lick this yourself," Phyllis continued.

"I've got another doctor coming to see Mark in the hospital for a second opinion. Perhaps they missed the diagnosis."

"Diane, do you know what magical thinking is?" she asked in gentle tones.

I could guess, but didn't really *know*. "No, not really."

"It's denial, it's Pay No Attention, It'll Go Away. It's quack cures, it's the fast fix. It'll be your biggest obstacle to fighting this disease," she said. "I know, because I refined it to a fine art with John. It's insidious, comforting, and easy. Beware."

I considered her words. But I certainly wasn't denying Mark's problems. Wasn't I educating myself and consulting specialists? We ended our conversation with words women use to console each other. I was to call her when I returned to Connecticut. I didn't know if I would or not. Her bald truths left me with a sense of dread.

That evening I trekked back to the hospital, hoping Mark would be awake. I'd bought him a gift to make his face light up with the joy of possession and gratitude for my being so thoughtful.

He was dressed but still curled up on his bed, staring at the wall. I put my package on the bed and sat in the only chair.

"Why have you put me in here?" he asked in a flat, colorless voice. His eyes did not stray from the wall.

"Mark, you were out of control. We're trying to help you." My response rang hollow. "What are the greatest lies of all time? I'll love you in the morning . . . the check is in the mail . . . I'm from the IRS and here to help you." That was how I sounded. Contrived, untrue, false. I had no answers and no faith that this place could help Mark. Yet I had nothing else to offer.

"I brought you a warm-up. It'll be just the thing to wear here." The words were out before I could swallow them back. What an inane thing to say. This wasn't camp. This wasn't something one dressed for. Magical thinking? I shoved the idea aside. My carefully crafted Visit-to-the-Hospital brightness evaporated.

"Take it away. I don't want anything from you. Get me out of here. I—want—to—go—back—to—school." The last said through clenched teeth under dark, glowering eyes fiercely boring into me.

"I'll see you tomorrow." I hesitated in the doorway. "Mark, I love you. I want you well, I want you happy again, I want all this to go away too. Believe me." I still hesitated. "I'll be back first thing tomorrow morning. I have an appointment with Dr. Lee." A thick pane of glass separated us, and my words fell soundlessly to the floor. He remained impassive on the bed staring at the wall. The visit was over.

MARK

Drugsdrugsdrugsdrugsdrugsdrugsdrugsdrugsdrugsdrugs. In their eyes. Eyeseyeseyeseyeseyes. I can see it. Where'd you get them? What'd you take? Uppers, downers, sideways? What do you smoke? Put anything up your nose? Do you use needles? Ever swallow Black Beauties, White Crosses, Purple Hearts? Even granddad. He said he understood. He said everything was going to be Okay. I'mnotgonnacry, I'mnotgonnacry, I'mnotgonnacry.

We've got to show them, Mark. Show them we're clean. "Excuse me . . ." I hold out my cigarette for the duty nurse. She smiles automatically. Nothing to do with me.

"Thanks. You must get tired of being the keeper of the flame." Smile back. Be cheerful. She didn't expect that. No one here smiles or talks. Just babblebabble or crying all night.

"It's no trouble," she says. She's remembering to put a note on my chart. Someone yells at the TV, and she writes it down. Her mind is so simple. I can read it like a postcard.

Smile. Head up. Don't shuffle. Walk with a purpose. Pick up that dirty Kleenex, Mark. Drop-kerplop in the wastebasket. Gross. Straighten those playing cards. Neat piles.

You gotta get out of here, Mark. Back to Boulder. She's watching. Sit up straight. Smile. Show her you don't belong. THE SHOW MUST GO ON.

Seven clubs, four clubs, jack of spades, and my angel, my guardian, QUEEN OF DIAMONDS. A gem, a jewel, what a fool. I know why she's here. It's a message. It's time. I must get back to Boulder. Time to begin my quest. Memememe. I'm the one. Chosen, frozen, a quest for only the best.

Empty your ashtray, Mark. Keep things tidy. Smile at the cow with the keys and matches.

Young Nixon's starting again. What a nose. I'm sure he catches it on his sweater. Someone's going to get pissed. PISSED OFF, PISSED PISSED PISSED. Zingzingzingzing. Roger ZING ZANGED his coffee cup at him this morning but no good. He stares at ONE AND ALL.

What do you think, Mark? Can we make this guy twitch, make him itch? We'll show him the power of a real B-R-A-I-N. My eyes are boring into him like lasers. He's made of glass. I'll make him turn, make him squirm. Don't let go, Mark. Boreboreboreborebore. AH HA, GOTCHA! You crazy bugger, that'll teach you.

Smile at Nurse Ratched.

In gardening, weeds often spring up after the soil has been tilled. Turning over long-undisturbed dirt buries the natural grasses and flowers, and brings forth dormant, noxious weeds. The weeds flourish—unwanted, unbidden—and squeeze out the carefully cultivated plants. Mark's condition brought forth feelings and thoughts I had forgotten. Things buried deep.

It was 1966, and I was in a room full of officers' wives at Reese Air Force Base in Texas. Chris had just started flight training, and the pilots' wives were being introduced to their husbands' commanding officer. We were all ridiculously young, most of us recently married and pregnant with our first children. We were still wearing our wedding trousseaux and getting up after our husbands were asleep to roll our hair on bristle rollers.

Vietnam was heating up, and we knew that our husbands were headed there—if they were lucky. Only those who finished far down in the class standings were assigned to the safer and less exciting tankers, bombers, and transports. The aerial bus drivers would never see real action. We sat in the darkened room in proper dresses, some with gloves, and listened to the major.

"During your husband's flight training, it is important that he leave the house in the morning with a complete breakfast and, *most important* [this with a dramatic pause], nothing to distract his attention from flying. He will be maneuvering high-performance aircraft that will require all of his concentration. It is your job to see that he is able to do his best. That means no domestic distractions, no fights, no late hours with a crying baby. The consequences of losing a second's concentration in these aircraft *can be fatal.* We don't want any pilot-error accidents."

We shifted uncomfortably. He didn't say it, but every wife in that stuffy room balancing a coffee cup clumsily on her lap knew that what he really meant was not "pilot-error accidents" but "wife-error accidents." We were very clear on the message in the message. Mark's condition made me remember wife error. Had I committed mother error? Had my attention and devotion to my son lapsed? Should I have spent more time with him? Disciplined him more, disciplined him less?

Dr. Lee was a staff psychiatrist for the hospital. Mark had been admitted during his watch, so we were his charges. His office on the ward was whatever small, windowless room was available. Airless and cramped, these rooms were furnished with a metal desk, the ubiquitous plastic chairs, and a hard, unforgiving overhead light. No papers on the desk, not even back issues of *Today's Health*.

Dr. Lee was Chinese, and spoke heavily accented English that, although understandable, was missing random prepositions and articles. His almost exclusive use of the present tense gave an odd timelessness to his medical remarks, and his limitations with descriptive English left his observations without context and color. He was a small man with heavy glasses, and wore the same dirt-brown suit and yellow shirt of the day before.

"Mark most probably have manic-depressive disorder," he began without preface. "I start him on lithium right away. He need to see a doctor immediately when he go back to school. The lithium levels in his blood have to be monitored constantly. I feel he not cooperate if we keep him here past three day. Some patients only have one episode. Maybe Mark one." He paused and studied me momentarily, his eyes enlarged by the thick correction in his glasses. I felt like Exhibit A in the Case of Mark Wakefield.

"Can I give you something?" he asked suddenly.

I was reluctant to barrage this doctor with a catalog of questions. "Pushy, domineering mother," he would think. "No wonder this child is in the psychiatric ward." All of my carefully developed patient-as-a-consumer questions vanished in a wave of self-doubt. Do I voice my opinion and take the chance that my child may suffer subtle retaliation, or keep quiet? I uncrossed my arms and shifted in my chair. Body language—psychology was the study of nonverbal meanings. He was probably taking mental mother-error notes for Mark's file.

"I beg your pardon?"

"Pills, sleeping pills. You look tired."

"No, no, of course not," I said. I must have looked as ragged as I felt. *But, yes, Doctor, you can give me something. Give me what you know, what you see for Mark, what your hunches and training tell you. Pretend you can be candid and give me what I really need, information.*

"Are you saying that Mark is to be released tomorrow to go back to school?" I asked, incredulous. "He doesn't seem in any shape to go back to school."

"Mark say that all he want to do is go back to classes. Biggest problem with manic-depressives not diagnosis but their cooperation. If he not cooperate, then no help, no improvement. I talk with Mark and he say he understand. He be discharge tomorrow. You pick up his records when he leave and take them to next doctor." He made a motion to rise.

"Dr. Lee, wait, please. I don't understand what I'm dealing with here. What is the prognosis for Mark? What should we be doing? Can he handle school?"

I took a breath and blurted out, "What about schizophrenia?" PBS had just aired an hour on schizophrenia. Patients humming tunelessly in corners, nodding their heads, families emotionally and financially devastated by the incurable illness. A living nightmare.

"Can't really say now. Always a possibility but maybe fifteen-percent chance. Have to wait to see." He stood up. "I meet with you and Mark tomorrow before he leave. Ten o'clock." He nodded politely, looked covertly at the clock over my shoulder, and headed for the nurses' station in short, rapid steps, Mark's chart under his arm.

"The doctor says I get out tomorrow," Mark said. We were sitting at the large table in the common area of the ward. "You can't keep me here. I want to go back to school."

I eyed him carefully. He looked better. His hair was wet from a morning shower, and he had put on the clean things I brought him. The lines of anger in his face had softened, but his eyes were still flinty and cold. He studied my face intently. I held the keys to this place.

"Dr. Lee feels you should be released tomorrow. I'll book a flight for first thing Friday morning for you. In the meantime, I'll find you a doctor at Boulder to monitor the lithium levels." I rattled on about the mechanics of his departure and medicines. His eyes wandered over my shoulder to the television behind me. "I'll pick you up tomorrow morning. We can go to lunch after." Mark walked me to the door as I was leaving. I leaned over to give him a hug. He stood impassively, arms slack at his sides, and said he would be ready in the morning.

MARK

Dr. Lee wants to Talk. WE'RE OFF TO SEE THE WIZARD, THE WONDER-
FUL WIZARD OF OZ. I know what: Test results! The truth is out! The
American Dream is restored. THE GENIUS is no dopehead. HEZ JUST SO
FUCKING CREATIVE NO ONE CAN FOLLOW HIM.

My file is in front of him: Thisisyourlife. Some life. Dr. Lee looks like a
bug-eyed fly.

"Your drug-screening tests are all negative, Mark." He pauses. Maybe he's
waiting for me to applaud. Forget it, you cretin. I can READ your mind too.

"So can I go?" Give him the God's Eye. That'll make him let go.

"It's not a good idea, Mark. You are sick. From my preliminary diagnosis,
I think you are manic-depressive."

Manic depression? Manic? DEPRESSION? He's saying I'm CRAZY. A label.
A white, sticky label. Looney. Wacko. Mad. I-N-S-A-N-E.

How can this be? Fly-eyes only talked to me twenty minutes. Questions
about sleeping. He shoulda asked about my dreams. It's not right. How can I be
crazy? I've been chosen. I'm going on a quest.

The rest of the day was spent on the telephone to Boulder. Bob
King, the attorney in Boulder for Mark's pending felony charge, gave
me some names. The doctors I could reach had no room in their
schedules, and the rest had officious recordings. "If this is Tuesday, I'll
be at the hospital" sorts of things. Finally, a doctor called back and
agreed to accept Mark as a patient. I made a Monday morning appointment for him with a Dr. Klein. There was no screening process, no
evaluation of academic credentials. I was desperate to find anyone to
get Mark started on some sort of treatment.

I was at the medical-records office in the hospital the next morning
at nine o'clock, and wasn't due to meet with Mark and Dr. Lee for an
hour. I filled out the request forms, paid the copying charge, and
waited for my name to be called. Taking Mark's file to the cafeteria next
door, I sat with a cup of coffee to hopefully get more information than
my abortive session with Dr. Lee had produced.

There was a page and a half of single-spaced typed material. Descriptions of Mark physically and the doctor's impressions from his
interviews with him. My son was vivisected on the page. I came to a

paragraph about Mark's sexual fixation about his mother and stopped reading. This was keyhole peeping, opening mail, going through secret drawers. I couldn't read on. I also couldn't believe Mark would unburden himself to this strange, uncommunicative man. How had he unearthed this information? I closed the file and finished my coffee.

To be mentally ill is to have no secrets, no hidden self, no self separate and private from the eyes of others. It is to be constantly under glass, every move scrutinized and studied and evaluated. How many of us could stand up to such scrutiny? I felt guilty and remorseful for having put Mark in this place where one's very soul is dissected and written about.

Our discharge meeting with Dr. Lee was in another of the Spartan rooms that passed for offices at the hospital. This one was larger and featured a vinyl sofa against the far wall. Mark and Dr. Lee were waiting when I arrived. Mark sat at the far end of the sofa, arms crossed on his chest, a burning cigarette dangling loosely from his fingers. The overhead fluorescent light cast a cold, bluish light on his face, accentuating the pallor and shadows beneath his half-opened eyes.

"Mark understand about his lithium," Dr. Lee began without introduction as I pulled a chair around. "He need to see another doctor as soon as possible to check blood levels." I told him about the doctor in Colorado, and he nodded vigorously. "Good, good," he muttered.

"Is that all right with you, Mark? You understand all this?" I turned to him. He was as rigid as the plastic furniture.

"Yeah, I guess so," he answered impassively.

The first thing Mark said after we left the hospital was, "I want to go to Oak Knoll." Oak Knoll was Mark's grammar school in Menlo Park. He hadn't been there in years.

When he was four and too young for school, he hung on the fence, longingly watching the children play. We lived next door, and the teacher would regularly call me to take Mark and his black Labrador home. Now, he found his old spot and paused, watching. Almost immediately a woman rushed out of the classroom door over to him. She looked alarmed, and motioned for him to leave. Mark, eyes downcast, came back to the car.

"That was Miss Knight, my kindergarten teacher. She didn't recognize me. She told me to leave or she would call the police," he said quietly. I could hear the pain behind his words. Miss Knight had been Mark's favorite teacher. "I only wanted to see my old room," he added wistfully.

"I know," I said. I couldn't tell him that he looked ominous and threatening, a strange man lurking around the schoolyard.

That afternoon we went to the supermarket together. Mark wandered off as I picked over the pineapples. Hearing a loud banging, I turned to find Mark rhythmically slamming the carts together, oblivious to the stacked displays nearby. His face was set in the grimace I remembered from the hospital. I dropped my produce and guided him out of the store. He didn't resist. A hand-wringing store manager had materialized, and gave us a worried look as we bustled out the door.

"Mark, why? What were you doing back there?" I asked him. He shrugged.

Mark's flight out of San Francisco was at 8:00 A.M.

"Mark, this duffel, what have you in it?" I lifted the dead weight into the trunk. I was suspicious of everything about him.

"Some books of mine I found," he replied, opening the top to show me. I could see children's picture books crammed inside. He must have brought them back from the beach. A few were old ones Mark and Robert had owned, but most belonged to Kate's three-year-old children. I said nothing.

I pulled up to the United terminal, and Mark got out and grabbed his bag from the trunk. "I'll call you. Don't come in. I'll be fine," he said. A flash of the old Mark. He strode toward the automatic door with his distinctive long-stepped, bouncy walk. I could always identify him in a crowd by his determined gait. I watched his blond head bob above a roiling sea of morning passengers as he disappeared into the terminal. I was memorizing the departing sight of him, I realized with a jolt. I wanted to freeze his image within me to keep him close.

I could no longer hold back my misery. The wire I had managed to keep taut all week sprung loose, and choking sobs consumed me. I felt that I would never see him again. He seemed so fragile, so vulnerable, so utterly alone. For the hundredth time I asked myself if I was doing the right thing. Should I have found him another doctor and another hospital here, or taken him back to Connecticut with me?

This Mark was so different from the eager teenager we had packed off to college. The last time I saw the healthy Mark, what psychiatrists call the "baseline personality," was in Boulder about a month after his classes had started.

Colorado in early fall vibrates with golden aspen against royal-blue skies, the air warm with a hint of snow to come. Mark met us at the coffee shop of the off-campus hotel. The lobby was full of middle-aged football fans in gray-and-gold Buffalo baseball hats.

"My bike is outside. You just have to see the rest of it." Mark gave me a hug as he sat down and reached over to pick the last french fry off my plate.

"It's great to have you here. There's so much I want to show you. Isn't it a beautiful day? You'll have to meet my friends." He was tan, the ends of his blond hair bleached white, wearing shorts and a miner-style long-sleeved shirt. His legs were muscled from miles of bicycling.

We stopped first at his room, a subground-level with a view of passing feet. The room had a cell-like quality typical of college dormitories, and the beds were neatly made. I smiled inwardly. His room at home had never been so tidy.

Mark then led us around the central quadrangle through the lengthening shadows of afternoon. The faint sounds of a band practicing on a nearby field drifted over us. Students hurried by, girls smiling hello to Mark. "That was So-and-so," he would say to my questioning look. "She's in my writing class."

After the campus tour, Chris and Mark stopped in Stella's delicatessen on the Hill to stock up on groceries to munch while studying. They came out laughing and ripping into the chips even before crossing the street. I glanced over my shoulder at the bags. "Not an honest calorie in there," I remarked to Mark, who grinned back. We decided to have dinner extra early so Mark could get a jump on the evening's studying. Chinese was the unanimous choice.

"Did you know these restaurants come from do-it-yourself kits?" Mark quizzed us as we sat down. "A friend told me that you can order an entire restaurant from Hong Kong: menus, pictures for the walls, matches, everything. That's why these places all look alike. He said they even take the shipping crates and make counters out of them." We surveyed the pagoda-tasseled lights and the black framed plastic jade trees around us. Mark loved Chinese food. Just a whiff of sesame oil in the house was guaranteed to bring him to the kitchen.

Chris ordered for the three of us; his Southeast Asia time had earned him the lifelong privilege of being the designated Oriental-food orderer. Mark expertly dug into the Mu Shu pork with his chopsticks, his left-handedness showing in his inverted fingering.

"They never give you enough plum sauce," he groused as he rolled the first pancake around the pork mixture. "I don't know what I'm going to major in yet. I really like my anthro class. Lots of *National Geographic*–type stuff. You'd really like it, Mom." He chatted and ate with equal enthusiasm. "I'm thinking of going through rush. Robert, Dad, Grandad—everyone in the family has belonged to a fraternity," he reminded me. "Can't be too bad an idea. I'm not sure though."

"I've got a lot of work to do tonight. I can't study in the dorm, so I have to go to the library. If I don't get there early, all the good spots will be gone."

"You go ahead. We'll finish our coffee and pay the bill." I gave him a hug. "We won't see you tomorrow. Our flight is early." He put his hand out to Chris, who started to shake it good-bye and then changed his mind and embraced him. I watched Mark grab a handful of mints from the bowl by the door and stuff them in his pocket as he breezed out.

That was the last time I saw my Mark.

I flew home to Connecticut, and over the next two months Mark called only twice. He refused to get a telephone, said he didn't need to talk to anyone, so we depended on his calls to us. They were disjointed conversations, with him flying from subject to subject and finishing before I could convince him to come home for Christmas. I had mailed tickets to Bob King to give to Mark at their weekly appointment. Bob had become a surrogate parent for Mark, at three hundred dollars an hour, I thought wryly. Mark's last call was to inform us he was spending Christmas in Vail with a friend. I pleaded with him to come home, but he was unmovable. "I can't come home," he declared without elaboration.

MARK

Listen! You hear that, Mark? SHE'S HERE! OUTSIDE THE DOOR! Hear the brain waves! LISTEN! Any second now she'll walk in. I just KNOOOOOW it.

We're ready. yup. Cashisinthestash, we'regonnahaveabash. Magic in Mexico. I didn't need those things. Skis, grandfather's watch, bike, boots. Wish I had more, is $355 enough? Do angels need money?

LISTEN!

Nothing. She went away. Maybe it's not time. Turn on the radio, Mark. She may be sending a message. Like yesterday through Iron Butterfly. I'm tired of waiting. Soooo tired. They said, she said a quest. A mission with an angel. She trained to become an angel. They said I'm a latecomer. I need to go to Mexico. To gain powers.

NOT FAIR! I'M READY, I'M READY.

Aaaagggh . . . OH YES! I HEAR YOU! I DO love you. Idoldoldo. I can prove it. Gimme a chance. Please, please, please. I can I can, oh man, I can!

Quick, Mark. She's in pain. We MUST do something. Out the door. Down the stairs. Nighttime. Blackness. Cold. Now WHAT??? SNOW! Yes, the snow. Make her pain yours. Bury yourself. In the dirty white cold. Take the pain. In your HEAD! Your BRAIN is STRONG. Coldsting. Stingstingsting. Don't move. It's her pain.

My sacrifice for yoooooooooooooou.

"He's legally an adult," Chris coldly pointed out. "There will be many holidays when he will be somewhere else. You had better get used to the idea now." I nodded silently and went upstairs to take a shower.

I set the faucets for my second shower of the day. The shower had become the perfect place to cry unobserved. I could let the misery and tears flow, all evidence of self-indulgence washed away. The sounds of weeping lost in the noise of the splashing spray against the curtain and tile.

I went through the motions of putting up decorations and shopping for the boys. Mark's presents were wrapped under the tree beside Robert's. Their stuffed stockings were tucked into a closet for Christmas morning.

He's going to come walking in the door anytime now, or he'll call from the airport with his Here-I-am voice. Then we'll all have a coming-home feast, laugh around the table after a wonderful meal and settle in with a funny movie on the VCR. Mark will look back with wonder at his tough first college semester—like a bad dream, he'll say—and then we will talk of next summer together in Idaho and set the date for vacation. He and Robert will stay up late laughing and playing gin rummy in front of the embers of a dying fire, the lights from the Christmas tree creating elongated squares slanting away from the mullioned windows on the fresh snow. Chris and I will hear their laughter from upstairs in bed and snuggle closer under the blankets, cat purring on our feet. That was my fantasy.

*   *   *

"This is a really harebrained idea," Chris muttered as we pulled from the driveway in a cloud of fine, blowing snow. The Christmas garlands I had wrapped around the lightposts in front of the house were coming untwisted in the wind, and the snow fence angled away from the drifts. "You couldn't have picked a worse day to go to New York. I would much rather sit and read by the fire. Hell, I would rather shovel snow than drive a hundred twenty-five miles to New York to see some musical I don't even care about."

"When I bought these tickets six months ago, they didn't say I could return them if the weather was bad," I snapped. This was supposed to be our day in the city with the boys for shopping, lunch, matinee. I had four tickets to *Starlight Express*, but Robert was immobilized in his knee brace and Mark had not come home.

We edged our way to Rockefeller Center to view the lit-up Christmas tree. The holiday crowd pressed against us, and we turned toward Fifth Avenue and an early lunch before the matinee.

"Lady, quarter for coffee?" I cast a glance sideways. An unshaven man of indeterminate age with a greasy shawl wrapped around his head and gloves without fingers stretched his hand toward me. Our eyes met for a millisecond. His had a wild, crafty look, the look I had seen in Mark at the hospital. The troll under the bridge. I turned away and pushed Chris ahead of me into the sidewalk melee. I was still shaking when we found a small northern Italian restaurant.

"You look like you've seen a ghost," Chris remarked casually as we sat down. "At least we can have a good lunch. I like this place." He scanned the rough brick wall with a large fruit-and-cheese display against it, and the Saturday crowd of out-of-town shoppers. Maybe his mood will lift with a good lunch, my mother's old trick.

"I want Mark to find a job if he won't be in school next semester. When will we know whether he'll be suspended or not?" Chris asked over anchovies and peppers.

"The disciplinary committee will decide after he appears in court next month. Bob King says he'll probably be suspended but will be able to go back later. He can stay in that apartment off campus until we know what's going to happen." Chris and I hadn't talked much about Mark. Our conversation always ended with a fight over our different points of view. So I kept Mark to myself.

"What about that doctor he's seeing? I can't see where lying on some quack's couch talking about how your dog died when you were six is of any use. It's a waste of money." He reached for another piece of bread.

"From what I've read, Mark's illness is chemical. That's why he's on lithium. There are different options from the doctors and researchers," I reported quietly, trying to keep my voice from the other diners.

"As I see it, Mark has a behavior problem, and the doctors are dressing it up to make a buck. Call it a disease and they can charge people like you to treat it. What a racket." He sounded authoritative and factual, but he knew even less than I.

"Chris, this is not just a 'behavior problem,' and I resent your implying that I've been duped by a bunch of charlatans. Granted, there's a lot of talking therapy out there that is totally useless and simply adult thumb-sucking. But manic depression isn't something you treat by merely sitting up straight and flying right." I mingled my sarcasm with anger not only at Chris's ignorance but also at his shoving me into a corner to defend the psychiatric profession.

"If this is just a chemical problem, what's he need Dr. Klein for? Why doesn't he do like the addicts in Britain, and line up at a clinic for his weekly dose of methadone or lithium or whatever? You can't have it both ways, Diane. It's either chemistry or psychiatry."

Chris paused while the waiter set down two platters of white-clam-sauce spaghetti. I was grateful for the small break. Chris made eminent sense, and I needed to marshal my thoughts.

"No, it isn't 'either/or,'" I declared. "Mental illness is not a black-and-white disease. It's all grays. Mark needs both. His personal chemistry needs regulating, and he needs therapy. Jesus Christ, Chris, he's going through hell—roughed up by the police, thrown in jail, committed to a psychiatric hospital, probably kicked out of school. Don't you think his mental health—his self-image, his confidence—could use a little support? Professional support, from experts who know how this disease affects people, especially kids." That little speech felt good and true.

A sad look came over Chris's face. "Maybe that's what parents are supposed to do," he began. "Maybe if we had taken more time . . . moved less, or just asked him how he felt about all those new schools. . . ." His voice trailed off. He twirled the spaghetti, his eyes unfocused as if watching an internal movie of the years of missed opportunities passing before him.

"I know, I know," I said helplessly. "Don't you think I've relived all the times I wasn't home? And replayed all the conversations I didn't have time for? I remember one afternoon in Spokane, after school, when out of the blue he asked me who my best friend was, and did I keep in touch with high school friends. I think I quipped that I only had time for family, then dashed off to a tennis game." I forced a bite of pasta into my mouth to halt my teary choking.

"We just assumed he would adjust. He always seemed to do okay. I guess he wasn't as adaptable as we thought." Chris pulled away from the self-recrimination. "But that doesn't mean a shrink can do the job."

"We're dealing with lots of unknowns here. I don't know what the doctors can do, but we have no choice. Anyway, it may be an academic point. Dr. Klein says Mark has been missing his appointments." I didn't add that we were charged for missed appointments.

"What are you going to do about that?" he demanded. Mother error, again. He had put down his fork and was looking intently at me.

"What can I do? Mark is in Colorado and not calling us." I pushed my food around my plate, appetite gone.

"Look," he whispered, leaning across the table. "I love you, but I cannot sit here and lie to you to make you feel better. Mark is out of control."

"I don't see why you can't just tell me everything is going to be all right. It's not against the rules to give comfort with less than the full truth. I don't understand why you take such a cold and uncompromising position. Your standards of truth wouldn't be compromised by words of love and understanding. You make me feel that it's my fault." I reluctantly added, "I hurt so much." I was pleading now, and felt tears ready to gush. It was just as well we were in a restaurant and not at home. This would have been a three-shower fight. I took a deep breath and held it.

"I'm out of it. You do what you want. I won't object. The thing that makes me so mad is that Mark is ruining my life with you. I have a hard time forgiving him for that. I just don't believe this illness stuff. It's sloppy, fuzzy thinking. Shrinks have created a whole industry by codifying human misery and offering expensive cures." We finished lunch in silence.

Starlight Express, a roller-skating fantasy with an elaborate track looping around the audience, couldn't have been a worse choice. The leering carnival faces of the skaters, the loud music, the noisy crowd of Christmas matinee-goers, made for a long afternoon. Chris sat stoically through the production. No comments, no complaints. When we finally got home, he took his book and went to read in bed, and I escaped into the shower.

MARK

"Has Will been around? Large black." She's ignoring my question. She doesn't like us taking up a booth all night. She thinks we're queers. Bums. She coughs every time we light up. Maybe if I bought a chocolate cream doughnut. Fuck it. He'll be here.

By the window. That's our view. Our classroom.

THERE HE IS! Gray hair. Lines on his face. He walks like a professor.

"Hey, Alex, had your dinner yet? What'll it be: Lemon creme or maple nut? Personally, I'm leaning toward something healthy tonight. Fruits. Blackberry, cherry, strawberry."

I like Will's smile. He sees me. After he slides in across the table, he props up his feet next to me. He likes me. Should I tell him I'm really Mark? Better wait.

"I've been thinking about what you said last night. About planetary paths and interstellar trajectories and how they affect different cultures and countries. Like in Scandinavia, how their attitudes about themselves and their environment—you know, their liberal approach to survival—is affected by their position on the globe, and really, in the universe."

Will's listening real close. I can tell because he stirs his coffee one circle each way, back and forth, back and forth, until I'm finished. I'm saying something new. Stuff he hasn't heard before. He's here to train me for my destiny. To explain everything the voices can't.

"Certainly planetary positions help to interpret the different schools of philosophical thought. Existentialism, behaviorism, nihilism. Calvinism too. You going to finish that doughnut? I'm really bummed out tonight. I lost the key to my apartment. Ten bucks. Stinking landlady wants ten bucks for another one."

Will stares out the window.

"You can stay with me. I got lots of room. I mean, a mattress on the floor, but it's real comfortable. And a cat, a kitten really. She's real smart. This sounds crazy, but I think she understands me, like sort of telepathy. I mean, she's

always at the door when I come home, like she knows I'll be there right at that
moment. And when I feed her, I know exactly what parts of her food she likes
best and if it's too cold for her. But sometimes she plays mind games with me.
Tries to stare me down. Really pisses me off. I might get rid of her."

"Yeah, well. You got any cigarettes?" Will's still looking out the window. He
sees things nobody else does.

Mark never came home for Christmas. Our holiday was bittersweet, with Chris, Robert, and me pretending it was normal. I often
stood in the window watching the driveway, trying to will Mark's
familiar form walking up to the house. I would freeze when the telephone rang, and constantly glimpsed the back of his head disappearing around street corners or in stores. I was on the verge of calling
the police to report him missing when he called three days after
Christmas.

"Things are great," he said. "I'm working for the Park Service in a
volunteer job up in the mountains. They train us and everything." No,
he hadn't called over Christmas because his friend's parents' telephone
hadn't been working. Lots of snow in the high passes. Had a great time
skiing. No, he wasn't going to see Dr. Klein anymore. He didn't feel he
needed it. His court date was set for January 28. He was going to look
for a job.

"I feel terrific, Mom. I need some money to get me through the
week." Here it is at last, the reason for the call. Almost immediately, I
felt guilty for the cynical reaction and agreed to send fifty dollars
through Bob King. His apartment was in a seedy part of town, and I
didn't trust the mail there. A financial short leash, at this point, was my
only guarantee of regular contact, and it was better than nothing. I
didn't tell Chris about the financial punch line of the conversation. His
cynicism would swallow me whole.

Phyllis called and insisted we meet at Loehmann's before our tennis
game. "It'll give us some inspiration to work off those Christmas cal-
ories."

I hesitated. I didn't want to reject the offer of friendship, but Phyllis
reminded me of my troubles with Mark. Phyllis was already in the Back
Room trying on things with beads and bits of fur when I arrived in
Norwalk.

"The tennis shoes make the outfit," I remarked as I came up behind her. She had taken off her warm-up but not bothered with the leather tennis shoes and high socks.

The Back Room was full of the usual mix of Westport Junior Leaguers, older women escaping retired husbands who want company for lunch, and welfare mothers. We pawed the dress racks, fingered the fabrics, and tried to read the cut-out labels.

"So how goes it?" she inquired neutrally, studying a dress to find the front.

"You have to try it on. Can never tell by looking," I told her. "Actually, fine. Things are going fine." Not raising her bent head, she rolled her eyes at me.

"Really fine, or just sort of fine?"

"Sort of fine. Mark goes to court in a week. He has stopped seeing his doctor. You know, they may have missed this diagnosis completely. He really sounded upbeat when I talked to him."

"John used to lie to us all the time. We believed him at first, but his stories always had small inconsistencies he couldn't explain. He'd get times wrong or forget what he had said before. I refused to believe he was lying until the evidence was overwhelming," she volunteered.

"Mark has never lied to us. I have a hard time not believing him. He has always placed such a premium on being truthful."

"Look," she said, putting the dress back and turning around to face me. "I can't know what Mark's situation is, but you need to be aware of the possibilities here. The doctors never tell you. Nothing would make me happier than to have everything I have said be unneeded and wrong. But I care about you, and should your situation be *anything* like mine, you need some preparation. Some armor. These problems just don't go away. They submerge only to resurface again, larger and more fierce."

"I don't know what the truth of anything is anymore," I sighed.

"How's Chris taking all this? Husbands are usually the last to understand these kinds of problems. It took Bill literally years. I know you must feel that you have to choose between husband and child, but hang tough. The good ones come around. Just takes time. Don't crowd him, he'll catch on soon enough."

She held up another dress. "Is this thing too much like wallpaper?"

I studied the cabbage roses and nodded. "My mother has a sofa like that. Anyway, I don't have much choice these days. Without Mark at hand, there is very little I can do. Hopefully, I can convince him to come home where we can get him some help. He's too big to physically drag back."

We meandered out to the main room. "It's not my day here. Let's grab a sandwich before tennis." We exchanged our tokens for our coats and left.

I had been putting a great deal of energy into not looking too closely at Mark. My textbook sat unopened on the shelf. I couldn't bring myself to read about symptoms because I saw in Mark everything from a mild personality disorder to paranoid schizophrenia. I had caught the faint scent of something burning and managed to convince myself that it was my imagination.

I hadn't heard from him in ten days. He didn't have much money and had not kept his appointments with Bob. Next time he calls, I resolved, I would do everything to convince him to come back to Connecticut. His court appearance was in three days, and after that there was no reason for him to stay in Colorado. He had been suspended from school for a year and was living month-to-month in a fleabag apartment.

The next morning I had a nine o'clock doctor's appointment for a checkup.

"You have a heart murmur. Probably prolapsed mitral valve. Very common and nothing to worry about. Everything else seems fine." Heart trouble? The irony made me smile.

"So what is it really? You look like you're not sleeping well."

"It's Mark." I gave Dr. Davis the miniseries version of Mark's story, and he listened without comment. I could feel my throat thickening, tears pushing at the dike. I hated this teary, self-pitying person I was becoming. My problems hung out like a ripped skirt lining. I wished I could disguise my misery better.

"Psychiatry is not my area at all. I can give you some names of people I know, but not much else. How about you? Have you considered seeing someone for yourself?" he asked with quiet kindness.

I had thought about making an appointment for an office visit with a therapist and even inquired anonymously about a doctor recommended by Phyllis. But I discarded the idea. My problem wasn't me, it was my son. Give me Mark back in one piece and I'll be fine. I had settled on talking long distance to my sisters Lisa and Kate almost daily, throwing the I Ching, reading May Sarton and Christopher Lloyd, and playing lots of tennis.

The idea of sharing this saga with a stranger revolted me.

"I have thought about it, but I see treating *my* problems with this as a luxury."

The red light on the answering machine was flashing when I returned home around lunchtime.

"Well, here I am," Mark announced on the machine. His voice was faraway and thin, almost ephemeral. "I'm just checking in," he said with a sigh. "I'll call back later. Bye." Gone before I could grab him, an electronic impulse on a wire. The machine paused and beeped for another message.

"Diane, this is your father. I'm going to need that partnership tax return soon. How are you doing on it? Give me a call at the office." Click.

The house was cold. I hadn't bothered to turn the heat past sixty. Snow was starting to fall again. I went to the cupboard and dug out the *I Ching* Kate had sent me.

I stood midway between my sisters on the emotional spectrum. Kate, six years younger than I, was what the rest of us described as "touchy-feely." She possessed an intellectual conviction of the existence of the unseen universe, the world beyond normal senses. Lisa, on the other hand, was here and now. No funny business for her. If you could see and touch it, it was real. Otherwise, sorry, no. I vacillated between them. Mark's situation was nudging me toward Kate and, sensing the readiness of a convert before the font, she had mailed me her favorite touchstone, the *I Ching*.

I intended to politely thank her and push it into the bookcase, but I came across it one white night at the terrible 3:00 A.M. hour. The apparently random passage that I had pulled out was so uncanny that I continually found myself drawn to the book. The *I Ching* is a book of sixty-four passages on universal subjects. Through a random toss of coins, one or two are selected. The passages are the distillation of thousands of years of Chinese philosophy and common sense. They create order out of chaos, sanity out of madness.

I drew Number 12: Stagnation. It read: "You may be adrift in a sea of misunderstandings and miscommunications. Hold courageously and unobtrusively to your values and inner confidence, for these times will certainly pass. This is true in matters of health as well. Self-reliance will see you through." Curious comfort from an odd source. My mother would claim that church offered the same thing, but organized religion never worked for me.

For over ten years in California, I had had a tax-preparation business. When we moved, I sold it. While I missed the tidiness of the numbers work, jousting with the IRS, and the independence of my own income, I did not miss the stress and pandemonium of tax season. In those days, I usually completed more than five hundred returns between January and April. Now, I was having difficulty getting one measly family-partnership return completed.

Mark didn't call again that evening, and with Chris gone, I had let things slip. The laundry piled up, the floors were full of footprints from the pets, and the walks unshoveled. I found some cookies in the cupboard and called it dinner.

I dug out my graph paper, garden books, catalogs, and plotted, for the fifth time, my herb garden and flower beds for the spring. It seemed like such a hopeful thing to do. Gardening had become the only way I could manage the chaos around me, the only nature I could control. I would get so immersed that I would be momentarily disappointed when I saw the bleak winter landscape out the window.

I was just sliding into sleep when the telephone rang.

"I think I want to come home," Mark began without a hello. I sat up in bed, and with shaking hands fumbled for the light. His voice was flat and without emotion.

"I'll Federal Express tickets to Bob King tomorrow." With deliberate slowness, I added, "I think that is the right thing to do, Mark. Back here, we can help you get back on track."

He paused. Had I leapt too fast at the chance of getting him home? "Okay. Could you send money too? I'm broke."

"Yes, yes. Of course. Mark, I love you. I want you home." I silently cursed the impulse that made me add the last remark. Had I frightened him off?

"I have to go now. I'm outside in a phone booth, it's cold here. I'll go by Bob's office tomorrow afternoon. Bye." Click. Gone.

Relief washed over me. Mark home, where I could take care of him. I put on my robe and went downstairs, pausing at the window on the stair landing to look at the full moon illuminating the snowy landscape, the apple-tree skeletons casting long shadows across the path to the garage.

I wondered if Mark could see this same moon from his phone booth. I found the *I Ching* and tossed the coins. Number 52 came up. "Meditation, keeping still . . . hold your thoughts to the present and attempt an unprejudiced view of the situation." Good advice.

I began the next morning with an energy I hadn't had in a long time, and set about finding a doctor for Mark. Phyllis's doctor couldn't take any new patients but gave me a name. In scavenger-hunt fashion, I tracked down a psychiatrist who would consider talking to me about Mark. As with the doctor in Colorado, I grabbed whoever I could find. For all I knew, he had a mail-order degree, but I was desperate. Mark was due to arrive in two days.

Dr. Anderson's office was in an old house in Torrington. In his early thirties, he wore a drip-dry shirt and baggy suit. The psychiatry business didn't appear to be flourishing.

He listened without comment to my tale. I could hear my voice galloping over the events of the past few months with an assurance I didn't feel. When I reached the substance of Mark's last phone call and finished, he made no immediate motion to respond. Maybe, I thought sarcastically, this is a medical-school technique they teach psychiatrists to extract all possible information from relatives.

He was earning an A in eye contact. What was he thinking? That this mother certainly messed up her child and she wants me to make it right? Still no comment. He hadn't so much as blinked.

"Well," I said as neutrally as I could manage, "what do you think? Will you take Mark for a patient?"

"Yes, I will," was his careful response. "I charge one hundred dollars per hour and will charge for missed appointments. I can see him next week." He took a small calendar out of his pocket and consulted his schedule. "Friday at two. Your son, not you, will be my patient, and our communications will be privileged. I bill monthly." He rose from his chair. The interview was finished.

He showed me to the door without further comment. No Mr. Small Talk here. I stifled my negative reaction. This was for Mark. My feelings were irrelevant.

Chapter 4

DRUGS AND OTHER ANTIDOTES

A Chemical Revolution

The modern era of drug therapy for mental illness is relatively young. Not too many years ago, mental illness was treated like a physical ailment. The symptoms were patched and soothed with ointments and preparations, and everyone hoped the disease disappeared. In the 1940s, the three most common treatments for mental illness were convulsive therapy, fever therapy and prolonged-sleep treatment. And if these remedies didn't work, there was always prefrontal leucotomy—surgery to remove part of the brain's white matter suspected of causing psychotic behavior.

We can pinpoint exactly when modern times began for drug therapy: September 3, 1949. On this day, an Australian psychiatrist named John Cade published the surprising results of his experiments with lithium salts among his manic-depressive patients. Lithium was the beginning, and while the United States vacillated for twenty years before embracing lithium treatment, the medical establishment plunged into the development of other types of psychiatric drugs.

Today, doctors have a pharmacopeia of medicines to fight, calm, and curb mental illness. For manic depression, lithium remains the mainstay among a very few drugs aimed solely at both poles of this disease. Yet families of other drug attack facets of bipolar illness, subduing the mania, relieving the depression, or dispelling the psychosis.

These drug families are antipsychotics (also called major tranquilizers or neuroleptics), antidepressants, anticonvulsants, and antianxiety drugs.

Drugs, while usually the first and best line of defense against mental illness, are not the only weapon. Some remedies from the past, especially convulsive or "shock" therapy, still help certain types of patients. While our pharmaceutical armaments have become increasingly sophisticated and diversified, we have not totally abandoned other approaches. Drugs are not a panacea. They have truly opened Pandora's box, for drug treatment has a price. In exchange for the wonders of chemical modification, patients risk serious, sometimes frightening, and occasionally devastating side effects.

Patients often feel that their medications, while quelling psychosis or lifting depression, make them a different person. They say they're less energetic, more quiet, less spontaneous, and physically uncomfortable, and often suffer from constant thirst, nausea, or blurred vision. Yet these drugs enable them to hold jobs, manage money, and keep family relationships intact.

Side effects quickly become complicated and confusing. They are frequently indistinguishable from symptoms of the illness, so they're elusive targets. Then there is the power of self-fulfilling prophecy—how much of a patient's discomfort is the result of knowing a certain drug slows thinking? Furthermore, many manic-depressives take two or three drugs that interact with each other and can produce unexpected feelings. Treatments for side effects can cause other side effects, and so unearthing the original source is a twisting, looping search.

Psychiatric drugs are so potent that doctors watch their side effects as closely as they do their curative powers. Harsh side effects not only make a patient uncomfortable, but may compel someone to stop treatment.

Patients stop taking medication for lots of reasons, often very good ones. At times, side effects become unbearable, especially if a patient is feeling relatively healthy. A remission in a manic or depressive episode can easily persuade a patient that lithium isn't worth the constant thirst, the extra twenty pounds, and the hand tremor that never goes away.

Emotional reasons also reinforce some patients' refusal of drug therapy. Drug treatment brings a bitter, sad truth. "To patients, taking medication is a daily reminder that they are chronically mentally ill, that they might become psychotic again, and that life is nowhere near what they or their families hoped for or expected," concludes psychiatrist Ronald Diamond.

Stopping medication is very common among manic-depressives. Doctors report that one third to one half their patients, at some time, stop drug therapy. A patient who feels better because of drug treatment may stop the medication, suffer a relapse weeks or months later, end up in the hospital and again begin taking medication. It's a vicious cycle for thousands of patients.

Which Drug?

Within the various families of drugs (except for lithium, which is in a class of its own) doctors have numerous choices. Deciding exactly which drug to prescribe can be a combination of applying a formal medical protocol, clinical experience, trial and error, and personal observations about an individual patient.

One of the first goals of drug therapy, and for which there are reams of studies and data from pharmaceutical manufacturers, is controlling the symptoms of the illness. Drugs do not cure manic depression, they simply relieve its symptoms. For the fortunate, drug use can deliver a lifelong remission. For the unfortunate, the symptoms will return, regardless of which medication they're on.

Sometimes manic depression is life-threatening. Upward of 15 percent of manic-depressive patients commit suicide. Doctors have to be careful in prescribing medication for two reasons: If their patient is suicidal, they need a medication that will quickly ease this symptom, and they need to monitor the patient in case he tries to overdose on the drug. So the prescribing physician works up a "safety profile" that suggests certain types of drugs for a certain type of patient.

In recommending a specific drug, doctors weigh the characteristics of what they call the "index episode." One of these is the patient's predominant symptom, be it mania, depression, or psychosis. Next, doctors try to assess the individual's metabolism and rate of drug absorption in the blood, age when symptoms hit, other complicating illnesses, and any family history of mental illness.

Then it's wait and see. Despite all the science, studies, and laboratory data, doctors have learned that frequently the best way to determine which drug is most effective is to see how a patient reacts to it over weeks and months.

Experimental Drugs

Patients and families are always hearing rumors or reading snippets of news about experimental miracle drugs. Drugs that cure; drugs with no side effects; companies hoarding drugs because they can't make any money on them. Like many rumors, the miracle-drug tales are mostly wishful thinking wrapped around grains of truth.

Drug manufacturers are experimenting with potentially break-through medications, and some are being given to patients. Yet new drugs for mental illness are coming on the market slowly, and they're often just chemical variations of existing medication. New drugs for manic depression are few and far between.

The federal Food and Drug Administration (FDA) controls the evolution of these drugs, and their journey through the bureaucracy is watched closely and is extensively documented.

Before drugs can be approved by the FDA and deemed "safe and effective," they must go through a gauntlet of tests. The entire process, from early research to sale in the United States, takes an average of ten years. The human-testing stage, called the clinical trial, happens at the very end of the process—after pharmacologic research and animal testing. Psychiatric patients may hear about experimental drugs during this final stage.

All drugs undergo clinical trials—three phases of testing with increasing numbers of volunteer patients. In phase I, a small group of healthy volunteers takes a medication to see if it's safe. In phase II, a larger group of volunteers who have the target illness take the drug to see if it's effective. In phase III, the test group is expanded to hundreds, sometimes thousands, of patients who provide details about dosage levels, schedules, and side effects. In each clinical trial, some volunteers unknowingly take a placebo, and their reactions are compared with the drug takers'.

Rumors about "miracle" drugs involved in secret experiments may really be about phase III clinical trials at a single hospital. Exactly who participates in clinical trials depends on researchers and doctors. A drug company generally arranges with individual doctors, hospitals, or research centers to test a drug and report on patients' reactions. Sometimes the National Institutes of Health in Bethesda, Maryland, conduct trials. Patients taking the drug first sign an informed-consent form stating they know their medication is experimental. Clinical trials can last for three or four years if doctors are looking for long-term effects.

Or trials may take just months if earlier tests show the drug is very safe, very effective, and vital for a life-and-death illness.

When a drug is finally approved by the FDA, it's labeled for treatment of specific condition—for instance, as an antidepressant. However, once it has the government's stamp, doctors can prescribe it for anything. This is common among the psychiatric drugs, particularly when a remedy approved for treating one kind of mood disorder can help manage another and the drug's patent has run out, leaving a company little incentive to conduct expensive studies simply for FDA approval of the drug for new symptoms.

Read, Skim, and Come Back

The information in this chapter is general and summarized. Each one of the drugs mentioned has been studied, examined, and written about at length. The information here is a starting point. Insist that a doctor recommending or prescribing a medication talk about the reasons behind the choice, side effects—both immediate and long-lasting—interactions with other drugs, and what might happen if a dose is missed or a patient goes off the medication.

The drug names will overwhelm at first. They're long, hard to pronounce, and contain tangles of Greek and Latin roots. And many of them look and sound alike. Eventually, you will acquire the vocabulary, probably after skimming this chapter many times.

The Miracles and Mysteries of Lithium

Lithium carbonate, a naturally occurring mineral salt, is probably the most powerful drug available to fight mental illness. It quiets mania in up to 80 percent of patients who take it. Even more wondrously, it reduces relapses. One study comparing patients on and off lithium reports recurrences in just 25 percent of the lithium group versus 61 percent of the nonlithium group.

Yet this potent drug was discovered by accident, and doctors still can't figure exactly how it works.

In the late 1940s, Australian psychiatrist John Cade was experimenting with uric acid to see if it affected the behavior of guinea pigs. He used uric acid's lithium salt as a test compound. To his surprise, the animals became lethargic. After tasting the solution to make sure it was safe, Cade immediately switched his experiments to test the lithium component of his preparation on patients.

The results were stunning. Severely agitated psychotic patients who hadn't known an hour's peace for years grew calm and controlled. Some, after years of institutionalization, even returned to jobs and homes.

Writing in the *Medical Journal of Australia*, Cade acknowledged the huge leap he made from guinea pigs to manics: "It may seem a long distance from lethargy in guinea pigs to the excitement of psychotics . . ." But the evidence was overwhelming. Ten patients, each with a history of mania stretching for years, relaxed and grew calm within weeks.

Scientists agree that Cade ushered in the modern era of psychopharmacology. The significance of his breakthrough is especially poignant in light of the treatment for mental illness at the time. Cade concluded in his landmark report: "Prefrontal leucotomy [brain surgery] has been performed lately on restless and psychopathic mental defectives in an attempt to control their restless impulses and ungovernable tempers. It is likely that lithium medication would be effective in such cases and would be much preferred to leucotomy."

But Cade had the misfortune of unlocking the miracles of lithium in 1949, the same year America was in hysterics about the naturally occurring salt. Reports of people using lithium as a salt substitute and being poisoned virtually guaranteed that no one would listen to Cade's claims about the mineral.

The American psychiatric community also rejected lithium salts. Steeped in psychoanalytic dogma about the origins of mental disorders, doctors refused to consider the possibility that a chemical could alleviate an illness unresponsive to years of psychotherapy. Almost twenty-five years passed before the United States approved the drug. In 1968, the Food and Drug Administration cleared lithium for the treatment of manic depression.

Lithium does double duty in its battle with manic depression. First, it modifies and curbs violent mood swings. Imagine a heavy pendulum moving through a long arc. One end is mania and the other depression. Lithium chops off the ends of the arc so that a person's moods stay within a shorter, less changeable range. (Lithium's ability to curb two mood extremes is part of its mystery. Other drugs attack just one mood.)

Second, lithium acts as a prophylactic or preventive. Daily doses of the drug keep moods in check and inhibit recurring outbreaks of mania and depression. Regular lithium treatment for some manic-depressives keep them virtually symptom-free for life. It doesn't cure the disease, and mania or depression sometimes breaks through the lithium safeguard. But it does soften the attacks.

Lithium has also helped in establishing the diagnosis of manic depression because it relieves mainly mood disorders, not usually other types of mental illnesses (unless combined with other drugs). In the 1950s and 1960s, psychiatrists in this country frequently mislabeled bipolar illness as schizophrenia, especially among patients who were delusional or hallucinated. With the approval of lithium by the 1970s, doctors could use it to aid in distinguishing manic depression from schizophrenia, depending on how a patient reacted to it. However, not all bipolar patients improve with only lithium, so this is by no means a foolproof test.

Scientists have only suspicions about how lithium does its remarkable balancing act. The latest research suggests the drug works within brain cells—not at the edges, where neurotransmitters send and receive signals. This theory proposes that lithium acts as a kind of security guard, halting the movement of unique proteins that set off a chain reaction leading to mania or depression. One reason this theory appeals to scientists is that it explains why the drug does not tamper with a person's normal moods, but acts only to block abnormal reactions.

Lithium is usually taken in tablets or capsules at least twice daily and in varying doses, depending on the severity of a patient's symptoms and how a person reacts to it. A typical daily dose ranges between 600 and 2400 mgs. Getting started on lithium is complicated because there is a delay from when the drug is first swallowed to when it begins its magic. While the drug readily works into the bloodstream, it doesn't show results for days to weeks. Very manic and depressed patients usually take, along with lithium, stronger antimanic or antidepressant medicine to better control their symptoms.

Once lithium reaches optimum levels in the blood, it is constantly monitored. Arriving at an individual's ideal lithium level is a delicate maneuver. Initially, this means blood samples about twice weekly. Once the lithium reaches a steady concentration, a patient's blood is tested much less frequently.

Another reason for closely watching lithium levels is that overdoses can be dangerous. The biggest danger is to the kidneys because the drug is excreted through these organs, as are other salts. If a person's fluid intake is low or the fluid balance is askew, the kidneys may retain lithium, which could build up to toxic levels. The only food restriction for a lithium patient is to avoid a low-salt diet, which would decrease the amount of lithium excreted.

Lithium: Side Effects

The side effects of lithium, compared with other drugs, can be relatively mild. It's not addictive and doesn't cause drowsiness. The most common complaints are that it increases thirst and may cause frequent urination and diarrhea. The most troubling side effects are hand tremors, acne, stomach cramps, weight gain, and fuzzy thinking.

It sounds like a rewarding trade-off: the devastation of manic depression for the annoying side effects of lithium. But lithium's side effects are the number-one reason most patients cease medication. And fuzzy thinking—meaning poor concentration, confusion, slowness, temporary loss of memory—is probably the biggest offender in provoking patients to discontinue lithium.

The weight gain also aggravates patients. The gain can be sizable: Studies report average first-year increases of nine to twenty-two pounds during a two-to-ten-year period of lithium treatment. Some researchers theorize a patient gains weight in response to shedding pounds during previous, untreated mood swings—the body compensating for earlier weight loss. Nevertheless, experts think they know how lithium adds weight, and how a patient can fight the extra pounds. They point to added calorie consumption because of the constant thirst. Surprisingly, increased appetite does not seem to be the main culprit. Thus, to help patients stave off the extra weight, they suggest low-calorie ways to quench thirst along with dietary suggestions for eating fewer carbohydrates.

Hypothyroidism is a less common side effect. Its symptoms are fatigue, puffiness, dry skin, muscle aches, and hair loss. Unlike other side effects, hypothyroidism can not be managed through lithium dosage adjustments, and usually requires adding thyroid hormone to a patient's regimen.

The fallout from lithium does not touch all lithium patients. Most endure at least some of the side effects, but predicting who will feel what is a guessing game.

Lithium is one of the true wonder drugs. Everything about it—Cade's accidental discovery, its simplicity as a naturally occurring salt, its miraculous attack on both mania and depression, its profound preventive effects—seems to contribute to its mystique. It even has spawned an educational establishment (the Lithium Information Center, Madison, Wisconsin, 608-263-6171) accessible to anyone's questions.

Rest of the Medicine Chest
Not everyone responds to lithium. About 30 percent of bipolar patients need additional or alternative medication to control their illness. Patients in the throes of acute mania, for instance, do not respond quickly to lithium. Doctors have a large medicine chest of drugs to treat lithium-resistant manic depression and smooth a patient's moods. The most common alternative is an anticonvulsant drug called carbamazepine (trade name Tegretol).

Anticonvulsants

Carbamazepine (or Tegretol), like lithium, is an all-around drug that eases not only mania and anxiousness but also depression and feelings of despair and hopelessness. While data are incomplete, doctors suspect that, as with lithium, regular use of the drug can trim the frequency and seriousness of manic-depressive episodes. Carbamazepine is an anticonvulsant (i.e., it calms abnormal brain electrical discharges), and was originally designed for epilepsy.

Like lithium, it needs one to two weeks to begin working and is successful in half to two thirds of patients. Doctors frequently combine it with regular lithium doses in the hope of achieving a "synergy" or improved combined effect.

Carbamazepine is a relatively new treatment for manic depression—studies about its good deeds first appeared in the mid-1970s. Today, it is widely prescribed for the 30 percent of manic-depressives who do not immediately respond to lithium and the up to 50 percent who may suffer relapses even on lithium-maintenance treatment.

Doctors find it is especially effective with manic-depressives who haven't improved on lithium and who are rapid cyclers (i.e., have at least four mania or depression cycles in a year). Often these two types of patients are the same people. Other patients who improve on this drug have no close family history of mental illness, have a very severe initial depression but one that doesn't last long, experienced their first manic episode early in life, and undergo very violent, delirious manias. Some doctors also believe that anticonvulsants are useful in controlling what is euphemistically called "behavioral disinhibition," meaning aggression and problems relating to people especially in patients with abnormal brain injury or mild retardation.

Average daily doses of the drug range from 400 to 2000 mg. Remarkably, doctors see little relationship between dose levels and how a patient responds. The assumption that more is stronger and better doesn't apply here. To discover the right dose, a doctor uses a wait-and-see approach. While some patients say they feel better within days of taking the drug, others find it may be weeks before they feel the full effects. Early signs that the dosage may be too high include dizziness, sleepiness, double vision, slurred speech, and loss of body coordination.

Carbamazepine generally has fewer side effects than lithium. It can cause dizziness, drowsiness, double vision, nausea, and headaches. It also is more prone to cause a variety of allergic reactions, such as rashes or dermatitis, and makes its takers sensitive to the sun. Doctors say skin rashes may be signs of more serious problems, and carefully watching for this type of side effect is essential.

The most serious side effects materialize not in how a patient feels, but in laboratory tests of patients' blood samples. These can reveal a marked lowering of infection-fighting white blood cells or platelet counts, which measure the blood's ability to coagulate. If this happens, doctors usually discontinue treatment to prevent a potentially fatal outcome.

Valproate, also known as sodium valproate, valproic acid, or divalproex sodium (trade names Depakene, Depakote)
As with other anticonvulsants, this is used to treat acute mania, especially for rapid-cycling patients who don't improve on lithium. It dramatically slows a patient's manic thinking—the grandiose thoughts and fast speech—and like lithium, may act as a preventive. Daily dosage varies from 750 to 3500 mg. It may be less effective with depression, and side effects appear in only a small percentage of patients (15 percent in one study). The most common are sleepiness, drowsiness, nausea, upset stomach, mild tremor, and weight gain. In rare cases, valproate may poison the liver, with potentially fatal results, so doctors do regular liver-function tests.

Calcium Channel Blockers
This class of drugs, first used to treat heart disease and hypertension, includes only one—verapamil (Calan)—reported to ease the symptoms of manic depression, especially mania. The jury is still out on this

drug, but if shown to be effective it would be a boon because of its extremely mild side effects.

Antipsychotics

These medicines fall under the heading of either "antipsychotic" or "neuroleptic" drugs. (Occasionally, they're called major tranquilizers, but doctors avoid this term because they differ by much more than degree from the so-called minor tranquilizers.) This family is comprised of many drugs, some low potency, some high potency, but none plainly more or less effective than another. Since their strength varies so much, so too do suggested doses. There's no average daily dosage for the neuroleptics, although there is a trend lately toward those of lower doses.

Much of our knowledge of neuroleptics comes from their affects on schizophrenia. Nevertheless, they are widely used to treat mania and severe, psychotic depression, and research shows they help.

When neuroleptics are used for mania, they calm agitated behavior, hyperactivity, sleeplessness, delusions, and hallucinations. With severe mania, they sometimes seem to work better than lithium and are either taken alone or combined with the salt. Quite often they are prescribed when patients "break through" lithium therapy. In curbing mania, they usually quiet a patient faster than lithium, so doctors give them to manic patients for several weeks until lithium or other drugs can kick in. Some psychotic or manic patients don't get better with neuroleptics, so researchers are constantly studying groups of patients, looking for clinical predictors or signs indicating response to a particular treatment. This is frustrating work but it has generated information about several new treatments, including the anticonvulsants and clozapine.

Antipsychotics are powerful chemicals and can produce dangerous side effects. (Doctors call them "neuroleptics," a Greek-derived term meaning "to clasp the nerve cell," because of their effects on parts of the nervous system regulating involuntary movements.) In some cases, they may seem to worsen depression because of their sedative effects. Their most serious long-term side effect is tardive dyskinesia, a syndrome of involuntary movements of the lips, face, tongue, and limbs (more on this in the next section). The drugs also can mimic Parkinson's disease, causing a masklike expression, stiffness, a shuffling gait, and tremors.

Since side effects are reversible, doctors commonly prescribe "anti-

Parkinsonian" drugs to moderate them. The most common such drugs are amantadine (trade name Symmetrel), diphenhydramine (trade name Benadryl), benztropine (trade name Cogentin), biperiden (trade name Akineton), and trihexyphenidyl (trade name Artane). Like all the others, these also can produce disturbing side effects such as rapid heartbeat, drowsiness, dizziness, blurred vision, dry mouth, and nausea, so doctors limit their use and dosage.

Another dangerous possible side effect is called "neuroleptic malignant syndrome." Although rare, it can be lethal. It usually attacks soon after a patient begins taking neuroleptics, and strikes men more than women. Symptoms are rigid muscles, stupor, and fever.

Any number of less dangerous, sometimes temporary side effects may also surface from neuroleptics. These include dry mouth, blurry vision, constipation, impotence, other sexual difficulties, weight gain, and sensitivity to the sun.

An all-too-frequent side effect of the neuroleptic drugs is akathisia, a syndrome of physical restlessness, anxiety, and discomfort which may affect 50 to 70 percent of patients treated with these drugs. Some doctors speculate that this feeling may be the most frequent reason patients stop taking antipsychotic drugs. Treatments for akathisia exist but are limited in efficacy. Doctors may use low doses of the low-blood-pressure drug propranolol (Inderal) or low doses of antianxiety drugs. No more than half of patients benefit from these treatments and akathisia remains a curse to be tolerated by anyone who needs long-term treatment with neuroleptics.

These are the more common neuroleptics:

haloperidol (trade name Haldol)

chlorpromazine (trade name Thorazine)

perphenazine (trade name Trilafon)

thioridazine (trade name Mellaril)

fluphenazine (trade name Prolixin)

molindone (trade name Moban)

trifluoperazone (trade name Stelazine)

loxitane (trade name Loxapine)

thiothixene (trade name Navane)

mesoridazine (trade name Serentil)

clozapine (trade name Clozaril)—this is a relatively new drug on the market, and is attracting attention for a number of reasons. It doesn't seem to produce tardive dyskinesia or affect involuntary muscles. It is often tolerated much more easily than neuroleptics, as it rarely causes akathisia. This drug may treat the psychotic symptoms of one third to one half of previously treatment-resistant patients, making it a true miracle for them. Side effects of the drug include drowsiness, rapid heartbeat, and excessive salivation. It is used in doses from 25 to 900 mg. daily. The drug's most frightening side effect is possible lowering of a patient's white blood-cell count, which can be fatal. At present this medication is only available through a cumbersome and expensive system of distribution and blood testing, and many insurers are loath to pay for it. Remarkably, Medicare, the insurer of last resort for patients with chronic illness (the sort most amenable to clozapine therapy), will not cover its use and monitoring. This is a national tragedy.

Minor tranquilizers. The medical name for these antianxiety drugs is "benzodiazepines," better known as the drug class of the popularly prescribed Valium and Xanax. Doctors sometimes prescribe minor tranquilizers or antianxiety medication for a short time to calm the agitation, irritability, and restless behavior of mania. They are also used in some emergency rooms to treat a threatening or possibly violent patient when a doctor is worried about side effects of other drugs. While most of these drugs are known for their calming effects, alprazolam (Xanax) is also useful in mild depression.

Recently, these antianxiety drugs have been tested for possible treatment of manic depression when combined with neuroleptics and lithium or carbamazepine therapy. Their big attraction, particularly when compared with neuroleptics, is their milder side effects. These tranquilizers are far less dangerous than their predecessors, barbiturates, but overdoses can still be fatal. Their primary side effect is drowsiness, and they are sometimes used as sleeping pills. Their biggest drawback is possible addiction and withdrawal symptoms when they are discontinued. Doctors, however, know about these possibilities and keep a close eye on dosage levels.

These are the more common benzodiazepines:

alprazolam (trade name Xanax)
chlordiazepoxide (trade name Librium)

lorazepam (trade name Ativan)
oxazepam (trade name Serax)
diazepam (trade name Valium)
triazolam (trade name Halcion)
clorazepate (trade name Tranxene)
clonazepam (trade name Klonopin)
midnazolam (trade name Versed)

The Shadow of TD

A discussion of the neuroleptics, or any other antipsychotic drugs for that matter, raises the specter of a possible side effect called tardive dyskinesia. Literally, the term means late or delayed ("tardive") abnormal movements ("dyskinesia"). It generally surfaces six months to several years after a patient begins taking antipsychotic medication and appears as involuntarily twisting and grimacing of the face, tongue, and body. Sometimes arms, neck, and hands become twisted or rigid. Although not painful, TD can be permanently disfiguring and embarrassing.

To diagnose it, doctors look for four kinds of movement: tremors, jerks, tics, and abnormal posture. It shouldn't be confused with the slight hand tremors that may appear soon after a manic-depressive patient begins medication.

Tardive dyskinesia scares patients and families, for it can radically distort a person's face and body. It represents the ravages, and stereotype, of mental illness. Yet as disfiguring as it can be, it is not as pervasive and overwhelming as people assume. As with most stereotypes, many of the underlying beliefs are founded on myth and misperception.

Researchers theorize there are different types of TD depending on the exact body movement, how quickly or slowly the syndrome advances, and how severe it becomes. These varieties are involuntary eye movement (blepharospasm), rocking, foot movement, restlessness (tardive akathisia), and head or trunk twisting (tardive dystonia).

TD sometimes spreads rapidly, and can be first noticeable by slight, involuntary chewing motions, tongue twitching, or eye blinking. The signs may be subtle, revealing just hints of symptoms. It may progress in fits and spurts, as it were, making identification more elusive. Sometimes it's masked by other treatments and symptoms. No tests or criteria exist for diagnosing it with absolute certainty, so we can only watch for clues.

Antipsychotic drugs are the main suspect for instigating TD, but not the proven villain. Instances of TD appearing in people who have not taken psychiatric medication and patients ingesting antipsychotics for years and never contracting TD confound theories about its causes. Current thinking about its origins leans toward a mixture of influences: drugs plus the character of the disorder plus how a person ages.

Not all antipsychotic patients get TD. Twenty to forty-five percent of drug-takers are stricken over the long term. Sufferers are usually older (over fifty-five years), and are more likely to suffer from manic depression or psychotic depression than schizophrenia. One study reveals that patients taking neuroleptics for more than six years are more than doubly vulnerable. Experts seem divided on whether it afflicts men or women more, although older women may be more at risk.

Scientists aren't certain of the causes of TD, but they know that it often subsides when a patient is taken off medication. Also, young patients recover better than older ones. And patients who develop it slowly tend to show milder signs over the long haul than patients who are stricken quickly. Some doctors suspect smoking may aggravate it.

Once spotted, TD can be curbed through lower doses or a change in medication. Paradoxically, lowering the dose or discontinuing the suspicious drug usually briefly *worsens* the symptoms before they calm. Similarly, *increasing* the neuroleptic may briefly improve the symptoms before they again worsen. Taking a person off stronger drugs, such as haloperidol or fluphenazine, may ease the symptoms. This remedy sounds like common sense, but some patients, because of their illness and their chemistry, are better off sticking with their original treatments, even if TD appears.

The consensus among psychiatrists is that *all* neuroleptic drugs bring a risk of TD, and this risk has to be weighed against the benefits of the drugs. As discussed above, the recent approval of clozapine, which does not appear to bring out TD, is a potential boon to patients who would otherwise be stuck in a neuroleptic treatment.

Another ploy in retarding the course of TD is giving highly vulnerable patients "drug holidays" from regular antipsychotic medication. These breaks are short so as not to unleash a psychotic episode but long enough to give the patient's body time to resist the onslaught of TD.

However, the long-term effectiveness of this approach has not been proven.

While TD can be calmed and its damage halted or slowly reversed, it often can't be cured, and complete reversals of its symptoms are rare unless it is caught very early and neuroleptics are discontinued. Thus, conscientious doctors scrutinize patients carefully and are quick to take action if telltale signs appear.

The Antidepressants

Antidepressants are the target of intense research—more than even antipsychotics—for a number of reasons. The most obvious is their life-and-death necessity. Depressed people are frighteningly prone to commit suicide. Among all mental illnesses, the suicide rate for manic-depressives tops the list. So concocting an antidepressant that a patient will take regularly, and that works, is vital.

Another reason for the persistent probing is that researchers have not yet come up with an antidepressant that has long-term preventive qualities as powerful as lithium. Unlike other psychiatric medications, the antidepressants don't stop recurrences. The drugs ease the symptoms, but a patient may continue to suffer bouts of major depression for many years. For many patients, however, maintenance treatment with antidepressants improves the quality of life by soothing and shortening their spells.

And there is a certain commercial incentive behind their proliferation: More people despair from various degrees of depression than any other mental illness. The potential market for a highly potent antidepressant with few side effects and lasting preventive qualities is enough to excite any drug manufacturer. While this may sound like criticism of the pharmaceutical industry, it is not. Researchers say that experimenters are currently examining more than seventy-five antidepressant drugs. Any incentive that spurs the industry to create safer, more effective drugs, regardless of its motives, helps everybody.

The early patent-medicine-based antidepressants were crude, consisting mostly of mixtures of opiates or alcohol bases. The problem, as everyone knows, is that they raise the spirits only temporarily and they're addictive; over the long haul, both of these drugs make depression worse. For a time in the forties and fifties, doctors used barbiturates and other sedations for depression with mixed results.

Even modern antidepressants are imperfect. Controversy continues to swirl around the question of whether a heavy dose of them can trip a manic episode in some patients and set off a series of rapid cycles. This flip-flop from depression to mania is called "switching," and medical heavyweights are deeply divided over whether antidepressants can set it in motion. Doctors who believe antidepressants do cause switching cite clinical experience, patient studies, and common sense. They insist, "intuitively, it seems to make sense that a treatment which lifts patients out of depression could cause an overshot into mania."

On the other side, a group of researchers at Western Psychiatric Institute in Pennsylvania studied 230 depressed patients on antidepressant medication and found that less than 3 percent developed mild symptoms consistent with mania.

The debate persists, but for patients it's useful to know that their antidepressant medication just might change their moods.

Remarkably, although some antidepressants are almost forty years old and much newer drugs are on the market, they all behave in the brain more or less the same way. Most act to boost levels in the brain of the neurotransmitters norepinephrine and serotonin. This points to a chemical imbalance as a probable cause of depression.

Antidepressants fall into three categories, depending on their chemical structures and to some degree, when they were introduced. The groups are the monoamine oxidase inhibitors, the tricyclic antidepressants, and the second-generation drugs.

The Monoamine Oxidase Inhibitor

The first really successful antidepressant was discovered in the 1950s by doctors who saw that tuberculosis patients treated with a drug called iproniazid became mellow and relaxed. This drug spawned a class of medications called monoamine oxidase inhibitors or MAOIs. MAOIs work by blocking the activity of the enzyme monoamine oxidase. This blockade prevents the chemical breakdown of norepinephrine and serotonin in the brain, and so increases their levels.

The MAOIs proved to be an imperfect elixir for depression. Their main drawback is that they interact with certain foods, causing a reaction that raises blood pressure to dangerous levels and can induce strokes.

Called the "cheese reaction," this lethal mixture comes about if patients eat such foods as aged or unpasteurized cheese (pasteurized cheese is okay), yeast extract, smoked herring, salami, and fava beans. Patients are also limited in the amounts of other foods they can eat, such as avocado, bananas, most alcoholic beverages, fermented meats (e.g. bologna, pepperoni, salami), caffeinated coffee, chocolate, and cola. Obviously, staying on MAOIs is no picnic.

Some researchers say patients taking MAOIs rarely have hypertension—fewer than one percent react this way. Nevertheless, the ban on certain foods remains. In smaller groups of patients, spontaneous episodes of elevated blood pressure may arise. This family of drugs also clashes with a number of drugs, namely decongestants, sedatives, amphetamines, and hypertension medication. Not surprisingly, many patients have a hard time sticking with a MAOI treatment program.

Yet sometimes patients don't have a choice, because the MAOIs are often recommended for treating unusual kinds of depression. Patients with high anxiety, panic attacks, phobic reactions, excessive sleeping, or great lethargy do well on these drugs. Also, they can be a savior for patients whose bodies disagree with other types of antidepressants or who don't improve with other types of antidepressant therapy.

If there is a dangerous reaction, the symptoms of hypertension appear quickly, often just one or two hours after eating. These warnings are a pounding headache in the eyes or temples, light sensitivity, choking or a racing-heart sensation, feelings of dread, and a stiff neck.

Normal side effects from these drugs are difficulty sleeping or disturbed sleep, low blood pressure, dizziness, dry mouth, drowsiness, sexual dysfunction, weight gain, and excitation. While none of these sounds pleasant, they can be relatively mild. And the absence of any strain on the heart's electrical impulses makes the MAOIs the antidepressant of choice for some older patients.

Researchers are actively investigating a new generation of these drugs that they hope will be more palatable. For now, these MAOIs are available:

isocarboxazid—trade name Marplan

phenelzine—trade name Nardil

tranylcypromine—trade name Parnate

selegiline—trade name Eldepryl

Tricyclic (Three-Ring) Antidepressants, More or Less

This family of antidepressants was discovered soon after the MAOIs. Like those drugs, these too set off a series of chemical reactions that ultimately increase the amount of neurotransmitters in the brain. They're called tricyclic antidepressants (TCAs) because their chemical structure looks like three benzene rings in a row. Since their discovery, chemists have tinkered with the formula, adding and subtracting rings. So although they are called the tricyclics, heterocyclic or multicyclic are more accurate names.

The reasons behind their creation, and where they depart from the MAOIs, is in their side effects. TCA-treated patients can eat pretty much anything, without worrying about possible hypertension. In this respect, TCAs are a great improvement. Still, they're not the best medicine for all patients, and not everybody feels better on them.

Doctors have identified the kinds of depressed patients that TCAs perk up most. Generally, these people more often exhibit disturbed sleep, early morning awakening, motor retardation, loss of appetite, weight loss, and loss of interest in work, hobbies, and sex. And these patients tend to feel better in the evenings. This syndrome is called "melancholia" and is the most common, classical kind of depression.

Today, the TCA medicine chest is loaded, with researchers inventing new ones all the time. But although they have multiplied, there remains a mystery in their story. Doctors have no way of knowing which TCA will connect best with which patient. Unless a patient has taken TCAs before and responded well or poorly, only a trial run will produce the TCA that will do the most for a patient. Complicating this trial run is the infamous lag time for these drugs (as with most psychiatric drugs). It's a good two to eight weeks before these potions begin taking effect, and even then improvements may be gradual.

Often doctors start treatment with one of the more common TCAs—such as desipramine or nortriptyline—then shift if the patient doesn't improve or can't stand the side effects. None of these drugs is free of side effects, and at times side effects and symptoms may blur. With antidepressants especially, side effects and the symptoms of depression may closely resemble each other.

The more common side effects are called "anticholinergic." They include a dry mouth, blurred vision, high blood pressure, rapid breathing, constipation, and difficulty urinating. Patients say these feelings are more a nuisance than a major worry. Other side effects from TCAs include dizziness, low blood pressure, sedation, fatigue, tremors, sweating, agitation, weight gain, and sexual dysfunction. Because these drugs can alter heartbeats, they're kept away from people with heart disease. Furthermore, an overdose of a TCA can be fatal, so patients with ideas about suicide should be given limited quantities.

Some heterocyclics have unique side effects or risks. Amoxapine is

WE HEARD THE ANGELS OF MADNESS

known to have neurolepticlike properties, so that it may cause akathisia and put a patient in danger of tardive dyskinesia. Naprotiline may cause epilepticlike seizures at higher doses. Unfortunately, even the tricyclics that are less likely to do this still have about a 1-in-1000 chance of causing this potentially devastating consequence.

Here are the better-known TCAs:

amitriptyline—trade name Elavil

amoxapine—trade name Asendin

trimipramine—trade name Surmontil

doxepin—trade name Sinequan

desipramine—trade name Norpramin

imipramine—trade name Tofranil

maprotiline—trade name Ludiomil

nortriptyline—trade names Pamelor, Aventyl

protriptyline—trade name Vivactil

clomiprimine—trade name Anafranil (especially helpful in obsessive-compulsive disorder)

Some patients taking TCA don't improve, but doctors don't know why. Sometimes misdiagnosis is the fault; other times doses may be too low or not maintained long enough, and patients may not take their medications regularly. But even when these don't apply, about 30 percent of patients still don't get better. When this happens, doctors usually move on to more powerful drugs, such as MAOIs or second-generation drugs, or supplement the treatment with our old friend lithium, the addition of which may help more than half of tricyclic-resistant patients.

The Second Generation
Researchers continue to tinker with chemical formulas and concoct new antidepressants. The new generation of drugs usually acts on the neurotransmitter serotonin. Researchers had hoped this second generation would exhibit fewer side effects than its predecessors, and this seems to be the case. The newer-generation drugs produce mild or less frequent side effects. These can include stomach upset, nausea, vomiting, cramps, diarrhea, insomnia, anxiety, weight loss, and restlessness.

Perhaps the best known of this class is fluoxetine (Prozac) which is widely prescribed for moderate depression. The main reason it's so popular is not only its effectiveness in relieving depression but also the absence of serious side effects. At this writing, a study in the *American Journal of Psychiatry* (February 1990) has linked Prozac with suicide attempts, citing six patients who developed self-destructive ideas while on the drug. Many doctors are taking a wait-and-see attitude toward Prozac's possible side effects and note that the evidence so far is anecdotal. Given the millions of patients on Prozac, researchers are following it carefully and new studies will keep coming. Fluoxetine is largely prescribed for depression, although it is also used for obsessive-compulsive behavior, bulimia, and anxiety. However, for treating manic depression, it joins the other antidepressants as a possible but not necessarily preferred medication.

These drugs are still young, and only three are readily available in America. Here are the more common second-generation antidepressants:

fluoxetine—trade name Prozac

fluvoxamine—(under research)

trazodone—trade name Desyrel

bupropion—trade name Wellbutrin

When Drugs Fail: Electroconvulsive Therapy

Drug treatment doesn't work for everybody. Physical complications, such as pregnancy or heart disease, or simply an intolerance of the powerful side effects of the standard drugs render many patients unable to take psychiatric medications. About 20 to 30 percent continue to suffer despite regular doses of antidepressants or lithium. A standard second line of attack is shock treatment or electroconvulsive therapy (ECT).

People outside the world of psychiatric hospitals and mental illness think ECT is primitive, painful, and damaging. But among those who have had firsthand encounters with it, ECT combats mental illness as well as the best tools of modern medicine. Doctors and patients respect it as therapeutic and, unlike most drugs, quickly effective. The people who make treatment decisions know that ECT saves lives and alleviates misery, and that it is no more primitive than an injection, and even less painful. Although ECT has been controversial since the day it was conceived, experts agree that it improves depression in 70 to 80 percent of cases.

ECT was devised in the 1930s to treat schizophrenia. Doctors believed that schizophrenia and epilepsy rarely occurred in the same person, and that somehow epileptic seizures warded off schizophrenia. To test this theory, researchers injected the blood of schizophrenic patients into epileptics, hoping to reduce their seizures. It didn't, so Hungarian neuropsychiatrist Ladislas Meduna reversed the experiment by *inducing* grand mal epileptic seizures in schizophrenics. It worked. After five seizures, a man who had been catatonic for four years miraculously got out of bed, dressed himself, talked to doctors, and started living an apparently normal life again.

Meduna, after experimenting with various chemicals, used injections of camphor to generate the seizures. Electricity was introduced into the process four years after Meduna's experiments. He and his colleagues reasoned that exactly *how* a seizure was triggered, whether by electricity or medication, was not important. The seizure was the thing.

Meduna was roundly criticized for his discovery. Ironically, the medical establishment's enlightened belief that schizophrenia was a hereditary disease compelled it to conclude that Meduna's treatment could not "cure" the illness. He was accused of being a money-grubbing charlatan. But the attacks on Meduna could not hide the success of the treatment.

By the early 1940s, ECT was applied to all sorts of mental illnesses, including mania and melancholia. It was a preferred treatment until the emergence of various psychiatric drugs in the 1950s. Then ECT began to wane, especially for schizophrenia and mania. But studies pitting ECT against drugs show shock treatment is just as, if not more, potent.

Today, ECT is a common treatment, particularly in private and university hospitals, where its stigma among the public is less likely to interfere. A survey of hospital patients in 1980 reports it's used on just under 3 percent of the patients, who are the most seriously depressed.

Typically, the ECT patient is deeply depressed and hasn't responded to antidepressant drugs. While ECT is applied more often to crippling depression, it's also used in mania, especially in violent and delusional patients. Another group of likely ECT patients are pregnant, elderly, or have heart disease and can't tolerate the side effects of antidepressant medication.

One special indication for ECT is in treating patients bent on suicide and so determined on it that doctors cannot wait the several weeks necessary for medication to begin acting. ECT is especially forceful in combating an acute manic episode. And the worse the manic episode, the better the response to ECT. Studies conclude that sometimes it's more effective than lithium.

Nevertheless, experts acknowledge that ECT is never the first line of treatment. Doctors resort to it when other remedies fail. One reason for its limited use is the expense. Applying ECT requires numerous professionals and special equipment.

Like many medical procedures, ECT is done in the psychiatric ward or a hospital's operating or recovery room. Usually, three or four people are involved, such as a psychiatrist, an anesthesiologist, a nurse, and a nurse's aide. Although practices vary widely from hospital to hospital, and depending on state laws (which usually require a patient to sign a consent form and specify who does the treatment), here's how it's typically done.

A patient is given an anesthesia, usually a quick-acting barbiturate, and then injected with muscle relaxants to prevent spasms during treatment. Doctors place electrodes on the right temple and the front of the head or on both temples, and attach a blood-pressure cuff and oxygen mask to monitor the patient's breathing and heart rate. A bite-block is put into the sleeping patient's mouth. The electric shock takes about one second, and the resulting seizure lasts half a minute to two minutes. However, none of this activity shows unless the patient is hooked up to an EEG monitoring brain waves. The patient lies still and sleeps.

Fifteen minutes later, the patient wakes up. He'll probably be groggy and disoriented, with a headache and sore muscles. Most of these side effects disappear in a few hours. The most serious outcome may be a loss of short-term memory. A patient can't remember events and conversations that happened days or weeks before. Generally, complete memory returns within weeks or months after treatment has stopped but patients may still have memory loss for the time of the treatment.

ECT requires a series of seizures to be effective. Typically, a patient undergoes grand mal seizures three times a week from two to six weeks. At first, the patient may not respond. But repeated seizures kindle electrical and chemical changes in the brain, stimulate the nervous system, and release hormones. Researchers are not quite sure how ECT works. They do know that it dramatically alters brain chemistry in a number of places, but are uncertain as to which exact action helps a patient.

Thus, researchers are always learning more about ECT. They are experimenting with various techniques—placement of the electrodes, length of seizures, the administration of drugs to help the seizure—to understand how seizures affect a patient's language, thought process, moods, behavior, and to optimize treatment response.

Of course, ECT is not recommended for all patients. It has obvious limitations. Most notable is its inability to prevent recurrences of a patient's symptoms. It's an immediate solution to an urgent problem, whether deep depression, the threat of suicide, or a manic episode, but unfortunately its impact doesn't last. It's an addition to drug therapy, not a replacement.

Cocaine and Alcohol: Self-medication?

As the crisis with drug addiction and alcohol abuse worsens, medical experts have suggested some addicts may have a mental illness that they are unconsciously subduing with these substances. Our very public problems with substance abuse are mirrored in the psychiatric community. The number of "dual-diagnosis" patients—people suffering from mental illness and alcoholism or drug abuse—is startling. As many as 60 percent of mental-illness patients also grapple with substance-abuse problems. (A vital distinction must be made between people who use alcohol and drugs to self-treat anxiety, depression, or mania and the much larger group for whom substance abuse is their primary illness. This group can lead normal lives when not abusing drugs.)

Addicts don't randomly choose their drugs. They may gravitate toward alcohol or variations of cocaine, heroin, or morphine in part because of how these drugs quell their psychiatric symptoms. Narcotics like heroin and morphine quiet restlessness and aggressiveness, even violent behavior and anger. They also can calm mental chaos and disorganized thinking. At the other end of the emotional spectrum, stimulants like cocaine and amphetamines seem to dispel feelings of depression and fatigue. They may also prolong euphoria or help people calm down and concentrate on a single problem or project.

Cocaine addicts can be very focused people. Doctors studying self-medication describe their patients before their cocaine addiction as impulsive, emotionally unstable, full of feelings of hopelessness and despair, with low self-esteem. With the drug, however, they concentrate better, work harder, and have better personal relations and improved self-images, at least in the short run. In the long run, their original problems return and grow worse with the drug.

Alcohol acts on the brain like a minor tranquilizer, relieving anxiety, restlessness, and hyperactivity. Most everyone knows how alcohol slows you down. For the manic or psychotic, this effect may be even more dramatic, and more welcoming.

None of this is meant to suggest that anyone should attempt self-medication or addiction. Aside from moral or ethical problems, there are serious medical drawbacks to self-medication. As one doctor puts it, "Such efforts at self-treatment are eventually doomed, given the hazards and complications of long-term, unstable drug-use patterns."

Odds and Ends

These are the new directions and side roads of various treatments. While they have shown promise, most of them have been tested on only small groups of patients, so results are limited and conclusions uncertain.

Sleep Deprivation. Psychiatrists have known since the 1960s that depriving a depressed person of sleep sometimes interrupts the cyclic disorder. In one study, 70 percent of depressed, bipolar patients responded to sleep-deprivation therapy. However, these results are as short-lived as they are dramatic. Sleep deprivation works, but not for long. One night of sleep and the depression returns. So doctors are trying to refine the treatment by partially depriving depressed patients of their sleep.

One theory explaining why this works centers on body temperature. Sleep deprivation lowers the body temperature while, at the same time, stimulating certain hormones. Antidepressant medications also lower body temperature. But why lower body temperature may inhibit depression is still conjecture.

Unfortunately, sleep deprivation can also trigger a switch from depression to mania. Manics are notorious for days of sleeplessness, and their midnight energy apparently fuels their manic outbursts. Mania and insomnia become intertwined in a vicious cycle. Needless to say, research continues.

Cold Wet-Sheet Packs. Although rarely used and outdated largely by psychotropic drugs, cold wet-sheet packs have been known to calm manic patients. This technique involves wrapping and restraining a patient in cold, wet sheets for up to two hours. Few hospitals use it, but it has been proven effective in quieting an extremely agitated patient without any harmful side effects.

Light Therapy. This is a novel treatment based on the premise that some depressed and manic-depressive patients sink into downswings as sunlight decreases in intensity during the fall and winter. Many manic-depressive patients suffer from seasonal variations in their symptoms (see Chapter 10). So-called "natural spectrum" light shining in a depressed patient's eyes two to six hours daily seems to help at least the depressive symptoms in some patients.

A Dictionary of Side Effects

The medical profession frequently talks in a kind of code that patients and families need a medical encyclopedia to decipher. In treatment, much of this arcane language surrounds the multitude of side effects from drugs and therapy. The following list includes some of the more common terms doctors use to describe what a drug or treatment does to a person.

   agranulocytosis—loss of white blood cells

   akathisia—restlessness

   akinesia—listlessness

   alogia—absence of thought or speech; "poverty of speech"

   amenorrhea—absence of menstruation

   angioedema—skin swelling

   anhedonia—inability to feel pleasure or happiness

   anhidrosis—dry skin and eyes

   anorgasmia—inability to have an orgasm

   anticholinergic—a collection of symptoms that include dry mouth, blurred vision, drowsiness, difficulty urinating, constipation, and rapid pulse

   aphasia—inability to speak properly because of brain injury

   arrhythmia—irregular heartbeat

   ataxia—lack of body coordination

   bradycardia—slow heartbeat

   bradykinesia—very slow movement

   catatonia—an apparently awake state, unresponsive to the world around the patient

chorea—abnormal, spontaneous dancelike movement of arms or legs

diplopia—double vision

dysarthria—unclear speech

dysphagia—difficulty swallowing

dysphoria—an intensely unpleasant feeling; worse than anhedonia

dystonia—muscle spasms or abnormal posture

dysuria—difficulty urinating

euthymia—a normal mood; not depressed or manic

extrapyramidal—involving involuntary muscle activity

hypernatremia—high sodium level in the blood

hyperphagia—tendency to eat too much

hypersomnia—long, deep sleep

hyponatremia—low sodium level in the blood

logorrhea—tendency to speak too much

myasthenia—muscle weakness

paresthesia—skin tingling

Parkinsonian—like Parkinson's disease, meaning tremors, rigid muscles, difficulty moving, and unresponsive expression

petechia—tiny red spots on the skin

phototoxicity—skin and eye sensitivity to the sun

polydipsia—excessive thirst

polyuria—frequent urination

priapism—painful, persistent erection (a rare side effect of trazodone)

tachycardia—fast heartbeat

teratogen—causes birth defects

tinnitus—ringing in the ears

Chapter 5

SATANIC WINTER

January

"Where are your skis and bike?" I asked Mark as he dragged his duffel off the revolving carousel. I didn't recognize him at first. His hair was longer and uncombed, and his clothes baggy and worn. In the space of a few months, he had lost the awkwardness of gangly youth and acquired Chris's chiseled features and serious blue eyes.

He had a resigned air about his homecoming. No smile, no warmth to break his morose expression. The edgy, crafty look of Thanksgiving was replaced by a dogged, haunted frown accentuated by dark shadows under his eyes. At least he didn't shrink away when I hugged him.

"My apartment was broken into. All my things were stolen. Everything I own is in this bag," he replied in a flat, colorless tone, glancing at a lumpy canvas tube.

"No matter," I said offhandedly as we walked out of baggage claim to the car. I felt a sharp pang of distress at the theft. It seemed bitterly cruel that not only had he lost his sense of self, but also the few possessions he cared for had been stolen. The ski equipment and bicycle represented many hours of after-school work in a deli and birthday and Christmas gifts. He prized these things and would return from a day's skiing upset when someone had stood on the ski tails in a lift line.

"I have some dinner for you at home. You have to be hungry. We can have a late Christmas. Your presents are waiting for you. Even the stocking." He shrugged.

We climbed over dirty piles of snow tinged salmon pink by overhead mercury lights bordering the parking lot. The urge to talk to him, to touch him, to comfort him, was overpowering. He sat in the car hugging the passenger-side door. The night air had a hard, cold bite to it, and our warm breath steamed the windows. I flipped the heat on high and rubbed my hands together as we waited in line to pay for parking. Without a word, Mark rolled down his window and, like a dog on the open road, pointed his nose into the wind. We rode for some miles in the subfreezing air. My teeth were chattering. He didn't seem to notice the cold.

"Mark, I'm going to freeze." I felt whiny. He hadn't been home an hour, and already I was nagging him. He fixed a long, suspicious stare on me and slowly rolled up the offending window.

How was I supposed to act? What was the right way to behave toward him? There must be a correct and an incorrect way to act, and I was instinctively making the wrong one at every turn. Like the computer game Adventure, where the player makes a decision, Y or N at every fork in the road, I was making small move on top of small move, all sending me farther and farther into the dungeon.

Nevertheless, I had Mark back. The fates had placed him into my care, and now it was up to me to meet the terms of the bargain I had made at Christmas.

At Christmas, as I set three places at the holiday table, I had resolved that if Mark made it home again, I would not submit to petty irritation, anger, and annoyance about his habits. I would ignore his messy room, his absentmindedness, his ability to sit for hours in front of MTV.

To convince him to come home, I promised to leave him alone. "No hovering mother telling me to cut my hair and clean my room," he demanded. No menial household chores, no persistent questions about what he was doing or thinking. He would have quasi–guest status in the house in exchange for living at home and seeing a doctor regularly.

"I just need some time to get myself together," he insisted. "Just leave me alone for a few months. I'll take care of my room and do my own laundry and food, but I won't take out trash, haul firewood, or do yard work." He was on two-year probation in Colorado, and required to perform forty hours of community service and see a mental-health professional. Those were the only demands on him. I readily accepted his terms.

Maybe this was my chance to quiet my worst fear—him taking off and becoming a half-crazy, panhandling street person living out of garbage cans or ending up in jail during another manic episode. To me, Mark's protection was a life-and-death matter.

Battling all of Chris's instincts and experience, I had persuaded him to go along with this jerry-built arrangement. In Chris's childhood, money was short, and both of his parents always worked. If Chris had a summer job, he paid rent to his parents. Saturdays, he scrubbed the kitchen floor and did yard work. For Mark to return home as an honored boarder and contribute nothing, even by gesture, was contrary to everything Chris believed. But Chris acquiesced.

I could not shake the guilt of being partly responsible for Mark's condition. At three in the morning, when sleep was gone, I recalled when the boys were small. I tried to remember how I felt back then.

In 1974, Mark entered kindergarten. He happily ran down the street to school clutching his nap blanket and cookie snack, and I decided to work. Night-school classes and half-days grew into a full-time accounting practice by 1980. Chris was not a house husband, so laundry and meals were done on a pickup basis. The boys usually dressed for school in front of the dryer, where their clothes seemed to live. I left dinners in the oven on a timer, missed soccer games and school plays, and scrawled instructions magneted to the refrigerator with a hasty "I love you." I'd call home most days at four to talk with the boys and hear about their day.

I never doubted my ability to manage family and work. I knew I could juggle them. My plans always worked in the past. Why should this be different? The boys and Chris seemed merely inconvenienced. Nothing more.

Mothering was no big deal for me. I had watched my mother manage a fifth child at age forty-two and took notes. "Don't worry about the small things," she told me. The mothering end of my life was completely under control. Until Mark disintegrated.

Now, I found myself reexamining all those small things I had ignored, wondering if I had missed some clue to Mark's illness or, worse yet, whether I had somehow caused it. I pawed through the memories and tried on various sizes of guilt. I thought about Mark's childhood—his intensity, his verbal quickness, the teachers who were charmed by his devilishness and infuriated with his thoughtless disorganization. No clues here.

And the guilt didn't fit either. The imperfections in my mothering—missing back-to-school nights, nagging him about his messy room, devoting Saturdays to a stranger's tax returns—weren't weighty enough to make me feel that I had brought about Mark's mental illness.

Although I rejected the mantle of mother guilt, it didn't disappear altogether. It continued to hover at the back of my mind—it still does—insisting that I keep trying it on. Today, I can say firmly that my childrearing did not make Mark sick. I'm pretty sure I'll feel this way tomorrow. But I'm not absolutely certain about much anymore.

Tail wagging, Jake greeted us at the door as we hung up coats in the mudroom. Jake's golden-retriever temperament made him an intimate family member but a worthless watchdog. Mark loved animals. When the boys were growing up, he was the one who cared for the dog and cats, combing their coats, cleaning their messes, and worrying about their eating habits. The cats returned his affection by having kittens in his closet, and the dog by waiting patiently at the end of the driveway for his daily return.

Mark and Jake had not met, but Jake took one look at Mark and slunk out of sight. Dog biscuits couldn't induce him back into the room. Even the cats disappeared down the cellar stairs. Mark ignored them all. Not a second glance.

I brought out the Christmas packages, and Mark wordlessly tore away the wrappings and ribbons. The bright foil packages embossed with laughing Santas and tied with perky bows underscored that this was an imitation of the real event. Mark said he needed the clothes but wondered if he could return the other presents. He dumped the contents of the red-and-green knit stocking with MARK woven into the top and idly poked through the playing cards, candies, toothbrushes, and dime-store toys.

Mark had always been very sentimental about Christmas rituals. When I replaced the large colored tree lights with small white ones a few years back, he objected. "That's a designer tree, not a Christmas tree," he argued. On cold December nights, he often sat in the living room in front of a dying fire with only the Christmas tree lights on, dreamily soaking up the pine scent and magical images.

What had I expected? The silly toys that make everyone smile Christmas morning over their cranberry juice now seemed cheap and awkward. As I was cursing myself for smothering him with selfish sentimentality, Mark looked up.

"Thank you," he said formally, and shoved the gifts into a pile. "I'm tired. I think I'll go to bed. I'm not hungry." With those words, he vanished upstairs.

Mechanically, I picked up the torn wrappings and ribbons. This charade had been for me, not him. I had to face the fact that I had staged the mini-Christmas to cauterize my own wounds for the holiday my son had missed.

I slept dreamlessly and without awakening for the first time in months, and was up by seven. The insides of the storm windows were frosted, and the winter cold had penetrated all corners of the house. Zipping up an old down robe, I checked on Mark. He had pulled the quilt over his head until only his shaggy blond hair poked out. I stood soundlessly in his doorway, listening to the soft rushing sound of his breathing. His bag was under my feet where he had dropped it, and after a moment's hesitation, I picked it up to wash his things.

For breakfast, I dug out an old recipe for popovers that was Mark's favorite. I dumped his clothes into the washer with a double dose of soap and bleach. After some ritual straightening up, I left to run errands and to give Mark time to himself.

MARK

One two three, turn. One two three, turn. Stay to left on stairs. Watch out, shadowy corner. Dragons on the rugs, faces on the plates. Don't step on 'em, don't look. Orientals are not to be trusted. Demons all. Beware, Mark, this place will get you. This is a scary house. Satan's in the air, I can feel it. I wish we were in California. Big rooms, big windows, nothing hidden.

Kitchen's new. It's safe. But not her food. The food chain, that's how she'll overpower you. She wants to take over your mind, squeeze out God. Tricky bitch, we'll fool her. I'll eat only my food. Mash-it-in-the-trash.

Where were we? Photographs, yesterday, a little boy. Was I ever really happy? Try to remember laughing. What's going to happen to us? A new life. A better life? We know more, don't we? And knowledge is wisdom. Are we wise, are we happy? Ask the cards—the Wheel of Fortune, the Devil, the Tower of Destruction. Show them the pictures. Find yourself. Where have you gone? The *old Mark is dead. Faded. Evaporated. A sad death. Stop crying. Was I ever there? What's left? Maybe the Magician knows.*

I returned late morning to find him sprawled on the rug in front of the bookcase, surrounded by family picture albums. Old photographs spilled out of the plastic holders and were scattered around. Popovers, eggs, and bacon had been scraped neatly into the garbage, untouched.

I paused as long as possible without appearing nosy. The open album was from his early childhood. Boys in Little League uniforms, in new clothes, frowning on their first day of school, peeking over candles blazing on cakes, proudly holding up six-inch fish or tiny kittens, perched in footed pajamas on Chris's lap. Family mythology created in pictures. Mark was intently studying the rows of pictures, slowly turning the pages.

His return, in spite of his behavior, reenergized me. I finally attacked the cleaning that had been just receiving a fast dust cloth. Mop, bucket, vacuum—I brought on the heavy equipment. I scrubbed the oven, dislodged high spiderwebs, cleaned under rugs, flipped mattresses, renested the pots and pans, and aligned all the canned goods.

Throughout my cleaning aerobics, Mark remained on the floor with the photographs. Coming down the stairs overloaded to save a trip, I brushed the end of the mop across the family pictures on the stairwell wall. The framed photographs cartwheeled down the stairs in a noisy cascade of shattering glass. Miraculously, only one picture was broken, a collage of Mark's school pictures.

I sat down heavily on the last stair and stared at the splintered images of my son behind broken glass, and cried. I usually laugh at superstition but cover my bets by avoiding walking under ladders and mentally noting broken mirrors. This time I was genuinely afraid for all of us. The almost corny symbolism of the broken picture deeply shook me. My family was as fragile as a sheet of plate glass.

After Mark scanned the albums, he proceeded to high school annuals and old school notebooks. That night, as I was emptying the garbage, I discovered the same notebooks, annuals, and pictures crammed into the trash can. I retrieved them, smoothing out the wrinkles and storing them in a back cabinet in the attic. But I said nothing to Mark about my furtive retrieval. Saving his things for a better time was a hopeful thing to do, even if I had doubts about when those times would return.

"How about a trip to New York for the day?" I proposed the next morning with brittle cheerfulness. Maybe city scenery would stimulate some change from this sober, silent stranger who had just moved in.

"Fine," he responded listlessly.

Our New York day became a monologue of my cheerful chatter as a counterpoint to Mark's gloomy silence. In his former life, a trip to New York was an adventure. He'd travel in on the train with a pal, hop the subway to Orchard Street, dig around for leather jackets or jeans, grab a cheap lunch off a corner vendor, and arrive home exclaiming about the wonders of the Big Apple.

This day Mark scarcely uttered a complete sentence. Even during the misery of Thanksgiving, he had talked. Mark loved to talk. He was always overflowing with observations and small discoveries and pushed them verbally around in casual conversation. He loved wordplay and had instinctive wit and humor. In short, he was entertaining company. If I was cooking, he would hop onto the counter, feet swinging, base-ball cap turned backward, and share his thoughts as he snitched bites of whatever I was dicing or sautéing. And he was a careful listener. "Why do you think that?" he would ask, grabbing a peeled carrot when I turned away.

Today, I had to fill the voids of silence. He trudged beside me, hands jammed deep into his pockets, shoulders slumped forward, face set in a mask of discontent and suppressed anger. My casual remarks were received with hostile silence.

"It's pinstripes," I responded to his lifted eyebrows. We were in the Museum of Modern Art. His choice. He wanted to see Monet's water-lilies. In front of us was a large canvas of charcoal gray with evenly spaced thin, vertical chalk stripes. "Like a business suit," I added. He nodded in understanding. We had been wandering through the display rooms separately, meeting occasionally in front of random pictures or displays. While Mark lingered in front of a Tide box sculpture, I meandered to some wood objects.

We ate lunch at a deli where all the patrons share tables and benches. Mark consumed both his and my pastrami sandwich with ferocious intensity. I obliquely watched the reaction of the other diners to Mark's single-minded approach to his meal and his inhaling most of the pickles from the common bowl. No one seemed to mind. But this was New York, where abnormal is normal and being odd counts for nothing. The waiter muttered under his breath and shook his head as he refilled the pickle bowl for the second time.

We headed out of town early in the afternoon to beat the thruway traffic. We occupied silent cocoons buffered by the space between us. My supply of observations and noncommittal remarks was exhausted.

"I think the existential painters and the discoverers of the religion and god are the way of hope and light in a troubled world and the philosophers of good and evil and the devil make us do things we don't want to do and the suffering and human misery of the universe should be redeemed by forgiveness and communion with the Holy Spirit and Oriental mystery." Mark's loud voice startled me.

"What did you say?" I jumped at the sudden sounds. His voice was higher-pitched than usual, and his words flew out in a torrent. The outburst was so abrupt I almost thought I had imagined it.

"The world of the spirit of god thinks sinners are doomed to worlds of red and yellow and eternal hell and damnation with angels and heaven," he added, not noticing my startled reaction.

I concentrated on the road, formulating the proper response to his first voluntary words since coming home. But his speech held no meaning. Maybe it was my perception of his sentences. Maybe all this stuff had a deep psychological import I should write down for Dr. Anderson. Was there meaning here I didn't comprehend and should? Were these profound thoughts from another level of consciousness, or random gibberish?

I tried to remember what the textbooks said. What was important: what he was saying or how he was saying it? Was it better to monitor or criticize, or should I be neutral and nonjudgmental?

"That's an interesting thought," I offered, glancing briefly at him. He was sitting forward in his seat and talking compulsively. Ideas, impressions, clichés, and phrases strung together in no apparent order tumbled from him seemingly beyond his control—a mindflight of ordered thinking. Gone was the open hostility of Thanksgiving, but in its place was a demeanor of superiority, as if only he could understand these esoteric concepts. He verbally circled his ideas, never able to nail them down.

At first I responded with but-on-the-other-hands and what-do-you-think-ofs, but quickly saw that Mark was not interested in conversation. The rest of the trip I drove without speaking, and his deluge of words continued to rain.

Mark's first appointment with Dr. Anderson was at the end of the week. To do something, I wrote out a summary of his medical history, family medical history, and an elaborate description of his behavior. Perhaps this would speed up the therapy process.

My package for the doctor also included samples of Mark's artwork, felt-tip drawings, and scribblings on poster board. He had sat by the hour at the kitchen table sketching complicated cartoonlike drawings of pyramids, lightning bolts, spheres, screaming profiles intricately intertwined with words and a Paisley of bright colors.

Some people are born doodlers. Their telephone messages, notepads, anything with an empty spot, are covered with random figures and drawings. Mark was never a doodler, while Robert had marked up every blotter at my desk doing high school homework or talking on the telephone. Not Mark. Nor was Mark particularly artistic. His skill was always in words, not images. His writing was superior; his artwork, average.

MARK

Moonlight, starlight, no light. Midnight is my hour, darkness my home. The night feels like a blanket, covering, hiding. House is black. They won't hear me, they never do. Asleep in another world, their world. Out here it's the nether world, my world.

A pot, a can, something to burn in. Think, Mark! The iron planter on the lawn. Too heavy. Everything's too heavy. My head hurts, he makes my head ache, he makes my skin crawl with spiders. I wish he'd go away. He shouldn't call me BOY. Take matches, wooden matches. He'll shut up if I do this right. Behind the garage. Rocks, collect rocks. Seven rocks, no, thirteen. What's the best number? Build the fire right, right angles for the positive and negative charges.

The sacrifice. Should I say something? He gave me no words. Empty your mind. Pentangle on flames. Don't blink, don't think. Eyeballs on flames. No words, no sounds, only senses. Flames eat the wooden points of my star. Like my brain. Melt it to red and black. To emptiness. Orange zigzags. The Magician's doing tricks in the embers. Sparks blink and disappear in the blackness. No words. Nothing. Save these stones. Hang them in the bush to protect their magic.

"Is Mark home for semester break? He answered the telephone when I called yesterday," said Pam as she zipped her racquet into its cover. I was sitting, soda in hand, with my Thursday tennis group after a couple of sets of doubles. As with my friendship with Phyllis, Pam Wilson and I had spent many hours on the court together, not too many off. Her polite question had thrown me into a maze of indecision. I played with the pull-top on my soda can, trying to assemble my feelings and thoughts.

How was I going to tell this tale to my friends? Will they think that Mark really has a drug problem and I am covering it up? Or will they think that we have a terrible family secret of madness and abuse now surfacing? Or will they nod sympathetically but think behind their concerned phrases, "Poor parenting. You know, she works—he travels."

The ego-saving lie has never come easily to me. I can get off the Lie with Purpose but not much more. I don't have the energy for deception. I went for the straight truth as Phyllis had over a year ago.

"He was suspended from school and is home seeing a psychiatrist. We think he's manic-depressive."

Silence. She looked down at her hands idly twisting her wedding band. Loud laughter erupted from the Coke machine across the room, and she briefly looked up. I regretted my openness, not for me, but for her discomfort. Casual openers usually don't result in naked revelations. She was probably as I was six months ago and didn't know what manic depression was.

"My husband is manic-depressive. Very few people in town know it. I know *all* about it." She whispered, her eyes quickly checking to see who was within earshot. "Plus, Wendy's oldest," she said, bobbing her head toward the raucous group, "has been in and out of treatment for years. This stuff's common as grass." We fell into a long talk about doctors and drugs. She had been through years of spending sprees, infidelities, depressions, and monstrous bills. I drove home that afternoon feeling lighter than I had since Mark arrived home. Confederations of misery are strong comforts.

I was digging flower beds and bundled up against the knife-edged winds. February had slipped into March, and in spite of the weather Chris and I were outside starting the spring garden work. He wandered along the wetlands behind the house, picking up stray bits of trash that had blown against the trees during the winter. Crystalline patches of snow lingered on matted brown grass in the shadows. Only on the calendar was it spring.

We had reached an accommodation with Mark home. We had

quarantined his bizarre activities into an isolated compartment of our lives. He was no longer the subject of bitter arguments; in fact, we didn't discuss the daily details of life with him at all.

I had developed tunnel vision about the mysterious, nonsensical items I found. Burnt candles, playing cards tucked into cupboards, torn pages from books of witchcraft, slabs of bacon stuck to the side of the house. Mark was furtive in his activities, slipping past me in the kitchen, clutching something, and vanishing upstairs to the bedroom. At night, I could hear him thumping around his room. He seemed to sleep very little, and insisted on preparing his own food.

Dr. Anderson had put him on lithium, but he stopped taking it after a few days, saying that it upset his stomach. I refused to interpret what these small signals meant. Chris's travel schedule had not abated, and he was gone most of the time. I didn't allow myself to examine the possibility that some of his travel might be by design.

"Come with me, I want to show you something," Chris directed.

I knew by the tone in his voice that I would not like what he had found. I reluctantly put my spade aside and followed him down the slope behind the house. He had stopped ahead of me at the end of an old stone wall. I could see a metallic glint from something in the ground.

"What do you think it is?" He pointed at a bucket of metal scraps in a hole in the ground. Extending upward from the bucket was a foil-wrapped hanger.

"It's my lobster pot!" I exclaimed with sudden recognition. I had been casually looking for it all winter and had given up, thinking that I had tucked it into some obscure, safe spot and that it would eventually turn up. Chris pulled it out of the ground and emptied the contents. Out spilled a large battery (*that's* where my large flashlight went) with exposed coils of film wrapped around it and a collection of rocks.

"What do you think Mark is doing here?" Chris was genuinely confused.

"I honestly don't know anymore. I'll ask him," I murmured, feeling the now familiar pain and queasiness in my stomach. Chris shrugged and shook his head in frustration. We stood for a moment gazing down at the contraption in the cold earth. It was ridiculously childlike. If Mark had been five, we would have proudly shown it off and wondered if he was headed for a career in science. With Mark nineteen, it was a tragedy.

"It's a lightning rod. I didn't want the house to be hit by lightning," Mark replied almost rationally when I casually asked him about the thing in the yard. Not having a proper response to him was not new to me anymore. I said nothing.

But just when I was on the cusp of a major decision to consider more drastic measures for Mark, even hospitalization, he would rise early, go jogging, eat a normal breakfast, and talk about his plans for summer. He had applied to the University of Arizona and was confident of acceptance. He debated majoring in biology. Although still shrouded in a veneer of anger at us, he seemed within the limits of normal. No one is exempt from bitterness about some aspect of their childhood.

MARK

Boil, boil, toil and trouble. Isn't that Macbeth? *It's so quiet, just the bubbling water. At night this house is mine, not theirs. We're in control now. Ha ha ha ha. Satan disappeared because of my powers. The voice has backed off. What a wimp! Played God, that's what I did. With my hands in prayer and my head bowed. He thought I was God. Who knows, maybe we are God. Light the candles, just in case.*

Water ready yet? Pasta, rigatoni, spaghetti, lasagna, bologna. Eye-talian delights. Fuck, I don't care what I eat. As long as it doesn't come off Diane's wooden spoon. She doesn't know I saw her I Ching. She's trying to overpower me, to make me her house pet, her household knickknack. But she won't, because I don't eat her food.

Ssshhhh! Feel something? Soft, warm air. From the porch, the cellar, where? Someone's touching my hand! I can feel it! Oh-so-gentle. Like making love. She's leading me! She wants to DANCE! An angel has come to dance! To glide with me and mix our souls. We twirl around the kitchen. My heart will break. Is this my happiness? Is this the end?

"Dr. Anderson, I'm calling to ask you about Mark's progress. You know he won't take the lithium. What do you think we should do?" I had vacillated on making this call, but after the lightning rod I felt I had no choice. It was Monday morning, and Chris was gone for the week again.

"Well, you know I can't really breach Mark's confidentiality," began Dr. Anderson. He was a small, soft-looking man with a timid voice.

"But if the diagnosis is correct, he may have another manic episode, and then maybe he'll be more agreeable to treatment."

"That's it? What about your sessions with him? Are you getting any clues about what else we can do for him? Is this all you can do?" I could hear my voice rise in anger. Exactly what is my hundred dollars an hour buying here?

"I can't really talk about our sessions together, you know they are private," he said evenly, enunciating every word as kindergarten teachers do to their pupils. He sounded like Mr. Rogers, the guru of children's television.

"Look, I feel Mark needs help, and what we are doing doesn't seem like much. I don't see a lot of progress. Do you want to know how he's doing at home? You never responded to the letter I sent you." I was on a tear now. Screw it if he thought I was a rash, pushy mother. This jerk was doing nothing that I could see to make Mark better.

"Calm down, Mrs. Wakefield. No need to get yourself all worked up," he replied placidly. If there was ever a response guaranteed to throw gas on the fire, it was "Calm down." But just as I was loading the cannons for a major fusillade, I took a deep breath and told myself to be smart. Telling Dr. Anderson what he could do with his ideas was dumb. I would be earning an entry in Mark's file as a part of the problem, not the solution.

"We'll have to wait with Mark and see how he does over a period of time. Have you and your husband considered family therapy?" he added.

Here it is again. The therapy answer to honest emotion and legitimate anger. Under no circumstances would Chris ever consent to open up to a therapist. He was intensely private. His lifetime habit of keeping his thoughts and emotions to himself was not about to be breached for a Dr. Anderson. The thought of Chris and me sitting in Dr. Anderson's dusty office dissecting frustrations like so many laboratory frogs was impossible to imagine. And I agreed with Chris. Venting my frustration and examining my feelings about Mark would produce nothing. I wanted information, results, not feel-good-and-learn-to-live-with-your-problems bromides.

"No, we don't feel that would address the main problem, namely, Mark's illness," I said testily.

"We'll continue with our sessions and see how he does," replied Dr. Anderson smoothly, neatly stepping around my anger.

"Fine, do what you think best," I mumbled. Later, at my Monday morning tennis game, I broke two strings, sprayed shots everywhere, and came home with a pulled muscle in my back. I blamed Dr. Anderson.

I tossed the mashed garlic into the hot olive oil along with chopped onion and celery. While the mixture sautéed, I diced red peppers. The sweet, pungent smell of garlic and onions filled the room as I poked the ingredients around the soup pot and watched the late-afternoon April sunlight slant through the water-spotted kitchen window. Chris silently stole up behind me in his ragg-wool-socked feet and encircled me with his arms, hands covered with dirt, held away. He'd been outside digging holes for his asparagus bed.

"What's for dinner? I could smell the garlic outside with the fan on. When do Tony and Ingrid get here? They're not bringing their cat, are they?" He rubbed his face against my cheek. "What are you going to do about Mark? He's not going to sit around acting weird all night, is he?"

"No, of course not. He's much better, and is looking forward to their visit. And no, Nutmeg's not coming. Ingrid said she's at the vet's getting her fur combed out. Himalayans get terrible fur balls. Tony's bringing his birthday present for dinner—a lasagna. I'm making minestrone to go with it." I poured in beef stock and tomatoes and reached over to chop more vegetables.

Tony was Queens-Italian and Ingrid was chic Canadian. They had met selling computer systems for IBM and married last year and were our closest friends. Chris and Tony used to work together. They came up from lower Connecticut for Saturday nights from time to time. I didn't even change the sheets between visits. Chris and Tony would go to the market and load up on beer and pretzels—sports-fan soul food, Tony maintained—and camp out in front of televised basketball. Ingrid and I took field trips through the abundant local antique shops and sifted for precious finds. Even Mark was looking forward to their coming.

"Tony got a lasagna for his birthday? His mother's?" Mark asked hopefully as he bent over the simmering soup for a sniff. Tony's mother's lasagna was the stuff of legend. Ingrid had been scheming for years without luck for the recipe. We planned to subject it to analysis this evening. I dumped the white beans into the pot.

We had just had the first warm week of the spring, and the change in Mark was dramatic. While he was still odd around the edges, he seemed more the way he was that weekend in Colorado six months ago. He had even offered to help with small jobs around the house and paint the picket fencing in exchange for a new pair of dark glasses. The grass was greening, the apple trees budding, and the daffodils exploding into bloom. The red buds of the maples were a faint blush on the distant hillsides. Even Jake's fur was growing back. He had neurotically chewed at his tail since Mark's return. While they still avoided each other, the dog didn't slink quite so much anymore.

"Mark seems to be doing well," volunteered Ingrid as she checked the temperature on the lasagna. Mark, Tony, and Chris were in the next room watching a basketball game. I could hear Mark's voice above the others just a bit louder than usual.

Open bags of chips littered the table, and empty beer bottles were scattered around. Ingrid and I had abandoned the room for the kitchen. The men had rebuffed our efforts to put the chips in a bowl and pick up the empties.

"He does seem better. The warmer weather has done wonders for him. Hopefully, we're out of the woods with this thing. Arizona says that if he has a B average this summer, he can enroll in the fall."

I could hear the confident tone of my voice, the hopeful coda at the end of my sentence. The in-control mother with her plans. "Why, yes," I was saying, "my child had a bit of a derailment from the College Track, but we're back now." I was settling into my assured replies as if nothing had happened. Then why did I still have this dark dread when I couldn't sleep or when Mark conjured up "the Look," that demonic black mood that descended on him from time to time?

Ingrid and I had waited until the basketball game was over, and put out the plates and food in the kitchen for everyone to serve himself. The table was quiet as we Parmesanned soup, poured wine, and dug for favorite chunks of the bread from the basket.

"Tony, this is great," said Mark, nodding vigorously, mouth full. "So who's going to win the NBA this year?" he asked, forking in another bite.

"Pistons look good."

"Maybe it's the whole-milk ricotta."

"His free-throw percentage is terrible."

"More Parmesan, please."

"Is that wine bottle empty?"

"Why three coffee beans in the Sambuca? Tell me again, I keep forgetting," Mark asked.

Conversation was batted around like a shiny beach ball, Mark inserting comments here and there, laughing and going back for thirds on lasagna.

I covertly watched him. Although he was not the person I remember taping *New Yorker* cartoons to my steering wheel or fertilizing "help wanted" into the lawn, he did seem almost a normal teenager. His edgy suspiciousness had evaporated. In the soft candlelight, as we shared food and talk, the past months seemed a bad memory.

"See you later," Mark shouted to Ingrid and Tony as we walked out to their car Sunday afternoon. He was shirtless, paintbrush in hand, radio perched on a post, slapping primer on the picket fencing. Working on his tan for Arizona, he said, although no formal acceptance had arrived yet.

MARK

enoughenoughenough. deadness, nothingness, blackness, senseless. time to know the truth. who are we, what are we, is there an end to this deadness? it feels like eternity. AAAggghh. i'm so tired, so sleepy. tired of the deadness. it never ends. maybe we're immortal. satan and i may live forever.

i don't like stealing, but i had to steal this. the test for immortality cannot be bought. weed killer. rat poison. they have greater purposes. it's destiny. i knew i wouldn't get caught, it's in the cards. the nursery man didn't see a thing. i'm invisible. should i stay in the truck or drive home? doesn't matter, i'll know the truth anywhere. pull over. park. "joshua tree" in the cassette.

they look harmless, ordinary: red and yellow. this is special though. made for me. ortho liquid sevin. it's a message. number seven. my destiny. and d-Con pellets. kills rats and mice. ha! rats. my life is crawling with rats.

here goes. pellet snack, cocktail chaser. maybe the pain will stop the deadness. deadness, immortality, no difference. tastes like sawdust and chemicals. now wait. is it over? again, more. nothing.

The flashing light atop the police cruiser made the scene of the accident easy to find in the dim, late May afternoon. The road was washed with a recent rainstorm, the red light casting an oscillating rosy glow on the faces of the officer and tow-truck driver. They stood in front of the smashed truck, assessing the damage. The wrecker, battered Red Sox hat in hand, was balanced on his beefy haunches, inspecting the front undercarriage, while the officer, a marine-recruit look-alike, was filling out a form on the hood of the damaged truck.

Mark stood off to the side, waiting for the verdict. The front end of the truck was sunk into the wood fence along the blind curve in the two-lane road. Telltale skid marks stretched for twenty-five yards.

Mark had called from a nearby pay phone. "I wrecked the truck," he declared without preamble.

"Are you okay?"

He hesitated for a second and slowly said, "Unfortunately, yes."

I assumed he was anticipating his father's anger. "I'll be right there."

"You the owner?" asked the wrecker as I approached. I nodded and felt my heart speed up. Mark looked unhurt.

"How bad is it?" I asked. He rubbed his stubbly chin, scratched his head, and craned his neck under the truck for another look.

"Frame may be bent. Could be totaled. I'll tow it to Leo and Al's and we'll see." I nodded again and turned to the officer, who was neatly separating carbons.

"I'll have to cite him again for the accident. No other vehicles were involved. He apparently took the curve too fast and hit the barrier. Reckless driving," he concluded, handing Mark his driver's license. Mark stepped closer to retrieve it gingerly. His look was impenetrable.

"Again?" I asked. "What do you mean 'again'?"

"I cited Mr. Wakefield just an hour ago for reckless driving. He was tailgating my vehicle over on Route Sixty-three."

I turned to Mark. "Is that so? What happened?"

"I wasn't doing anything but minding my own business, and he gave me a ticket," Mark said in a low, defiant voice. He folded his arms over his chest and looked at his feet.

"Why? I don't understand. Tell me why, Mark!" The pitch of my voice rose. The troll had peeked out again from under the bridge. I was about to break my bargain.

"Just what the hell were you doing here?" I shouted at him.

"He was very lucky. Apparently, he wasn't wearing a seat belt and only hit his head on the windshield," interjected the officer. Mark's forehead was bruised, and the truck window displayed a spiderweb crack. "I'm not going to cite him for not wearing a belt."

"I don't see any possible excuse for this, Mark. It was stupid care-lessness. How could you? You weren't even wearing your seat belt— you could have been killed! The truck is probably a total loss. Don't you even care?" I wanted to shake him, to slap him. He seemed so smug and indifferent, oblivious to the destruction he left in his trail. And I was always the one who cleaned up after him. He didn't give a damn about anyone else.

"I was trying to . . . I was . . ." he stammered in a small, thin voice, then paused midsentence. "Forget it. I'm sorry. It just happened, that's all. What do you want me to do now?"

"It's done. We'll talk about it later," I snapped.

I slammed the car door, making Mark jump, and we headed home. Mark slunk in his seat, arms wrapped around himself. "Put on your seat belt. Think you're immortal?" I said as I braked sharply for the traffic light, throwing him forward. He dutifully pulled the belt around him.

"I'm going for a walk," Mark said over his shoulder as he disappeared out the kitchen door after we arrived home. I was pulling food out of the refrigerator for dinner. Chris was due home in an hour.

"Where's the truck? Did you finally take it in for an oil change?" asked Chris cheerfully as he came in the door, tossing *The Wall Street Journal* on the table.

"No," I said flatly, not looking up from peeling potatoes. "Mark had an accident."

"He's not hurt, is he?" he asked quickly, the cheerfulness gone in an instant.

"No, he's fine, but the truck is not. The wrecker said it could be a total loss. No other cars involved. He hit a fence. Going too fast." I spit out the details in clipped phrases.

"Poor Mark. He must feel terrible. Where is he now?"

"What do you mean 'poor Mark'?" I lashed out. "He totaled the truck with his carelessness. And he doesn't give a damn."

Chris was startled. Normally, his temper far outpaced mine. He'd grit his teeth and coldly demand apologies and mete out harsh punishments. His wrath, although always in control, was fearsome. I wheeled around to the sink and finished the potatoes, ripping off large hunks of brown skin and white flesh and stuffing them into the garbage disposal.

"I'm going to go look for Mark. He may want to talk," said Chris as he went out the door.

Fifteen minutes later, Chris and Mark reappeared, walking up the hill to the house. The rain clouds had blown away, and the sky was pale pink in the twilight. Mark was walking, head down, hands in his jacket pockets, up the incline with Chris beside him, his hand lightly resting on Mark's shoulder. Chris was talking intensely, Mark listening. Watching them, I felt envious that Mark would not listen to me as he would to Chris.

Mark evaporated into his room as soon as he came in the back door. Chris came into the kitchen behind him, poured two glasses of wine, and handed one to me.

"I want to talk to you," he said softly. He took his glass and sat down at the kitchen table, pulling out a second chair for me. Reluctantly, I joined him.

"Up until today, you have been acting like Mother Teresa with a hair shirt. You feel that none of this illness with Mark would have happened if you were a better mother when he was small. Right?" I shrugged my shoulders noncommittally.

"So you have been trying to make up for what you think is twenty years of mistakes by joining the Order of Our Lady of the Suburbs." I ran my fingers around the edge of the wineglass, not looking at Chris, now leaning forward and looking intently at me across the table.

"You've probably been baking cookies and taking him on field trips," he surmised. "I know you think that I have been totally divorced from what's been going on, from what you've been going through and from Mark's troubles." His face softened, the chiseled lines smoothed. "I'm not, not at all. But you have grabbed on to this thing, like an angry dog attacking an intruder, and asked for no help. This has become your personal crusade."

He reached across the table and put his hand on mine. "I may not take four showers a day, Diane, but that doesn't mean I don't hurt too. You know me. I'm no good at dealing with emotion, or even talking about it. It's just not in me. But that doesn't mean I don't love you, and Mark, very, very much. And your pain is my pain."

He turned away to reach for the wine bottle and refill our glasses. "Mark needs both of us, but as adults, not as long-suffering mother and distant father. But I can't share this with you as long as you continue in the guilt thing and insist on trying to fix it on your own. You're going to drive me away and be of no use to Mark."

I was crying now, not delicate tears inching down my cheeks but red-face-swollen-eye-type crying that is beyond control. I could barely catch my breath between sobs.

"This accident—something doesn't make sense. I think he was trying to hurt himself, not wreck the truck," continued Chris.

His words stunned me. How could I be so blind? My only thought had been that Mark was trying to get even with us by smashing the truck. No other possibility had occurred to me.

"Mark didn't say it in so many words, but that was my feeling after talking to him. I think he got a good scare. Actually, my talk with him coming back to the house was the best we have had in a long time."

I rose and found a Kleenex to wipe my eyes and blow my nose. Chris came over and held me close to him. "The situation with Mark really will get better. I know it will." He stroked my hair. "You just have to have faith and not take all the blame on yourself. Can we send Mother Teresa back to the convent and pick up where we left off last fall? Mark still hopes to go to Arizona. He wants his life back again. I think we should let him have another chance."

I bent over to dig yet another rock out of the fresh dirt under my feet, backhanded it into the wheelbarrow, slowly straightened my stiff back, and surveyed the afternoon's work. Three more feet and my herb bed would be ready. The potted plants, lined up on the edge of the walk, awaited planting.

"Boo!" said Mark, appearing behind me with a clutch of mail in his hand. "Arizona, here we come! It's all set. I'm in. Here's the letter. Life begins anew." He sat down on the stone steps rereading the letter. "I start in two weeks."

"Mark, have you talked about this with Dr. Anderson? We should find a doctor in Tucson as a backup for you. What does he say?" I turned another spadeful of dirt.

"We've gone over all this before. Fuck Dr. Anderson. He doesn't know anything. I don't need a doctor in Tucson. There is the health service if I need it. Anyway, I'm just fine," he pronounced loudly. I quickly looked up.

"What now?" he demanded. "You're not going to start in on me again about 'my illness,' are you? I'm just fine, thank you. What I need is my own peer group, meaningful work, intellectual stimulation, a change of scenery. What I don't need is your doctors and pills and telling me I'm sick when I have never felt better in my life," he said angrily.

"You're right, of course. You need all those things. I just worry that we're not out of the woods yet," I offered in my mildest, least offensive tone, flipping another rock behind me.

"You've no faith in me. No faith in my ability to do things for myself, to get well and manage my own life. You just want to keep me around as a house pet to mother and bake cookies for." Was he right? I honestly didn't know.

"We need to get your clothes together for the desert. You'll need some shorts." I began smoothing the clods. Mark was orbiting around me, so we continued to face each other. He leaned forward into my face as I bent over the rake. A bit too closely.

"I can get my own things. All you have to do is get me a ticket to Arizona. The rest is easy," he said with finality, and retreated inside, slamming the door behind him. I continued my raking, cursing the intractable clods.

"Twenty-four years is a long time to be married. I like it though, this middle-aged comfort with the same person," Chris said, raising his wineglass for an anniversary toast. The windows of the restaurant overlooked the Boston Public Garden through translucent leaves on a late June evening. Swan boats floated among the lily pads on the pond on the far side, the lights from the surrounding buildings reflected in the water.

Mark had left for Arizona ten days before. We hadn't heard from him except for a short "I'm-here-in-my-room-making-lots-of-friends-like-my-classes" call. During the conversation, Chris had given me a knowing look that all was well.

Yet I was still uneasy. But as my father says: Why go looking for your problems? They find you soon enough.

Chapter 6

FINDING PROFESSIONAL
HELP

A Medical Maze

You are about to enter, if you haven't already, the labyrinthine world of mental-health professionals. Whether you're desperate for emergency medical help or searching for a therapist for regular sessions, you will find the mental-health profession bewildering and frustrating.

It's confusing because mental illness has spawned so many professionals—narrow specialists and those who offer a medley of care and treatments. Patients and families, on first meeting a psychiatrist, social worker, psychiatric nurse, or whatever, can't know exactly what this person does or how she might help. To pick your way through the maze, you have to ask lots of questions while also having a sense of where you're headed. We'll give you ideas on that in this chapter.

Knowing Where You're Headed: Meds and Therapy

A manic-depressive, especially someone new to the illness, so to speak, has two pressing needs: medication and psychotherapy. Doctors, patients, and families agree that medication is absolutely essential, even if it's limited to lithium. And the only people who can write prescriptions are licensed medical doctors.

The need for psychotherapy is much more debatable, even controversial. A host of mental-health professionals, some doctors but some with degrees other than M.D., offer therapy. In searching for a therapist, you're exploring a much larger universe than in searching for someone to dispense medication.

Not all manic-depressives need or want therapy, and experts clash over whether it does any good. Those against it say that medication alone is a much more effective, efficient treatment for curbing symptoms, and especially for preventing relapses. Another argument is that manic-depressives aren't responsive therapy patients—when manic, they don't listen and have little judgment or insight, and when depressed, they consider their condition temporary and part of a larger cycle, and would rather wait for it to pass than try to dissect it.

And some manic-depressives don't like the idea of weekly sessions that remind them of their mental illness, especially if they're feeling stable and their life is in control. We've talked to many manic-depressives who don't use a therapist—they see a doctor every month for their meds, and that's it for medical attention. They're happy with this arrangement.

But not all manic-depressives are so fortunate. We mentioned psychotherapy in the context of someone new to the disease—someone who's just been diagnosed or suspects he may have it.

Manic depression, particularly because it can strike so suddenly, creates enormous personal and social problems. Lives are ripped apart in midstream. A person in the turmoil of mania or depression alienates family and friends, ruins relationships, jeopardizes jobs and schoolwork, loses confidence, and undermines the strongest self-image.

Even after early episodes have passed and the symptoms have quieted, researchers have found that a manic-depressive may not function at the same level as before. The manic-depressive may have difficulty with work that was once easy, or with finding a new job and coping at home. Further complicating a patient's life is the possibility that he has acquired an alcohol- or drug-abuse problem along the way. Finally, a patient has to face the stigma of mental illness. Given a life turned upside down, psychotherapy or counseling, coupled with drug therapy, helps.

Furthermore, some people don't like taking drugs. Not only can they produce debilitating, even dangerous side effects, but they too are regular reminders of a person's mental illness. So these patients prefer talk therapy to chemical modification.

Psychotherapy will not cure the illness, and many experts believe the primary symptoms of mania and depression are better fought with medication. Therapy is helpful to combat the fallout from the disease—

the personal and emotional troubles it has created or that accompany it.

Doctors who advocate psychotherapy for manic depression give other reasons. Dr. Robert Benson, in an article in *Diseases of the Nervous System*, declares that psychotherapy for a bipolar patient: (1) keeps a patient motivated to continue lithium; (2) eases the fear and terror of manic episodes; (3) allows a patient to explore new avenues of creativity, and; (4) allows the therapist to monitor a patient's mood as an early detection of noncompliance or symptoms breaking through.

A Frustrating Relationship

Before explaining about the various mental-health professions, we want to begin with a warning. Many patients and families in their early dealings with mental-health professionals come away bewildered and angry. This isn't simply our suspicion or conclusion from talking to a few people. It's a documented fact of medical life, and has even been researched and studied. Studies have focused on families' reactions to the mental-health system, and here's what they found:

- Two thirds were given a diagnosis within two years of the relative's first episode; one third waited two to eleven years or received no diagnosis.

- Only one quarter of the families received an explanation about their relatives' treatment plan.

- Less than one quarter were told about possible side effects of drug treatments.

- Most families spent less than an hour a week with doctors or staff.

- Most contact with staff or doctors consisted of informal chats in the wards or corridors, or over the telephone.

- Three quarters of the relatives initiated the contact themselves.

One of the studies concludes, "There continues to be a general lack of professional awareness of and response to the families' needs, as evidenced in part by the growth of self-help groups for families and friends of the chronically mentally ill." (Support groups are discussed later in this chapter.)

The reasons for this troubled relationship lie in miscommunication and misunderstanding. Patients and families need lots of information about mental illness. Not just medical facts, but explanations about all the pieces in the puzzle of mental illness. They want to know what happens in a locked ward, what their insurance covers, whether a mentally ill person is violent, where a grown-up manic-depressive can live after hospitalization, and on and on.

They pose these questions to doctors and other mental-health professionals—people we expect to have answers and solve problems—and they don't respond. The answers aren't in one place or lodged in one person. Answers are scattered, and some questions seem to have no answers, which is even more infuriating. Mental illness is wrapped in mysteries and uncertainties. No one knows *exactly* what causes it, whether siblings will get sick, or who will try suicide.

But often patients and families look to a doctor or a social worker for support and hear only bits and pieces, and the result is anger and frustration. That's the misunderstanding—expecting mental-health professionals to know everything.

Then there's the miscommunication. Doctors and others are not very frank about the limitations of what they can do. They don't share with patients and families uncertainties, hunches, or knowledge gaps. And they may not explain treatments, drug side effects, or changed ideas about a diagnosis. Some are simply bad communicators—inarticulate, preoccupied, or uncomfortable with all the charged emotion around mental illness.

Another type of mental-health professional is reluctant to share information because she suspects that the family is at the root of the problem, that the attitudes, emotions, and atmosphere at home have stirred up the illness. Families, suspected as part of the problem and not the solution, may be distanced or cut off from a patient's treatment activities. Doctors may not share information, coolly deflect a family's questions, or even limit access to a hospitalized patient.

Other mental-health professionals may leave families in the dark because of patient-therapist confidentiality. While confidentiality is a necessary medical tool in the patient-therapist relationship, it's sometimes used to shield information a patient or family should rightfully hear, like medical facts and general treatment protocol. (We discuss the limits of confidentiality later in this chapter.)

We begin on this somewhat negative note not to discourage or malign, but to reassure patients and families that feelings of helplessness and uncertainty are typical. When you can't extract answers or identify the right doctor or are unsure what to do next, remember that many others have been there.

Even more important, in the end there's good news. While initial encounters with mental-health professionals may be maddening, patients and families who persist in their search for good professional help often find someone. Patients and families typically say that they hate dealing with mental-health professionals or doctors in general, but that they have found a psychiatrist, social worker, psychopharmacologist, or whatever who is absolutely wonderful. This person answers their phone calls, is truthful and forthcoming, is current on medical developments, and understands what patients and families need. These medical people are out there. You just have to be dogged and determined to find them.

Ways to Sift Through
To find this wonderful mental-health professional (or professionals—we'll talk about the team approach later), you have to ask questions and trust your instincts.

Individual names and referrals are available from a number of sources—professional medical or support organizations, family doctors, medical schools, hospitals, and friends. (The appendices contain referral sources.) Experts agree that the most knowledgeable professionals are attached to teaching institutions or hospitals. Contact the hospital or medical center associated with a university or college and ask to be put in touch with its psychiatric center or unit. From there, get the names of individual doctors and other mental-health professionals working with bipolar patients. A morning on the telephone can produce a long list of names. However, this list will probably be general and need culling.

To pare it down, look for practitioners with these qualities:

- Has clinical experience with manic-depressive patients similar to your case (e.g., adolescent manic depression, lithium-resistant manic depression).
- Has privileges to practice at an accredited hospital (preferably a hospital associated with a university or teaching institution).
- Recognizes the biological and chemical origins of the illness.
- Stays current on new research and findings. (These often come out of the National Institute of Mental Health, appear in profes-

sional journals such as *American Journal of Psychiatry, Archives of General Psychiatry, Journal of Affective Disorders, JAMA* [*Journal of the American Medical Association*], and *Hospital and Community Psychiatry*, or in seminars and continuing-education studies.)

- Is accessible to family members for nonconfidential information about the illness and the patient's treatment and progress.

You should meet and talk with the prospective doctor or therapist. This is probably inconvenient, but instincts, impressions, and personal chemistry are important in choosing a mental-health professional. If a patient doesn't like or respect a doctor, or is intimidated by him, the treatment can easily fail. The best way to judge a professional's style, philosophy, and treatment goals is to see and hear him.

In this interview, you should raise questions about key psychiatric issues for an idea of how the health professional treats manic-depressives. Regardless of the type of treatment offered, you'll want to know about treatment goals. There are lots of possible treatment goals. These are some, and their relative importance differs with each patient:

- Eradicate symptoms of the illness.
- Prescribe medication and long-term drug treatment.
- Understand origins and causes.
- Help the patient understand and accept the illness.
- Restore the patient to normal functioning.
- Prevent relapses.

Each of these is accomplished differently, and most professionals can't address all of them. The patient and his family should have an idea of what they want to accomplish immediately and over the long run.

Another line of questioning surrounds the professional's ideas about the origins of the disease. These beliefs may well set the course of treatment. Ask the professional how much he thinks a patient's past or childhood contributes to the illness. Does he think the illness is caused by the individual patient, internal conflicts, or outside stress and relationships? A therapist who believes the illness stems from bad parenting or deep-seated family conflicts and limits his interview to exploring this won't be much help in getting a patient whose syndrome does not fit his particular blueprint up and running.

Some people are uncomfortable quizzing medical people about techniques and beliefs, fearing perhaps the expert will dismiss their uneducated questions. Don't be reticent or intimidated in your search for help. How a mental-health professional responds and reacts to you says much about the person. Sensitivity, compassion, a knowledgeable understanding of the illness, honesty, and candor are just as important as a wall crammed with certificates.

Start with the Medical Doctors

You need a licensed doctor for medication. Although this person can be a nonspecialist like a general practitioner or family doctor, you're better off with a psychiatrist or psychopharmacologist. (Some psychoanalysts are M.D.'s, but their expertise usually does not include drug therapy or treating major mental illness.)

Telephone books are full of psychiatrists, but you are not shopping for someone who treats the "worried well." Many general psychiatrists do not have hands-on familiarity with major mental illness. They specialize in outpatient treatment, dealing with people whose lives are not severely disrupted by their symptoms. A manic-depressive needs a psychiatrist with firsthand knowledge of how to treat and medicate major mental illness.

A useful place to start your search is by contacting the experienced experts, the researchers in affective disorders and manic depression. Appendix A lists the doctors and institutions that have received grants from the Alcohol, Drug Abuse and Mental Health Administration to study psychiatric illnesses, particularly those related to bipolar illness. While some of these people are researchers only, they may point you to colleagues who are practitioners.

Why a Psychiatrist?

A psychiatrist is a licensed doctor who has attended four years of medical school, then devoted four more to residency training in a hospital, clinic, or other medical center. Don't confuse "psychiatrist" with "psychotherapist," which does not necessarily mean a licensed medical doctor. The term "psychiatrist" is a legal title.

The first year of residency is internship. You may encounter interns and residents in psychiatry in a hospital, because they work with licensed psychiatrists. Sometime after medical school and during residency, a doctor may take an examination given by a state medical board and receive a license to practice. A doctor can also earn a license by meeting the requirements of the National Board of Medical Examiners. He might do this if he's licensed to practice in one state and wants to move to a state where there is no reciprocity.

Following residency, a doctor can sit for an examination administered by an independent, private organization called the American Board of Medical Specialties, which issues certificates in individual specialties, like psychiatry. Certification is the paper proof that a doctor has gone beyond a state license and met requirements to practice a specialty.

Doctors establish their own professional guidelines through medical associations and certification boards that issue educational and training standards and certificates. These groups are like the American Bar Association and American Institute of Certified Public Accountants. They're private, voluntary, and nongovernmental. In medicine, the American Board of Medical Specialties (ABMS) is the largest such group, and is made up of twenty-three specialty boards.

Professional organizations can be confusing, even misleading, because some are simply membership groups while others impose strict education and examination requirements. A framed document on a doctor's wall may signify that he has completed three years of specialty training and is highly qualified. Or it may simply mean the person paid $150 dues to an association with an official-sounding name.

"Board certified" means a doctor has met certain requirements for a specialty as required by the ABMS. In general, these requirements consist of having a medical degree, completing residency, successful performance or competency, a couple years' experience in the specialty, and passing a written, and sometimes oral, examination.

Some doctors describe themselves as "board eligible," meaning they possess the qualifications for certification by the ABMS but haven't formally completed the process. The ABMS thinks the term is used too loosely and has become meaningless because virtually anyone can use it. If you encounter a psychiatrist using the term, you can't assume anything, so ask about clinical experience.

The ABMS certifies psychiatrists in the specialty of general psychiatry. For recognition in a subspecialty, doctors turn to a member board or organization of the ABMS. One such subspecialist is the consultation-liaison psychiatrist, who provides general hospital staff and doctors with diagnoses and consultations, and connects them with mental-health services outside the hospital. Another is geriatric psychiatrist, specializing in emotional illnesses of the over-65. A child psychiatrist does receive board certification after two years of training.

Combine or Separate Jobs?
A patient looking for meds and therapy may find a psychiatrist who knows the intricacies of drug therapy and is a skilled psychotherapist. But this may not be the case, and you may decide to separate the two functions. There are pros and cons for either option.

You may want to deliberately split the two functions. Some medical experts point out that a patient-therapist relationship can be tumultuous, sometimes even discontinued, and if a therapist is also dispensing the person's medication, then that treatment is also disrupted. On the other hand, the argument for putting the medication and therapy responsibilities with the same person is that psychotherapy may show the psychiatrist how well medication is working.

These functions may be separated if you find either a psychiatrist who is very knowledgeable about pharmacology but less adroit or interested in psychotherapy, or a therapist who is a skilled counselor but cannot dispense medication. You want an expert in drug therapy and someone whose psychotherapy will help you. This may be one person, two, or even more. It depends on whom you find and what kind of therapy you want. (We discuss types of therapy later in the chapter.)

The Drug Specialist
Called a psychopharmacologist, this person is a medical doctor who specializes in drug treatment. Normally, she is also a psychiatrist, either board certified or board eligible. This doctor prescribes various drugs and tests their levels. While psychopharmacology is a highly refined branch of psychiatry, it is not a board-certified specialty. In experience and training, its practitioners may differ greatly beyond their degrees. Their expertise lies in their experience matching up a particular drug treatment with a specific cluster of symptoms.

A psychopharmacologist attacks mental illness as a biological, not psychological, problem. This is a major demarcation line in psychiatry. Declares a special article in the *American Journal of Psychiatry*, "The splitting of 'pharmacotherapy' and 'psychotherapy' in particular has become a chronic (albeit changing) characterization of the field of psychiatry to the present day." The profession is visibly split between those who believe that mental illness is a biological, physical, chemical illness, best treated with the "somatic" therapies of pharmacology, ECT, sleep deprivation or biofeedback, and those who believe its origins are rooted in psychological, emotional experiences, and that psychological therapies are equally, if not more, effective.

This schism is not an ivory-tower argument. It has a direct impact on patients and families, for they must decide which advice to follow. There are no doubts where psychopharmacologists stand in this debate. While some psychiatrists may straddle this issue, placing more or less equal belief in medication and talking therapy, the psychopharmacologist is a firm believer in science and medicine. Patients know for certain the course of treatment—they take various drugs, frequently a combination of drugs, at different doses that may be adjusted along the way. The doctor will monitor the blood levels of the drugs and will meet regularly with the patient to talk about how the drugs affect symptoms and side effects. Through this trial-and-error process, they try to find the best mixture, and often succeed.

The Talking Therapists

The controversy about the efficacy of psychotherapy with manic depression centers on only particular kinds of therapy—therapy that attempts to eradicate the symptoms. The other kind of therapy, which tries to rehabilitate and bring a person back to normal functioning, is much less disputed. A layman might not be aware of this distinction at first glance. Typically, these two types are lumped together as "psychotherapy." A therapist's title or professional label may not tell you what kind of therapy she offers. Or a therapist may stage a two-front assault, trying to ease the symptoms and help a person become more functional.

The upshot of all this crisscrossing of goals and blurring of functions is that the patient has to talk to the therapist and make the decisions. A patient can choose either to follow a certain type of therapy or to opt for an individual therapist, regardless of her approach, trusting the person to apply the best treatment.

Here are some questions to ask a therapist when evaluating how this person would treat manic depression.

- What's your treatment philosophy—for example, analytic, cognitive, behavioral, or eclectic? (We explain these approaches later.)

- What experience have you had in clinical psychiatry and working with mental illness?
- How would you recognize signs that I am getting worse or better? For instance, can you detect the beginnings of tardive dyskinesia?
- Are you familiar with the clinical issues surrounding manic depression? (For instance, the initial grief reaction from the shock of learning about manic depression and the feeling of hopelessness that sometimes accompanies acceptance of the illness.)

We use the expression "talking therapists" to include a wide spectrum of mental-health professionals. They're a diverse group in experience and education. The list begins with the psychiatrist, whom we have already discussed. What follows is an explanation of the other kinds of therapists.

Psychotherapist
Anyone can call himself a "psychotherapist." It's a generic term, sort of like the title "consultant," which may be a fresh college graduate looking for work or an independent investment banker with three advanced degrees and twenty years' experience. The only information the title conveys is that a person practices some type of psychological therapy.

A psychotherapist's education, training, and qualifications range from a highly schooled medical doctor to someone with a bachelor's degree in psychology and a week's study at an obscure institute.

Psychologist
A psychologist has an academic degree in psychology (bachelor's, master's, or doctorate) and experience in counseling or psychotherapy. Like other mental-health professionals, the more qualified practitioners have been certified by a standard-setting organization, in this case the American Board of Professional Psychology. To be certified by this group, a psychologist needs a Ph.D. in psychology, five years' experience, and successful completion of its exam. The organization offers diplomas in six specialties: clinical psychology, counseling psychology, industrial/organizational psychology, school psychology, forensic psychology, and clinical neuropsychology.

Social Worker

Social workers are scattered throughout the mental-health field, offering counseling, formal psychotherapy, crisis intervention, and community-resource information. They fill gaps left by other mental-health professionals. You find them in public and private hospitals, and private practice.

Social workers reach different levels of expertise, with each step adding a cluster of initials to their names. A social worker who has earned a bachelor's degree uses the label BSW. A master's degree in social work confers MSW. The profession is licensed in most states, indicated by the initials LCSW or a variation (e.g., CISW, LMSW, BCSW, LISW).

The largest professional association for social workers is the National Association of Social Workers, which promotes ethical and educational standards and offers certification. Certification is indicated by the letters ACSW (Academy of Certified Social Workers) after a name. To be certified by the association, a person must have a master's degree, two years' experience, and pass an exam.

What Therapists Offer

Treatments offered by psychotherapists are a patchwork of methods. A report in the *American Journal of Psychiatry* cites a survey of therapy techniques that unearthed more than four hundred different approaches to psychotherapy. Ten years earlier, observers counted a mere 136 therapies. While some therapies follow recognized protocol, such as behavior therapy or psychoanalysis, most treatment is eclectic, employing a mixture of beliefs, assumptions, and techniques. Researchers estimate that one third to one half of therapists use an eclectic approach.

Perhaps one reason there are so many types of therapy is that no one method is superior. Despite what you might hear, no one can say unequivocally that one type of therapist or therapy is measurably more successful with manic depression. For one thing, it's impossible to measure and compare therapy sessions, the delivery skills of individual therapists, and patients' progress with contrasting therapies. Then there arises the quandary about patients who improve with any type of therapy, not because of the treatment but because of the cyclical nature of the illness. Doctors have discovered that regardless of the approach, given all kinds of psychotherapy and all kinds of nonpsychotic patients, patients improve about two thirds of the time.

The only certainty the profession espouses has little to do with psychological systems. Experts believe that successful psychotherapy depends not on a particular treatment method but on the personalities of patient and therapist, and how they get along. A special article in the *American Journal of Psychiatry* declares that "the largest variation in therapy outcome is accounted for by preexisting client factors, such as motivation for change, and the like. Therapist personal factors account for the second largest proportion of change, with technique variables coming in a distant third." In short, psychotherapy succeeds if a patient truly wants to get better and if there's good chemistry between him and the therapist.

The cardinal ingredients in psychotherapy are the attitude of the patient and his relationship with the therapist. How much a patient wants to get well and believes and trusts in a therapist's insights and suggestions set the tone of therapy. In all therapies, except perhaps psychoanalysis, patient and doctor forge an emotional relationship. The value and weight a patient gives this relationship determines whether the therapy helps. Some experts go so far as insisting the patient-therapist relationship is "the critical curative factor in therapy."

Psychotherapy offers a huge menu of principles, techniques, and goals. Some therapists tend to follow the guidelines of certain schools and methods, while others piece together an eclectic style. The therapies we describe here range from formal, psychodynamic methods, like cognitive therapy or psychodynamic therapy, to the very informal counseling that goes on in a support group. The common thread is they're all used with manic depression. Exactly which one you pick is your decision.

Cognitive Therapy
As the name suggests, cognitive therapy confronts the way a patient thinks, whether he's depressed or manic. Based on the idea that a person's thought patterns create and feed his problems, this therapy deals with the here and now. It doesn't delve into a patient's childhood or past to learn *why* someone thinks the way he does, but examines how a person thinks at present and how these thoughts interfere with depression or mania. It is a practical therapy that addresses immediate problems. It's also short-term therapy (twelve to twenty weeks), with the goal of helping a patient break free of churning emotions and stop their reoccurrence.

The cognitive therapist and patient work together to uncover and examine depressive thinking patterns, false assumptions, automatic thoughts, and negative self-images. This give-and-take relationship involves discussion, questions from the therapist, and reflections by the patient. It's like two people sharing a puzzle. Often the therapist makes homework assignments, directing the patient to look at a single thinking habit.

For a depressed patient, this process requires probing into negative beliefs about himself, his abilities, and his illness. Labeled "automatic thoughts," these ideas, say cognitive therapists, aggravate depression. The therapist pushes ahead on the assumption that if these bad thinking habits can be brought into the open and broken, the depression will fade. Here's an example, from the medical textbook *Depression and Mania*, of how this process unfolds for a patient whose self-criticism reinforces his depression.

Therapist: What is your goal in coming into therapy today?
Patient: I don't understand.
T: What do you want to do about your depression—increase it or decrease it?
P: Decrease it.
T: How will criticizing yourself for being depressed decrease your depression?
P: It won't. It'll increase it. But this is a mental problem, not a physical one.
T: How are they different?
P: You should be able to control your mental problems.
T: How are you going to control your depression? You already indicated that you didn't know how to do that—you don't know how to stop being depressed. If you were in a strange town that had no signs and you had no map and got lost, would you criticize yourself?
P: No. But I'd try to find someone to give me directions.
T: Isn't that why you're here—to find directions and get a map?

Someone caught in a manic episode also has distinctive thoughts that shape behavior and need to be corrected in order to control the illness. From the same textbook, here are examples of a manic's automatic thoughts.

Thought: All or nothing (example: "Everything I do is great")

Thought: Positive prediction ("I'll be a great success at everything I attempt")

Thought: Arbitrary inference ("He thinks I'm wonderful")

Thought: Selective abstraction ("I did so well on that one question")

Thought: Personalizing ("She's helpful like that only with me")

Thought: Magnification ("It'll be the greatest thing that ever happened")

Thought: Discounting negatives ("None of the mistakes count")

This therapy tries to show a patient how individual thoughts may ignite mania or depression and teaches him how to reverse those thinking habits, and so short-circuit the illness.

Interpersonal Therapy

This therapy technique builds on the principle that depression is fueled by interpersonal problems and flawed social relationships. Mental disorders, according to IPT practitioners, can be the result of stress and tension in personal relationships. Although stress and tension are not considered direct causes, they're accused of being contributors or triggers. Consequently, IPT's main goal is to help a person improve relationships.

IPT is a very structured, systematic therapy that was devised chiefly for depressed patients. In its strictest application, it doesn't grapple with mania as such, although it may tackle the consequences of mania in a person's relationships. Like the cognitive approach, it treats a patient's present symptoms and problem relationships. It also is relatively short term and tries to patch up a patient as soon as possible.

Treatment consists of an IPT therapist guiding a patient through three phases:

- Early phase: Assess problem areas and treat the immediate depression.

- Middle phase: Address problem areas surrounding relationships with family and friends. IPT therapists say these emotions and reactions are especially troublesome: abnormal grief, conflicts in close relationships, adapting to different social roles, and sustaining close relationships.

- Termination: Prepare to leave the therapist and handle problems alone.

Like cognitive therapy, IPT focuses on the here and now. A manic-depressive's problems are social and personal, and they can be solved by acquiring coping and social skills, like how to avoid arguments and maintain friendships. Instead of wrestling with the origins and symptoms of the illness, IPT isolates the disease and dissects its effects on a patient's relationships with family and friends. It then shows a patient how to repair, strengthen, and improve those ties.

Behavioral Therapy

Behaviorists believe that our emotions and moods are learned. Depression, in this scheme, is a reaction to inadequate support from a person's environment, mainly home life or upbringing. Just as we learn particular emotions or reactions, behavioral therapy teaches how to unlearn or change them.

This retooling or unlearning happens by directing attention to a person's actions, not his thoughts or feelings or relationships. With this therapy, learning is in the doing or deliberately not doing. Thus, a patient unlearns abnormal behavior, like the listlessness of depression or the hyperactivity of mania, and replaces these habits with new, positive ways of behaving. "Assertiveness training," a discipline popular in the seventies that taught women assertiveness by forcing them to act that way regardless of how they felt, is a kind of behavioral therapy.

Through positive reinforcement, such as rewards, encouragement, and coping skills (called "conditioning"), a patient learns new behavior. The relationship between therapist and patient is like teacher and pupil, with the therapist educating and training the patient to act in different ways.

At the beginning, therapist and patient discuss the exact behavior that needs to be changed—for instance, becoming anxious and not sleeping when under pressure. They then set specific goals for when and how this change will happen and start the conditioning program for the new behavior. The program may begin with muscle-relaxation exercises as teacher and pupil talk about reactions to fears and anxieties, and map out new responses.

This is not reflective therapy that explores a person's thoughts or past. Instead, it corrects by changing a way a person acts. But while behavioral therapy may help curb crazy actions, it can't completely manage manic depression alone. A manic person, especially, has little sense of appropriate or inappropriate behavior. So this therapy is often combined with medication. Many therapists combine the cognitive and behavioral aspects of treatment. They are somewhat compatible since one focuses on thoughts and the other on actions. Together, they encompass the mind and the body.

Eclectic Therapy

Upward of 40 percent of practicing therapists use an eclectic approach that combines procedures and methods tailored to the individual patient. For a manic-depressive, an eclectic therapist may try a variety of approaches, depending on what she thinks will help the patient and the patient will respond to. Their techniques vary in their use of questions, confrontation, suggestion, silence, homework assignments, empathy, and criticism.

For instance, a therapist may see a lot of negative thinking accompanying a patient's depression, and so apply cognitive-therapy techniques. In addition, she may think the patient needs help with his self-image because of his grandiose plans and unrealistic ideas about his talents. In attacking this problem, she may be confrontational, she may be supportive, or she may let the patient discover and develop for himself, through talking and selected insights, a more realistic self-image.

Another approach may be closer to the psychoanalytic method, which probes a person's childhood experiences and feelings to find the origins of a person's depression and mania. Some therapists believe depression stems from childhood difficulties with parents, and that mania is a way of denying this depression. Such a therapist may use lots of questions to help a patient understand his depression and mania.

There's no script for the eclectic therapist. What goes on between the therapist and a manic-depressive depends on the therapist's judgment and skills, and on the patient's motivation and trust.

Rehabilitation or Supportive Therapy and Groups

Supportive therapy is not any one technique, but simply a therapist or counselor talking with the patient, providing emotional support and advice. They share ideas and strategies for how a patient copes with the illness and returns to the world he lived in before the illness. The focus of the sessions is the present, with little delving into past problems or childhood experiences.

This therapy avoids exploring childhood traumas, conflicts with parents, or subconscious fears and desires. It's practical, here and now, aimed mainly at rehabilitating a patient to as close to being the person he was before the illness as possible. This is therapy for daily life.

The therapist may be a doctor, but more likely is a social worker, psychiatric nurse, or psychotherapist. She helps patients learn how to function in the world, giving advice, counseling, and practical instruction for such activities as finding a place to live, balancing a checkbook, managing money, cooking meals, keeping appointments, interviewing for a job, coping with employers, maintaining personal hygiene, and staying on medication.

Sometimes supportive or rehab therapy is given one-on-one, at other times it's delivered in groups. A therapy group is organized by a therapist or institution (such as in a hospital or halfway house) drawing from a pool of patients and referrals from other professionals or institutions. As a rule, these groups try to assemble similar people—patients with common problems, around the same age, and with similar economic and social backgrounds. For manic depression, the ideal is a group of manic-depressive patients. Yet sometimes patients with other types of mental illness—for instance, unipolar depression—are included.

Some doctors think group therapy is the best treatment for manic depression because it offers more than support or coping skills. A group of manic-depressive patients can be a powerful force in helping and shaping their own treatment. Their credibility with each other often far exceeds that of a therapist who has never suffered as they have. Their insights and advice for each other, which can be brutally honest and insightful, carry more weight because they know firsthand. The voice of experience is very persuasive.

One of the first things a manic-depression group shares is feelings about and reactions to various drugs. In some groups, lithium maintenance (checking to make sure everyone is taking his medication) is part of the group ritual. If someone is tempted to go off medication, the group may act as an enforcer and persuade the person to take the drugs. These groups tend to concentrate on immediate problems with jobs, relationships, or living arrangements, and so-called reality-issues rather than personal histories.

Another type of group therapy involves the family of a bipolar patient. Organized to relieve strains on a marriage, siblings, children, and parents, family therapy helps people to cope with the side effects of manic depression. These are usually denial of the illness and skewed feelings of dependence or independence.

Support groups—private organizations dedicated to counseling and helping patients and families racked by mental illness—are active in every state. Some are associated with university hospitals or research centers, such as the Depressive and Related Affective Disorders Association, which is attached to Johns Hopkins University in Baltimore. Others may be part of a national network of support groups, such as National Alliance for the Mentally Ill (2101 Wilson Boulevard, Arlington, Virginia 22201) or the National Depressive and Manic Depressive Association (Merchandise Mart, Box 3395, Chicago, Illinois). Appendix B lists support groups and state contacts for NAMI. Names and addresses for NDMDA support groups are available from the organization.

Postscript: The Limits of Confidentiality

Any discussion of therapists and therapy raises the question of confidentiality. What exactly is confidential, and what information about a patient might be passed on?

What is said between patient and therapist is largely confidential, with legal exceptions. State courts have ruled that if a patient threatens someone, the doctor must tell the police or the potential victim. The "duty to protect" precedent, or the Tarasoff decision, after a case in California, limits a doctor's liability by spelling out circumstances under which a potential victim must be warned by a care provider. Without this warning, a doctor may be liable for a victim's injuries.

Yet Tarasoff also creates a predicament for doctors because they must decide if a patient's threat is genuine, and what will happen if a patient's confidence is broken and shared with authorities. What if a patient has sought help to curb violent tendencies and assures the doctor that he will not act on them? If a doctor reports an empty threat, he'll destroy the patient's confidence in him and any treatment progress. Doctors also have the option of protecting potential victims and themselves by hospitalizing a patient they think is dangerous.

Most mental-health professionals, however, do not take such costly, extreme action. Instead, they may inform patients of the law (in some states, patients sign forms acknowledging that they have been told that a therapist may break a confidence under certain circumstances) and talk about it as well as informing the potential victim. Other legal exceptions to the ethics of confidentiality include reporting abuse of children, and elderly or dependent adults.

Confidentiality is essential. It guarantees the privacy and independence from the tensions and frictions within families that mental illness produces. Yet should confidentiality extend to every facet of the patient-therapist relationship? The canons of confidentiality should not be an excuse for doctors and medical staff to refuse to talk to a patient's relatives.

Families deserve and need information about a patient. A doctor ought to be able to tell them about treatment goals, possible side effects from medications and generally how a patient is responding to treatment. Most experienced physicians contract with a patient at the outset to keep the family informed about treatment progress. Most patients are usually pleased to give such permission; it's evidence that the family cares and is available. In the (not rare enough) case of a paranoid patient who refuses to give such consent, a dilemma may arise. But time and a treatment relationship usually allow some reasonable accommodation for both patient and family. Rarely, a family's interest does reach confidential subjects and could compromise the patient's care. In this situation, a doctor lets the family know in a nonpatronizing manner.

A doctor may hedge, in early treatment, at offering a diagnosis. This hesitation may not be an ethical reluctance but more a matter of uncertainty. Nevertheless, even if a doctor cannot confidently put a name on the patient's disease, he should at least explain to the families the possibilities—what realms of mental illness are being considered.

Similarly, a doctor may not be able to answer questions about a prognosis or what a family can expect in a recovery. The future, especially with mental illness, is a big unknown. Much depends on the individual patient, type of treatment, and the course of the disease. Not having answers about when a patient might be released from the hospital or be well enough to return to work usually has less to do with confidentiality than with medical doubt and caution.

Manic-depressive patients commonly suffer from two illnesses—the mental illness and a related or previous problem, such as drug or alcohol abuse. In this situation too, families are entitled to know how a patient is being treated and responding to both ailments.

Chapter 7

MUSICAL SUMMER

July

*I*knew for over a week that a large letter from Mark waited for me at
the post office. The yellow postage-due slip showed an Arizona zip
code. Every day as I passed the post office, I imagined that inside that
charming geranium-filled New England building in a back room something with my name on it ticked silently. I then fabricated a reason for
not standing in line to get my letter and hurried on.

Mark's first calls from Arizona were short and cheerful: The desert
was wonderful. It was hot as hell. Making lots of friends. Signed up for
some great classes. Miss you both. Will call next week.

It was like being worked on by a gifted salesman. You know you're
being hustled, but like the salesman and allow yourself to go along with
the pitch. It was so easy to be passive and black out the past. I drifted
along, accepting his view of school, and ignored the small warnings
along the path—the pitch of his voice, notched a shade too high,
responses a bit too animated. It all suggested a stage performance
geared for the upper balcony.

New England summer, that extravagant burst of leafing and flow-
ering glory that burns itself out in 120 short days, had captured us.
During the day, I worked at the real estate office, shepherding New
Yorkers around country cottages, then came home late in the afternoon,
dumping my flowered dress on the bed, climbed into jeans and boots

and attacked the yard. I dug, clipped, tied up and tied down, weeded, and puttered.

Chris did the same with his vegetable garden. I often found his tie in the garage, belt and shoes in the kitchen, shirt on the floor on the bedroom. Dinner was often a late-evening salad of current pickings. We'd collapse with the sun around ten and both be up at five-thirty, walking in the dawn light, coffee cups in hand, to see if anything had grown.

Mark was a taboo subject. We had mentally crossed our fingers for his success and were afraid to upset the cosmic balance with idle conversation and speculation.

"I am applying to Juilliard School of Music," announced Mark on the telephone one hot Sunday afternoon in early July. "I'm playing the piano and am doing concert-quality work," he continued matter-of-factly.

"You had six months of piano lessons that you hated when you were nine," I blurted out. "How can this be? Mark, what's going on?"

Take a deep breath, slow down, don't scare him off. Go along with him, find out what's going on here. "Tell me more about what you're doing," I said in my conversational, read-any-good-books-lately? tone, letting each word fade softly.

"This music, it just comes to me. I'm fantastic. There's a piano here. I play for hours and hours." His voice was high-pitched and excited. In the past, Mark's interest in music stopped at music videos.

"How are your classes going?" I wanted to change the tempo. "Do you find the work difficult?" I asked neutrally.

"Easy, easy, easy. I could do it in my sleep. These classes are really a waste of my time, but I'll finish up. I'm in for the fall for sure based on my summer performance. I'm getting all A's so far," he said dismissively. This subject was done, said his voice. "Let me tell you more about my music," and he did.

Chris was listening on the extension in the next room after I had motioned to him that Mark was calling. Through the door and down the hall, I could see him, face set in a deep frown, slowly shaking his head at the conversation from Arizona.

"Mark, have you seen any of the doctors at the health service yet?" I asked when he paused to inhale between sentences. "I think it would be a good idea to talk with them." *Say this quietly but firmly. Make him go in just to please me.* "Are you sleeping and eating okay?" Calm voice.

Just get him across the threshold of the clinic. Surely, they'll see he needs help.

"Yeah, that's another thing. I *did* go in to see the doctor. My spine is killing me. I know it's some sort of degeneration. They said nothing's wrong and sent me packing. What a waste of time. Those doctors were no help at all," he replied angrily. "Look, I've got things to do. I'll call you later." Click.

"What was that all about?" Chris asked after hanging up. "He sounds crazy again. Do you really think he's doing so well in school?" Chris eyed me intently, as if I had the answers.

"I don't know. Maybe he's slipped a bit. Could be it's just a bad day for him. It's a hundred and four degrees there now. Let's give him some time." Before Chris could detect my panic, I grabbed Jake's leash and took him for a long walk in the fields behind the house.

The genie was out of the bottle again and on a rampage. What trouble would materialize now? Should I grab the next flight to Tucson? Commit Mark based on one bizarre telephone call? Not enough evidence, so in the end I did nothing but wait and throw the *I Ching*. Number 18, said the *I Ching*: "The object of your inquiry is in a state of disrepair." Even my customary source of wisdom told me Mark was in trouble.

When I returned from my walk with a bouquet of wildflowers and a tired dog, Chris had retreated to his corner with the remainder of the Sunday paper. The Mark subject was closed again. The peace talks had broken down, and we were in another armaments buildup.

July 8, 1988

MOM AND DAD,

Surprise-surprise. I learned how to play the piano. I am sending you a tape for your listening enjoyment. I play by ear—I am very good—better than Amadaeus. The album plays upon my bad winter and progressive summer (two A's in college is the only way to Start Off). In general I HAD FULL COMMAND or ease with the Instrument. I ACT out the songs in my B-R-A-I-N . . . it all just comes so easy for me. The music is from the park in Colorado—very natural, flowing like a trickle in a frozen creek bed, it's fantasy music I think. I call it *Monday's* YEAH, it's brilliantly amazing . . . HOLY SHIT where did I learn to play like that? THIS IS MY ONLY COPY. Send back the original. I am thinking about the Berkeley

School of Music. I might do it again tomorrow.

Loveya, Mark Wakefield

I sat in front of the post office, car windows down to the heavy July air, tape in hand, and read the homemade labels stuck all over it. Mark's letter accompanying the tape was three pages of penciled words and flourishes. Some of the titles were illegible. I dreaded listening to the tape. My hands trembled. This was the evidence I couldn't ignore.

I pulled out of the parking space and headed north out of Litchfield toward Goshen, into countryside alive with growing corn, lush trees, and overflowing gardens. I slid the tape into the tape deck and waited. Scratchy noises, Mark talking under his breath, words inaudible. Then, music.

Lovely music, soft, flowing. Atonal chords, runs, sharp pauses. Building and suddenly relaxing. I couldn't stop shaking; I was braced for manic noise, hysteria, ugly sounds. They never came. The tape wound on and on without pause, music without punctuation, without beginning and without an end. It stopped abruptly after forty-five minutes.

I was far up the road by now, the acid green of the trees and fields surrounding me, the humid summer air swamping the car's air-conditioning. I turned around and shoved in the tape again. It was a piece of Mark capsulized on magnetic plastic. I had peeked under the craziness.

MARK

Hello? Someone's with me. I can't be playing this way by myself. How did I learn this? This is fantastic! My fingers fly over the keys and music flows. When they drift to the left, it sounds scary, like the Voice. But on the right it sounds like rain in a Monet forest, like lilies, angels. Rising-from-the-mist/He-seeks-the-sky/To-touch-the-wonder-of-Nepal. Not a bad voice, my friend. I'm a cinch for Juilliard but I don't know about New York. I gotta ask them.

The Mirror People know about New York. I don't need anybody. I've got six friends waiting in my room. Okay, Mark, so they're angles of me, but they're really different. The strong, dominant one doesn't talk much. But the weak one, we're going to help him with his problems, talk 'em out. New York's freaky. Angels floating along Fifth Avenue. Can I go back?

It's not so bad being alone. This place has cured my loneliness. Everyone's in Manzinetta dorm, so the piano here's mine. I think I'm starving, eating just oats and honey. It's cheap but it's eating away my spine.

"I'm coming to White Flower Farm next week to pick up some perennials. How about lunch?" I hadn't talked to Phyllis since our tennis game in January. I was eager to prove her wrong about Mark. Look, I wanted to say, we're different from your run-of-the-mill family. We've solved this mental-illness thing neatly, and without excess anguish. You were wrong in your dire warnings. But I hadn't called her. My "Be-a-Success" mentality had not allowed me to approach her with less than a victory. But I forgot all that with the sound of her voice.

"We'll have lunch at my house," I offered. "I'll meet you by the daylilies, and we'll go from there. It's been too long." I needed someone to talk to. My smooth, controlled veneer to Chris, the family, and friends was wearing thin. I should have called her long ago.

Chris and I were back to the start with the Mark Thing, so there was little discussion. I had not shown him Mark's letter or the tape. He would just glower and ask what was I going to do about it. Mother error again. To make matters worse, the University of Arizona had sent an interim grade card on Mark's progress. It arrived in the Saturday mail, and Chris had opened it. Two D's and an F. He had left the slip of paper on the kitchen counter without comment, just a "Do something" look at me.

As usual, Phyllis was early and already had filled her green wagon with plants by the time I arrived at the nursery. She was stretching to the back of the ranked plants for a choice sedum. The display gardens on the tiered slope above us were in full flower, and shoppers wandered among the achilleas and aconitums.

"Bill's the gardener. I just check things off his list as I buy them. He insisted I come all the way up here for these rock plants. Do you know what all this stuff is?" she asked, inclining her head at the plants lining the walkway as we ambled along.

"Most of it. It's my academic, compulsive nature to overwork a subject," I replied with a sigh. "I'm glad you came up. Things are not much better with Mark," I volunteered.

"Of course they aren't. This problem's a bitch. It's chronic. It doesn't just disappear." She fixed her honest, open gaze on me. "There's hope of recovery. That's what keeps you going day to day. You learn to take care of yourself, your marriage, and pray for your child. Medicine doesn't have much to offer here. I didn't want to ask. I know it's hard to talk about," she added.

"I'm getting better about it. Chris still expects me to fix things. We have this family division of labor. He does the insurance, I do the taxes. He does the mortgage, I do the household expenses. He does the American Express, I do the mental illness. We don't discuss Mark. What's to say? You know he's in Arizona."

I told her about summer school, the tapes and letter, the grades, as we walked between aisles of plants, Phyllis pulling her stock-laden wagon with its squeaky wheels.

"You know the worst is yet to come," she said softly, rearranging the pots in the wagon. She paused, fiddling with the plants, considering her next words. "How's your medical insurance?" Suddenly, her voice was businesslike.

"The usual stuff. Chris is covered with a group plan at work. I checked the pamphlet they sent us. It covers some psychiatric care. Half of Dr. Anderson's visits up to a thousand dollars, and sixty days' hospital," I replied with authority as we entered the shade-plant area.

She shook her head, the shadows from the overhead lath striping her like a prison uniform. "A joke what insurance covers. First you use your private coverage for medical care. If you're lucky, that is. You're very fortunate that Mark was under nineteen when this happened. If he'd been older, you might have been out of luck. Then you put a second mortgage on the house, borrow on your retirement, and cash in insurance policies and securities and hit up the relatives. When all that's gone, you cut your adult child loose, and he goes on public assistance, Social Security, whatever. John's medical care has cost us more than the combined cost of private colleges for the three other boys."

This was a different Phyllis. Hardened, bitter, angry. Bill, her husband, was a senior executive with a major New York investment-banking firm. But it sounded like his son was on welfare.

"I'm sure we have good coverage." I made a mental note to re-check it.

"Mental illness is the disease of John Hinckley and the Son of Sam—not Van Gogh and Nijinsky. When Jerry Lewis goes on his Telethon Labor Day with a crippled child, people rush to their check-books. Never mind that muscular dystrophy affects an insignificant number of people. No heartstrings are tugged by a crazy old man living in squalor on the street. People can't get away fast enough. No cans for pocket change for mental illness at cash registers. No appeals on the evening news. Charles Manson as the poster child? Sure. We're on our own."

She snapped out the words with anger. "Forgive me," she added, her face clearing after the outburst, "this subject really gets me started. Pray you never have to know these problems firsthand.

"What about your doctor? What does he say?" she asked.

"Not much. His sessions with Mark are private—he won't discuss them with me."

"How could I forget? The old medical-confidentiality scam. You're the only person who could really help him, and they don't talk to you."

After selecting and paying for her plants, Phyllis followed me home for lunch. We settled into faded chintz-covered wicker chairs on the back porch and dug into our salads.

"Tell me again," she asked between bites, "where is it you go in the summer? Somewhere out West. One of those 'I' states?"

I laughed. Phyllis was typical of the easterners who refer to Ohio as "out West." "It's Idaho, and it's nowhere near those other 'I' states. We bought a summer house there when we lived nearby in eastern Washington. Mark will meet us there in August after he finishes summer school. Robert comes over weekends from his summer job in Seattle." Here I was again, Confident Mother with Family Plans, as if there were no uncertainties. Could I convince Mark to join us?

Her straight look told me that Phyllis saw through my false facade. But she left my house of cards standing. "You have to have faith that things will get better, or you just give up," she said with finality.

The late-afternoon sunlight sparkled off the lake as we unpacked the rental car. After three changes of aircraft, seven hours of flying, driving, and stopping to buy food, Chris and I arrived in northern Idaho.

Mark's and Robert's old jackets hung on the hooks by the door topped with baseball hats. A faded snapshot of wet boys with a wet dog was pinned to the bulletin board beside a checklist for closing the house and a New Yorker cartoon about Idaho. An afghan knitted by my long-dead grandmother was draped over a ratty rocker.

"I'm going down to the dock to check the lake," shouted Chris from the steps as I unpacked the groceries. The refrigerator was full of beer and hot-dog condiments. Traces of Robert.

The house, originally a 1940s cottage, perched on a steep slope with a panoramic view of the lake and surrounding mountains. A catwalk stairway led to the floating dock where an old motorboat bobbed on a tether. We had bought the house and boat five years ago, after moving to Spokane from Menlo Park.

Spokane, a city of almost two hundred thousand, straddles the Washington-Idaho border. We found ourselves there after Chris took a job with a small computer company. The boys, at first glance, hated it. Compared with the shopping malls of northern California and the fast times at Palo Alto High, they disdained the quiet, rural pace and school activities led by the 4-H Club. Nevertheless, Robert immediately found a group of pals among the football team, easily fitting in with his tobacco-chewing teammates.

Mark was a different story. Because our house was just over the borderline of a rural school district, he was consigned to a year at a small country school. He felt dropped into *Little House on the Prairie*. Classmates were excused early fall afternoons to help drive the combines, swathers, balers, and harrow beds. The school vending machine dispensed bruised apples, the girls sewed their own clothes, and the boys had home-done haircuts. Mark's Bay Area worldliness and sardonic humor brought stares of incomprehension from his classmates.

Salvation came in the form of Axel English. Small, dark, and intense, he was the middle child of a successful local doctor. In the country-school environment, Mark and Axel stood apart from the farm children like a pair of truffle-topped pâtés on a table of noodle casseroles at the church social. They both read *Rolling Stone,* watched MTV, and had traveled beyond the bounds of wheat country. Like his accomplished parents, Axel was bright and possessed a dry wit about eighth-grade life in the country that brightened Mark's spirits.

During school months, they were a fixture in each other's houses. When Mark had a cold, Axel's physician father, Hal English, would send him home with a bottle of cough medicine. Sports-team physicals sometimes took place in the English kitchen. Axel spent many weekends with us at the lake perfecting his water-skiing skills. Their friendship was like that of wartime buddies.

Despite moving away from Spokane for his last two years of high school, Mark had stayed in touch with Axel and had planned to stay with him when he arrived from Arizona.

The telephone rang just as I reached the dock. Chris was at the house checking his fishing gear. The ringing stopped. It was Tuesday, and the tickets I had sent Mark were for Thursday evening. Maybe he was confirming his arrival time. While I waited for Chris, I removed the boat covers and started the engine.

After a few moments, Chris appeared on the dock, tackle box and new rod in hand. Fishing, particularly fly-fishing, was a lifelong passion for Chris. I didn't share his fascination, but went along for his company and to read or watch birds.

"We have a great night tonight," he said, throwing the mooring lines into the boat as he climbed in. "It's still and flat. I think the hatch is on," he said, expertly surveying the mirrorlike finish of the lake, broken only by the dimples of rising fish.

We put-putted to the far end of the lake in the dusk, cut the engine, and drifted with the breeze, line trailing behind us.

"Chironomids," he said to himself, digging into his tackle box. Chris's tackle box would have been the envy of a surgical nurse. He neatly tied the fly to the floating line leader, biting off the stray end with his teeth. The setting sun cast slanted shadows through the firs along the shore. Unseen cattle mooed from nearby fields. The green smell of the water plants drifted up to meet us.

"That was Mark," Chris said after a few tentative casts. He was standing on the bow trying to lay the yellow floating line like a feather on the motionless surface. "He's coming into Spokane Thursday evening. Said he wants to see a doctor Friday morning, something about his back. He's already talked to Axel, and will spend Thursday night with the Englishes."

His back was to me, and I couldn't see his face. Stripping more line off the reel, he added in an undertone, "He sounded terrible. Crazy again."

I watched the Purple Martins swoop and dip over the water, snatching insects off the water's surface. The sun had just set, leaving a luminous glow on the surrounding mountains. The tips of the cedars remained in sunshine.

Like the aura before a migraine headache, the signals of coming chaos were unmistakable. I felt a sudden chill and zipped up my jacket. My fingertips were numb, although the air was only a few degrees cooler. Chris's blunt words hit me as nothing had before. I shrank inward, harboring what grit I had for Mark's return. His back was still to me as he stood on the bow casting over the now-obsidian-colored water. We were silent.

"It's getting dark. Fish have gone to bed. Let's go home," I said quietly. He reeled in his line and carefully packed away his tackle. I was grateful that the boat-motor noise made conversation impossible on the ride back to the dock.

"Axel," I said cautiously on the telephone the next morning, "there are some things you need to know about Mark before you pick him up. He may not be the same as you remember him." I gave him a very abbreviated version of the last year, and felt like a traitor.

"I know he'll be fine, Mrs. Wakefield," he replied loyally. "I've talked to him. He sounds okay. He just needs to see his old friends again. We're having a party here Thursday night to welcome him home. I'll see that he makes his Friday morning appointment at the clinic downtown."

We chatted for a few more moments. Axel's open and uncomplicated nineteen-year-old conversation was in stark contrast to the convoluted, emotional encounters I had with Mark. Axel talked about college and his younger brother and his summer job with simple directness. I suddenly had an intense longing for the old Mark, an almost physical pain for his open laughter and corny jokes.

I hastily said good-bye and collapsed in tears beside the telephone. Just when I thought I was handling this well. Chris was at the store picking up a paper, and I washed my face so he wouldn't see I had been crying again. My tears made him even angrier at Mark.

MARK

The professor's talking about me. Positively. He doesn't use my name, but it's me. Psychology's basically a snap. These stages of development, it's me. My LIFE. This guy KNOWS. Telepathy. Maybe he saw me last night tending the bushes outside the dorm, all night, smoothing the dirt, throwing away weeds, clearing trash, until the sun came up. So I'm in shape to work hard in class.

I'm gonna get an A because I climbed the mountain with the big A on it. Took all afternoon but I sat right on top of it. I'll get an A for sure. It's preordained.

After class, I'll do my homework with crayons. A special assignment. The professor wants only me to do it. That's why he's talking in code. I understand. Scribblescribblescribble. Until I forget how to write, like a kid. Swirls and circles in red and yellow and black. Lower your mental age, Mark, and I'll have a higher IQ. That's what the professor's really saying. IQ is chronological age

divided by mental age times 100, so if I lower my mental age, presto, I'm
smarter. Then I'll do an Inference Paper. He'll really like that.

A chattering squirrel woke me early Friday. Chris had gone fishing
at sunrise. I slid into an old wool robe against the chilly summer
mountain air and made coffee. Mark had arrived late last night, and
Axel picked him up. I quashed the urge to call him. Hal English would
call me if something was wrong. He had been reassuring when I talked
to him yesterday. "He'll be fine," he had said. "Don't worry, I know Dick
Bright well. When Marks sees him Friday, if there's anything amiss, he'll
find it." Nothing like one doctor's assessment of another. My best
doctor referrals always came from doctor's wives. They all candidly
admitted that their husbands refused to recommend some of their
colleagues.

The phone rang.

"Mrs. Wakefield, this is Doctor Bright's nurse. Mark just stormed
out of here. He refused to stay for his appointment. Doctor Bright
would like to talk to you if you can come right in," she said. I told her
I was on my way, but that it would take an hour. We were fifty miles
away.

I quickly called Axel, searching for an explanation.

"He's not the same, like you said. He was up all night, pacing
around. He refused to talk to anyone, or he would shout to everyone.
He, he . . ." Axel stopped. "He really acted crazy."

"This isn't my field at all. Psychiatry and plastic surgery are miles
apart," offered Hal English when I reached him, "but Mark is clearly not
the same boy we saw grow up. He paced around the kitchen island for
hours. I tried to look at his back. He's complaining that his spine hurts,
but he was so irritable I really couldn't get near him. Something needs
to be done. Come by the office later this morning, and we'll work
something out."

Dr. Bright's nurse showed me into his office. Jungle animals gam-
boled around the wall, and the furniture was scaled down for the small
patients. Although Mark was on the outer limits of pediatrics, Dr.
Bright knew the healthy Mark and could make an educated judgment
about him.

I was comforted by the familiar sounds of babies crying down the
hall as they were vaccinated and the scummy fish aquarium illuminating a dark corner. I gingerly sat down across from the doctor's desk in
the back office and consciously took slow, deep breaths. Tears fizzed

inside me like soda in an agitated can. I was determined not to disintegrate into a soggy blob of emotion.

"Relax, relax, it's only me," said Dr. Bright casually as I started at his coming into the room. Here was the master at handling mothers. I inwardly released a small piece of tension and sat back. "Tell me what's happened. I only saw Mark for a moment, but didn't recognize him." I swallowed and took another deep breath. *Here it goes, Diane. Do it without tears.*

I galloped over details of the past year, wanting to elaborate but acutely conscious of his time. An anxious nurse with "Mrs. Smith and baby are ready in room four" peeked in during my monologue. My voice cracked and wavered, but I stayed above flood level.

"He needs to be in the hospital, or he will not get better. You can't treat his mania any other way."

Hard words, but oddly reassuring. This was medical advice, something I could understand. Not the vague, ambling platitudes of the psychiatrists. Dr. Bright dug into his desk and came up with a battered directory, from which he drew out some doctor and hospital names from Connecticut and Boston.

"Don't fool around with the bush leagues. Back East, you live near the best medical help in the country. Take Mark back, and we'll see what we can do to get him appropriate help."

The hot, dry August air whooshed through the automatic doors as I headed for the car to find Mark. He was on foot and had an hour's start. I called Chris and let him know what was happening. I had the only car, so all he could do was wait for reports fifty miles away. I drove south of town toward Axel's house in the country.

The English house sat on a basalt outcropping above wheat fields and surrounded by pine trees. A fleet of combines, obscured by dust and heat haze, were harvesting the crop nearest the long straight road up the hill. Shiny black magpies squawked from their perch on a sagging barbed-wire fence. The road was deserted except for a solitary thin man methodically trudging uphill.

I sped up the road, passing the walking man, and glanced at him in my rearview mirror. With an electric jolt, I hit the brakes with a squeal and a lurch and backed up as I reached over to roll down the passenger-side window. It was Mark. He had lost so much weight that his clothes hung limply on him, and he had shaved the hair over his ears. He had a wild, monkish cast.

"Mark!" I shouted, knowing he wouldn't recognize the rented car.

He continued his plod up the hill. "Mark, it's me. Get in, we'll go back downtown. Dr. Bright wants to help you."

I was now driving alongside him as he trudged. "Mark, *please*. Dr. English also feels you need to see Dr. Bright." He had not acknowledged me yet. I crept along beside him for some minutes. A standoff.

"Get out of my life. Leave me alone, bitch. Leavemealone, leavemealone." In one swift motion, he spun around, tore open the passenger door, and crawled over the center console to shout inches from my ear. I felt the force of his outburst and could feel his breath. Instinctively, I cupped my hands over my ears for protection. His face was contorted into a menacing grimace of hate and anger.

"I'm going to get my bag from Axel's and hit the road. To L.A. I'm going to hitch to Los Angeles and write music. Follow the Grateful Dead. And you can't stop me! *Get out of my life!*" He was out of the car as quickly as he had descended upon it, and returned to his determined march up the hill to Axel's house.

I turned around and headed back downtown, my heart pounding in my head, the vibrations of Mark's shouting ringing in my ears. The time for reasoned assessments with Dr. Bright was gone. Mark had to go into the hospital, and Hal could help me. This was an emergency.

I found Hal's windowless office in the warren of corridors surrounding the operating rooms. He was eating a sandwich over a stack of charts. He shoved folders and journals off the only chair and, mouth full, motioned for me to sit down.

"I have to commit Mark to the psychiatric ward," I declared, dropping into the chair. "I don't know how to do it. He's up at your house with Axel now." I felt leaden and numb; all emotions on ice. Tired beyond imagining. Playing out a losing hand.

"I'll call Axel. He'll get him down to the emergency room here at the hospital." He picked up the telephone.

"Mark is so angry at me, if he sees me nearby, he'll flee again, and we'll lose him," I added.

Hal arranged for Axel to bring Mark into town on some pretext, alerted the emergency room and psychiatric ward, and ferreted out the name of a psychiatrist from the head nurse on the ward. "Always ask the head nurse for referrals. They know where the bodies are buried," he shared with me. "We just wait now. Here," he offered, handing me the uneaten half of his sandwich. I shook my head. My stomach was already filled with hard burls of pain.

"I'm putting Mark back in the hospital," I told Chris when I called him.

"How are *you* doing?" he asked. He already sensed the truth that I was rediscovering. Mark was out of control—it was hard for me to say "crazy." He was unsurprised by my call. "Just hang in there. I wish I was there." His sympathy broke my last barrier to tears, and I collapsed into uncontrollable crying. Hal pushed the Kleenex box across the desk. I snuffled and went through swallowing and breathing aerobics for tear suppression.

"I'm going down to the emergency room to meet Axel and Mark," said Hal. "You wait here. I'll call you as soon as he's in the ward."

I leaned back in the chair, closing my eyes, and tried to push away the implications of what was happening to Mark. An hour passed. No call. What was happening?

"We finally got him into the locked ward," Hal said. I could hear the weariness in his voice. "As they were putting the restraints on him, he was shouting to everyone his theories about the Industrial Revolution. He also threatened to kill you. They'll do a drug screen immediately. I've been in medicine a long time, and he's as bad as I have ever seen. They had to chase him down the street. You need to go over to the ward to sign some papers. Dr. Harp is your doctor." I thanked him profusely. I knew I could not have negotiated the commitment alone. He had cut through the Gordian knot of hospital regulations as only a doctor can.

The adult psychiatric unit of Holy Cross Hospital is reached around corners, through doors, up elevators, and down featureless corridors. An errant patient would have to be in full possession of his faculties to find the exit. Maybe this was by design, not chance.

Unlike Mark's first hospital, this was all subdued lighting, new carpets, and soft colors. No scuffed-linoleum floor, stale cigarette smoke, and noisy television laughter. At first glance, I couldn't tell the patients from the staff except for the telltale heavy-soled shoes. I later learned this is a good sign. The unit was divided into locked and unlocked units. Mark was sedated in the locked unit. I didn't ask to see him.

"I need to ask you some questions," said a young man in street clothes with forms in his hands.

"I know," I replied, collapsing into one of the comfortable sofas. "I've been through this before." I knew the drill this time. My answers were concise. No surprises about Aunt Helen's psychiatric history. Was her spirit sitting on a cloud somewhere disturbed by all these earthly references? I had never seen her, but perhaps that errant gene of Mark's was her legacy. I was even able to find my insurance card.

Going down the corridor to the exit, I noticed a life-sized stone Madonna, sweet face and eyes lowered, surrounded with fresh flowers in an alcove. Maybe she would watch over Mark.

Wordlessly, I fell into Chris's arms when I returned to the lake. He gently stroked my hair and whispered, "It's okay now. He's safe," over and over. Hal had called him while I drove out to the lake and gave him the details.

I wanted to curl up into a ball and shut the world out and cry until I was out of tears. I crawled to bed at five and slept dreamlessly for fourteen hours and arose with the heavy-limbed, slow-witted feeling I remembered from college-finals week.

MARK

Fuck, I got to get to Axel. Axelaxel. He'll save me. We're blood brothers. She's after me, to shove me into the mountains at the lake. Thinks I'm crazy, doesn't believe in my music. Putting me on drugs like that lithium crap. Stupid fucking world. It's sick. I showed her, swallowed the whole supply in two days. Didn't do a thing. Some medicine. They believe everything. I don't care about the Grateful Dead. They're not even on tour. I just have to get away from HER. I need my freedom. My music takes me away, to rain forests and mountains. I soar like an Eagle. Rising to a pool of light.

IHATEHER, HATEHER, HATEHER, HATEHER, HATEHER

"Could I speak with Mark Wakefield, please?" I asked at the psychiatric ward the next morning. Chris said leave it alone, but I couldn't. I waited until he had gone out on errands before reaching for the phone.

"One moment, please," an unidentified voice said. Muffled sounds, whispers on the other end. "Sorry, I can't tell you if he's here. Who is calling?" I told her. "I'm sorry, I can't help you. You'll have to go through his doctor." She gave no hint about whether he was even there. Maybe he had slipped out, found the interstate, and was on his way to joining the legions of homeless children living on the streets of Los Angeles.

"If he were a surgical patient, would you tell me if he were there?" I asked.

"Of course," she replied. "That's no problem. But professional ethics and law dictate that psychiatric patients remain confidential." I hung up. Mark had vanished behind a curtain of shame and secrecy. I called Dr. Harp and arranged to see him later that day.

"You should have let him go," said Chris, who had quietly walked in while I was on the telephone. I felt as though I had been caught cheating.

"What do you mean?" I asked, knowing what he meant but not wanting to admit it.

"Let him find his own way in the world. It would have been good for him rather than putting him in the hospital."

"How can you say that? You didn't see him. Something is terribly wrong. You've talked to him, to Hal, about him. Mark needs medical help." My voice rose.

"What if, just what if, he's not mentally ill and just wants us out of his life? It happens," he offered.

"I refuse to believe it. Not Mark. You're still not convinced about the mental-illness thing, are you?" When I saw Mark on the road, I had no doubts, but now I wasn't sure. "It's just a chance I'm not willing to take, leaving him alone if he's sick. I would rather the error be on the side of too much control rather than not enough."

Chris silently burrowed into the morning paper. His freewheeling, "let the boy make his own mistakes" couldn't match my ferocious protection.

The wheat farmers were burning off the stubble from the recent harvest, and the smoke and haze lay like London fog over the charred fields as I drove to Spokane. I met Dr. Harp after his rounds in a room near the ward.

"I want to start Mark on lithium, but he resists taking pills. He's very hostile, but that's typical of a manic-depressive in the manic phase of the disorder. The staff is going to work on convincing him to cooperate," he said in clean, clinical fashion.

Dr. Harp had the misfortune of being a Don Knotts lookalike. He had a permanent "What?" expression on his face, in contrast to his soft voice. I leaned forward to hear him over the pages and noise around us.

"What then?" I asked. He shrugged noncommittally.

"It's a process. You just have to wait and see. I'll arrange for your calls to be answered. Call me anytime. I'll be seeing him every day." A mashed-potato sandwich. Smooth, bland, tasteless. I tried peppering him with questions—about Mark's physical health, how long he'd be in the hospital, other drug treatments—but received only solicitous shrugs.

"I'm sorry, Mrs. Wakefield, but he refuses to see or talk to you. He is very angry and difficult to deal with. Looks like he'll be on the locked side for some time," the nurse told me when I asked to see Mark. I returned to the lake and Chris, empty and aching.

Robert's car was in the driveway, and the entryway was blocked by a large University of Washington crew duffel stuffed with dirty clothes. Chris and Robert were on the dock, drinking beer. Chris's head was thrown back in laughter, Robert was leaning forward in the throes of a story. I hesitated before joining them. I was the black fairy casting a shadow on the magic of Chris and Robert's camaraderie. I was the reminder of Mark's condition, the keeper of the dark flame. I felt eroded by grief. Their guilt, momentarily shelved, at relishing the sun, the beer, and each other while Mark was locked up would reawaken with one glimpse of me.

"How is he?" Robert quickly asked after giving me a hug, all mirth drained from his face.

"Same as yesterday. Maybe the same tomorrow. He has finally consented to try the lithium. We just have to wait and see if it works on him." I dug a beer out of the cooler and unfolded a spare aluminum chair.

"I think I'll go in to see him tonight. Do you think he'll see me?" Robert asked.

"Perhaps. It's worth a try. You're still going back East next week?" I turned to Chris.

"Come home with me. Mark is well cared for. There's not much more you can do here." His words carried the sweet seduction of escape from my grief. It would be so easy and blameless to leave Mark in competent medical hands. After all, he was under legal and physical lock and key.

"You know I can't leave. Not just yet. Mark needs me." I heard the martyrdom in my voice.

"Hell, he's not even talking to you. You're being a fool," he growled. Robert looked on helplessly, reduced to innocent-bystander status.

"I know," I whispered.

The next day, Robert visited his brother. "It was terrible. Seeing him locked up like that. I had no idea it would be so bad. The place gave me the creeps. Crazy people wandering around talking to themselves. Real cuckoo's nest." Robert shuddered.

"I thought I could talk to him. Reason with him about acting sane. Mark was always so practical. We used to be close. Instead," he continued, full of self-recrimination and disgust, "I lectured him. I couldn't stop myself. I should have just taken a pack of cards and played gin with him. Like we used to. Sneaked in a beer. That would have been better. He's mad at me too, now. I've blown my chance to help." He flopped into a chair.

Comforting my healthy son seemed easy. "He's mad at everyone. It's part of this illness. It's not you, it's a symptom. You have to remember that. Give it time." Good advice for everyone, I thought.

MARK

We're in isolation, Mark, that's why they don't talk to us. Nurse doesn't say a fucking word. The Big Glare, the Big Silence. I'll talk anyhow: The-origins-of-Russian-theology-and-the-rise-of-atheism-can-be-traced-to-the-slaughter-of-the-royal-family-don't-you-agree? A granduesque theory, my Mank friend. Good brain work. More, more.

Gotta get ready for L.A. Craft lady thinks I'm sewing. Likes the swell things I'm doing with calico. I smile. I've played this game before. Fucking play school. She doesn't see it's a backpack. Today I'll do leather straps. Paint stars and diamonds on them. Lights to lead the way to freedom. Need food, food, food. Cat food's best. Cheap, easy to carry. No one will suspect.

I laid the pastel pencils and paper on the counter at the nurse's station and waited for someone to notice me.

"I know Mark won't take these from me," I told the nurse. "Just tell him that another patient left them behind." When I made my daily telephone call for Mark to refuse, a nurse said he was doing artwork. "But tell him I was here, that he's not alone. Sooner or later, that may mean something to him."

She nodded sympathetically, then in a low voice said, "He's been on the lithium for almost two weeks now. We may see some results soon. He's still irritable and angry, but more manageable. Dr. Harp has him on Thorazine. He's been very busy in crafts," she added cheerfully.

There was so much I didn't understand, like what she meant by "manageable," and how drugged he was, and why a nineteen-year-old college student would be doing crafts. I left the hospital, eager to look up Thorazine in the *Physicians' Desk Reference*.

I monitored Mark alone. Chris had returned to work in the East, Robert back to his summer job in Seattle. Mark still refused to speak to me, and reports from Dr. Harp were vague. Our encounters were all the same. I usually ambushed him after rounds in the hall with my written list of questions about Mark's progress. He would shrug at each one and say, "Let's wait and see," covertly glancing at his watch. Our consultations lasted five minutes. I felt like a starving man after one bite.

"Mom, it's me. Mark." The timid voice called late one afternoon. "Are you coming into town to see me today?" I sank into a chair and took a deep breath. He had been in the hospital for almost three weeks, and I had not heard this voice for over a year. Mark home from a long voyage.

"Yes, yes. I'll be in right away." I had been to visit him that morning, and the nurse again said that he refused to see me. "Can I bring you anything?"

"No," he said slowly, "I don't think so."

Time inched forward during the drive from the lake to the hospital. It felt like the trip to Travis Air Force Base to meet Chris, returning home from his year in Vietnam. But instead of my husband, this time I was praying for my son back in one piece.

Mark appeared from behind a locked door with a wire-reinforced glass window. "It's not so bad here. The food is all right, and the nurses are nice. Do you want to see my drawings?" A sharp-eyed nurse lurked within arm's length as he, almost shyly, said hello.

I tentatively reached out and touched his arm. He didn't draw away. "I'm glad you called," was all I could think of.

He was still thin. The khaki shorts and blue work shirt hung loosely on his frame. New Reeboks I had left for him a week earlier were on his feet, pristine white from never having been outside, laces untied. The socks were mismatched. His home-shaven haircut was growing out in tufts above the ears. On his wrists and around his neck hung strips of mustard-yellow calico fabric and leather strung with plastic beads. He had another piece of wider green calico tied, sushi chef–style, around his head.

"We have to go back to the locked side." He nodded to the nurse, who unlocked the door and held her hand out for my handbag. I followed him to a table in the center of a large dayroom. No other patients were around. Mark scurried away for his drawings as I sat down.

"I've been working on these while I have been here. What do you think?" he asked in a soft voice. No preamble, no conversation, but no anger or hostility. Just a vague sweetness. He didn't make any eye contact. The room was quiet but for the distant ringing of the occasional telephone and the rubber squeak of heavy-soled shoes.

"I call these my views of heaven," he said, opening a large sketchbook stuffed with loose paper. His hands fluttered like a pair of birds over the pages as he spread them across the table. He selected one drawing for me to see. The paper quivered in his trembling hands. I kept my eyes lowered to the drawing to hide my alarm at his shaking.

"They're very nice, Mark," I said. They were terrible. Stick figures, smudges of color, some pages with just a line or two, some completely covered with scribbles. Not every manic is Van Gogh.

"I'm glad you like them," he said with composure. He could have been the artist at a gallery opening, acknowledging the compliments of his patrons. "This one is a thought. It's an idea I'm still working on. It needs a little work, but I like it." He held up an indistinguishable muddy sketch, a stick figure with a smear of orange sky. He slowly turned each picture for me to see, sitting impassively as I leafed through the stack, commenting here and there on each.

"What else have you been doing?" I asked.

"Crafts. See my bracelet and headband? Also some ceramics. And playing the piano. They have a nice piano here. Do you want to hear me play? Did you like my tape? I've been using the piano quite a bit."

"I'd like that very much, Mark," I said. While he was putting his drawings back in his room, I wandered over to a blackboard by the door. The day's weather report: "Sunny and 95!!" A two-line, two-dot happy face in colored chalk and "Group today is at 3:00."

Mark's piano playing had stirred a heated family debate. After recovering from the shock of the melodic music instead of the manic noise I expected, I sent the tape to my sister Kate, an accomplished pianist. She thought the pianist was someone with musical training, not Mark. "Perhaps a friend did it for him," she suggested.

The old upright covered with dust and peeling veneer was in a dark corner of the dayroom on the unlocked side of the ward. He settled at the keyboard, tilted his head backward à la Ray Charles, eyes closed, and started to play. It was the music on the tape—chords and runs, minor-key melodic, bittersweet. He swayed side to side as his hands found his keys. I sat very still on the folding chair, as if watching a child's first music recital.

"Playing the piano makes me feel good," Mark said after he finished. "I think I'll have a cigarette. That's right," he replied to my quick look, "I still smoke." He pulled a battered pack from a shirt pocket and, with trembling hands, shakily lit it.

"Dad gone back to work?" he asked after a long drag. I nodded. "That's too bad, I wanted to see him." The dead air hung between us.

"Why the change? How do you feel?" I asked finally. "You must know how different you are now from when you were put in here. Do you still want to follow the Grateful Dead to L.A.?"

"Sometimes." A look of confusion crossed his face. "I don't know anymore." He rose. I had stayed too long. As I hugged him, I could feel his thin shoulder blades through his shirt. He seemed so frail, so fragile.

In a mild panic over what was to become of Mark, I called Dr. Harp the next morning. "Have you talked to the social workers yet?" he asked.

"Social workers? No one told me there were any social workers around," I snapped. "I've been at the hospital every day for three weeks, and none have materialized."

"Oh yes. There's an office just across from the ward," he replied. "Surely, someone must have told you."

"No, they didn't." Get on with it, Diane, this isn't the place for a skirmish. "What about Mark's tremor? Is that the drugs?"

"Lithium can cause that. It happens. Don't worry about it. Mark may be eligible for a group home when he leaves the hospital. You need to check with the social workers. Anything else? I can see you after rounds tomorrow," he said with finality. The meter was running.

"We have several group homes around town, funded by the state. We can legally commit Mark to one for ninety days after his hospital stay. We have a hearing here in the hospital where Mark is represented by a public defender, and then he is under legal restriction to stay or he goes to Eastern State Hospital." The social worker, Mr. Evans, talked as he shuffled amid the stacks of manuals while rummaging for Mark's file.

"I'm afraid that the hospital will release Mark onto the interstate, and he will disappear." I voiced my worst nightmare. "Mark may still run away if released."

"We'll set the group home up for him. He can see a counselor, work, whatever, under supervision for ninety days. I'll arrange for him to visit it when he's ready. That's about all we can do. If Mark leaves Washington State, we will have no legal control over him." We were stuck. Until I was sure he wouldn't flee, he had to stay put.

"What's all this going to cost?" asked Chris when I called him that night. I shuddered.

"I haven't asked." Silence on the other end.

"Not at all?" he asked incredulously. "You have *no* idea?"

"How could I? I just wanted to give Mark the best treatment available and find a way to pay for it later." My stomach twisted into its now-familiar knot.

After a second's pause, he said more evenly, "Don't worry, we'll sort it out later. Just take care of Mark." I relaxed a bit, but the money shadow hung over everything. I had been afraid to call the insurance company. What if none of this treatment was covered?

"Are you going to set up housekeeping in Washington?" Chris wondered. "Mark will be taken care of. Come home."

"I will next week. Give me some time to be sure everything is running smoothly here." Untangling the social worker from the hospital from the doctor from the public defender from the court-appointed trustee would take all week and more. I left the mechanics of Mark's hospitalization out of our conversation. Big picture was his department; detail, mine.

"How do you feel?" I asked Mark as we sat down. I promised myself not to start every conversation with "How do you feel?" It was enough that he now slept in the unlocked side of the unit.

"They let me sit in the sun today. It felt wonderful to be outside again," he replied evenly. The medication had rubbed smooth his sharp edges. Mark was passive, agreeable to everything. His hands still trembled, but he seemed unaware of it. "Did you find my Walkman in the duffel I left at Axel's?"

"No, I'll look when I get back to the lake. What are you doing during the day? Not watching television, I hope." Stupid, Diane. Don't nag.

"They won't let you," he replied, not noticing my carping. "I work on my ceramics, draw, play the piano." This was an improved Mark, but it still wasn't the ironic, witty Mark who would have been full of sly remarks about the hospital and anxious to get on with his life. The old Mark would have had some choice comments about the *Reader's Digest*-Wonder Bread atmosphere of the ward.

This Mark was aloof, distant, unreadable. He didn't smile. He let the conversation die and made no attempt to fan it back to life. He didn't ask how long he was going to be in the hospital or about Chris or Robert. He slithered easily around my crude questions about what he was thinking and feeling. Between my questions and his nebulous words, he gazed past me at nothing and waited for the next remark to come his way. Someone sat on the sofa next to me, but it wasn't Mark, only a transparent imitation.

Yet the anger that had created a mutation of his personality was gone. His rage had been extinguished by lithium and Thorazine.

"Is Mr. Wakefield represented by counsel?" asked the hearing officer.

"He is," replied a nondescript man in a rumpled summer suit half-standing from his folding chair beside Mark. The commitment hearing was the required legal procedure to keep Mark restricted for the next ninety days. The courtroom was a folding table with folding chairs in a naked, windowless room somewhere in the hospital. Instantly assembled and dismantled, ready anytime.

Mark agreed to living in a group home in Spokane for the fall. But his acquiescence looked shaky. Sometimes he had the scared-deer-in-the-headlights look that frightened me into sensing he might still follow his "destiny" to Los Angeles.

The legal proceeding was over in moments, a certainty before the gavel was hammered down. Mark sat on the edge of his chair beside his attorney, rail thin but tidy in new clothes. He replied in a low voice to the officer's questions, almost inaudible in the back row where I sat with my friend Janet, who held my cold hand. I glanced at her and saw tears filling her eyes as Mark's commitment history was read for the record.

"This is lousy for you," I whispered, swallowing hard.

"Life can be lousy. I'm fine. Don't worry." She squeezed my hand. After the hearing, I followed Mark into the hall.

"I leave this afternoon for Connecticut," I said as we stood in the corridor. I wanted to hold him, keep him close, not leave him in the clutches of a legal system three thousand miles from home.

"I know. I'll be okay, Mom. This group home won't be too bad. I'll see it next week and be out of here in about ten days, they say." This was a good morning for him. He was clear-eyed and alert in his sober, almost cheerful way. "Maybe I can get back to Colorado next spring."

Chapter 8

HOSPITALS TO HALFWAY HOUSES AND BEYOND

Getting Past Stigma

"Stigma has become the single most destructive factor in the care and recovery of persons with mental illness," declares a patient brochure from one of the foremost hospitals in the country, McLean Hospital in Boston. McLean should know. Affiliated with Harvard Medical School and Massachusetts General Hospital, it has been setting standards for the care of the mentally ill since 1811.

Mental illness is a double burden. Not only must people contend with a crippling illness, but also with public branding and rejection. Society accepts physical illness and disability of almost any shape. The biblical scourge, leprosy, is now referred to as Hansen's disease and treated openly. On daily talk shows, every crease and fold of myriad ailments are discussed and displayed.

But when it comes to mental illness, people turn away. Even being a recovered cocaine addict or alcoholic is more socially acceptable than being mentally ill. Thus, it's no wonder that the mentally ill recoil from admitting to their sickness, let alone seeking treatment at a hospital.

Just as the mentally ill must bear personal stigma, so too do mental institutions. Care and treatment of the mentally ill has been hidden away and overgrown with shame for so long that public knowledge about it is scanty and covered with clichés. People think they know about places that hospitalize the mentally ill: The staff wears white coats, male nurses all look like linebackers, everyone gets shock therapy or psychosurgery or wears straitjackets, drugs are used to silence and numb, and patients are locked away for life. Every now and then, these images are reinforced by sensational movies or books. The film *Frances*, for instance, dramatized the surgical destruction of an actress's mind.

The "good" places are private, always expensive, and tucked into a remote place where neighbors don't complain. The "bad" places are usually state hospitals with high fences and barred windows, and inside, filth, overcrowding, and warehousing.

These images linger, even though care for the mentally ill has changed dramatically. Today, technology and a slow dawn of public understanding, brought on in part by the sprawling increase in mentally ill homeless, has pushed the pendulum of change toward reform. Although the wretched conditions have not completely disappeared, they have become the exception rather than the rule.

Once Upon a Time

The history of mental-health care is marked by cycles of concern and abuse. The first mental institutions were designed only to confine the mentally ill and to punish antisocial behavior or curb blasphemy. Mental illness was not recognized as a *medical* problem until the late eighteenth century.

The Enlightenment brought major improvements to the care of the mentally ill. Prominent social reformers advocated humane treatment and pressed for the construction of private and public asylums. Yet their hopes that proper care would cure the mentally ill soon faded. Population growth, industrialization, and masses of urban poor overwhelmed social systems. Asylums became places to stash the indigent insane and untreatable "lunatics."

In 1908, Clifford Beers, a Yale student, described his nightmarish experiences in various hospitals in *A Mind that Found Itself*. His vivid depiction of the horrors of the asylum focused attention on the barbaric care of the mentally ill. The pendulum was poised to swing again toward reform. The early twentieth century saw the building of psychiatric medical centers. Led by Sigmund Freud and Emil Kraeplin, psychiatry as a medical and scientific discipline sprang forth and flourished.

Yet the burgeoning of psychiatry brought little permanent enlightenment. By the 1950s, more than half a million mentally ill were warehoused in barbaric, sad conditions. Among all the hospital beds in the country, the mentally ill occupied fully *half*.

A swing of the pendulum back toward reform in 1946 when the National Mental Health Act created a new government agency and a new arm of the Public Health Service—the National Institute of Mental Health (NIMH). The new agency's mission was twofold: Make mental-health care available to all citizens and lead research in the causes and treatment of psychiatric illness. In the 1960s, it funded more than 760 community mental-health centers. As a research institution, the NIMH conducts laboratory and inpatient clinical research and funds studies outside the institution.

The 1960s and 1970s also saw the passage of the Community Mental Health Centers Act as well as Medicare and Medicaid. In addition, Social Security disability programs (both disability insurance— SSDI—and Supplemental Security Income—SSI) expanded to help the mentally ill.

By 1980, the number of mentally ill inpatients had fallen to about 132,000. This decline reflected both the community health-care movement and the introduction of treatment with drugs such as lithium, antidepressants, and neuroleptics. In addition, some medical technology was now advancing toward distinguishing between genuine mental disorders and people with treatable organic disorders that mimicked mental illness.

One such illness was pellagra, which in the early 1900s accounted for as much as 10 percent of mental-hospital admissions, particularly in the rural South. Potentially fatal, pellagra exhibits a host of physical symptoms as well as dementia and psychotic thinking. While doctors knew it was seasonal, they did not discover until 1920 that it was caused by a dietary (niacin) deficiency. The winter diet of the rural poor—high in cornmeal, meat, and molasses—lacked the yeast products and vegetables necessary to prevent it.

Another example of a medically treatable illness that accounted for a remarkable number of psychiatric hospital beds until the advent of antibiotic therapy was tertiary syphilis. Today, as a psychiatric syndrome, it is virtually unheard of.

In recent years, psychiatry's advances have been in the area of treatment—more specific applications of new and old drugs, and therapies in more precisely defined diagnostic categories. Psychiatry is also honing its diagnostic imaging skills, and finding new uses for the

still-young technologies of computerized tomography, magnetic reso-
nance, and positron-emission tomography.

Ins and Outs of Hospitals

Psychiatric care is roughly divided into two spheres: inpatient and
outpatient. Inpatients obviously are in hospitals. Outside hospitals,
outpatients frequent an assortment of facilities, from a therapist's office
for weekly visits to twenty-four-hour residential care (sometimes called
a halfway or three-quarters-way house, depending on the level of supervision) to emergency care or crisis intervention delivered by a hospital.

Psychiatric hospitals specialize in mental-health care, yet their care
is different from that in a general hospital. Because doctors have no
handy lab tests to help make a diagnosis, they frequently admit a
patient to a psychiatric hospital to make a diagnosis by watching a
patient's behavior and moods. While a first step in many psychiatric
admissions is a complete physical examination and a battery of neurologic or endocrine lab tests, these activities may well be secondary to
simple observation.

Psychiatric hospitals are also skilled in sorting out patients suffering
from both psychiatric and neurologic ailments, meaning their psychotic or affective disorder is mixed in with organically based illnesses
stemming from localized brain injuries. Untangling these problems
usually requires four to eight weeks of hospitalization in what's called
a neuropsychiatry unit. Generally, such units that specialize in clinical
evaluation are located at research hospitals, and typically these hospitals are associated with medical schools, universities, and academic-
research centers.

While these institutions are on the front line of innovative research,
they do not care for the chronically mentally ill.

The Bogeyman: State Hospitals

Most patients, unless they have extraordinary financial resources, eventually spend some time in state (public) hospitals. For generations,
popular literature has crudely depicted and roundly condemned public
hospitals as state-sponsored snake pits. Our horrific images of mental-
health care—a skeleton staff caring for thousands of patients in crum-
bling buildings—come from stories about state hospitals. While this
picture has now largely faded, it persists. People still cringe at the

thought of someone relegated to a state hospital. Nevertheless, state institutions still care for the bulk of this country's mentally ill.

In 1983, about 273 state psychiatric hospitals were operating. Public-funding sources such as Medicaid and Medicare pay the patient's bills. The individual states administer and set standards for their hospitals, which are closely monitored and supervised. The catchall term for monitoring health-care services is "quality assurance." Public funding of medical care has created a flourishing secondary business—the monitoring and evaluation of that care. Quality assurance examines how resources are used and facilities are staffed. Hospital quality assurance in the United States is usually carried out by the Joint Commission on Accreditation of Healthcare Organizations (JCAHO), a private, voluntary organization, and by the federal Health Care Financing Administration.

Using a pass-or-fail rating, these groups compare actual care at each hospital with predetermined standards. They look at how medical records are kept (for example, does each patient have a treatment plan?), how units are staffed, the competence and qualifications of the staff, treatment conditions, and any extra resources.

A major aspect of quality assurance at these hospitals is the credentialing and privileging of the professionals who work there—that is, deciding who is qualified to practice at an institution. A credentials committee conducts this process, examining a professional's education, training, experiences, and licenses. Yet, remember, we are talking about mental-health professionals. Unlike other medical specialties such as surgery, which has specific procedures, techniques, and tests of competence, the mental-health field has a difficult time codifying exactly who should or should not practice. To date, it has developed no single set of professional standards.

Unfortunately, the details of professional assessment reports are carefully guarded secrets by the JCAHO (hence the pass/fail grade). So while accreditation by JCAHO or HCFA is not a guarantee of quality care, the accreditation is worth noting if you are comparing hospitals.

The Community Hospital
Over the past twenty years, the number of yearly admissions to the psychiatric units of community general hospitals has exceeded admissions to state hospitals. Community general hospitals have taken a major bite out of inpatient populations at the large state mental institutions. Psychiatric units at these hospitals keep materializing to meet

local demand. In 1941, there were only thirty-nine inpatient psychiatric units at community general hospitals. Thirty years later, they were found in more than seven hundred community hospitals. Today, almost any hospital with more than one hundred beds offers some kind of inpatient psychiatric care.

At one time, conventional wisdom, coupled with established practices, insisted that the mentally ill and physically ill could not be treated under the same roof. Mental patients were said to be too disruptive and their problems too chronic. All they needed, administrators believed, was custodial care. With the advent of drug therapies and extensive support services, patients who might have needed extensive hospitalization now receive care through a temporary hospital stay followed by careful outpatient monitoring and rehabilitation.

Inevitably, the question of dangerousness arises when debating the care of the mentally ill. While a legitimate concern, this question has been answered with drug therapy, which can moderate and tranquilize threatening behavior. Yet of late this question has arisen once more, this time because of recent laws giving patients the right to refuse drug treatment. Once again, people want to know. "Are mental patients dangerous?"

A recent study suggests that the answer is "Not many—and those that are can be spotted early." This study looked at all patients who had to be restrained (buckled to beds with full leather wrist and ankle cuffs) in the acute psychiatric units of two general hospitals. Researchers found that these potentially violent people were usually young, unmarried men with a history of violent behavior and previous psychiatric care. The researchers counted 1,457 psychiatric patients, but only 77 patients who had to be held down. Yet other experts cite studies that fail to find more criminal or violent behavior in large populations of psychiatric patients than in the general population.

Drugs are not the only calming influence among potentially violent patients. Researchers have discovered that the atmosphere and attitudes of the psychiatric units themselves seem to calm people. A study of thirty-one patients in a Seattle hospital found patients improving significantly in the psychiatric units within the first forty-eight hours of treatment, compared with improvements attributed to drug treatment, which took longer.

In this study, manic-depressive patients were divided into two types of care. One group was in open units where patients had roommates, mingled with the general hospital population and visitors, and had to walk around the hospital for meals and lab tests. The second group was secluded in the psychiatric unit. Here, patients had no roommates and little interaction with outsiders. Researchers discovered that patients treated in an isolated, nonstimulating environment improved more.

The Forensic Hospital

Forensic hospitals are for people involved in legal or criminal issues. They are usually operated in conjunction with corrections departments, and confine and treat patients referred by the courts. Sometimes their patients are potentially violent and must have safe, secure care. For these hospitals, unlike others, building security, fences, and locks are major concerns. They house the potentially dangerous, like John Hinckley or Charles Manson, who are kept separate from general psychiatric patients.

The Psychiatric Unit

The admissions process in a psychiatric unit is more complicated than in other parts of a hospital. The unit has to collect not only medical data but also extensive family and behavioral history. Thus, initial interviews are long, detailed, and personal.

Most psychiatric units, but not all, are divided into locked and unlocked sections. To a newcomer to the world of psychiatric care, a journey into a locked unit can be a disturbing experience. You're buzzed through heavy, locked doors covered in wire mesh and carefully scrutinized by the staff person tending the door. Sometimes you empty your pockets and offer your purse for inspection or leave it with the staff. Staff will also inspect any packages you bring in for anything potentially harmful. In short, the unit feels more like a jail than a hospital. But given the very real danger of suicide or violent outbursts, tight precautions are necessary.

Most areas of a psychiatric unit are not locked but open, and often indistinguishable from other parts of the hospital. People come and go freely, including some patients, with no inspections or challenges. These units operate on a system of privileges ranging from none to complete freedom. A patient's level of privileges depends on a medical assessment and how much a patient cooperates. This cooperation, sometimes referred to as a "contract" between a patient and the hospital, often entails attending required group-therapy sessions and helping with small housekeeping chores around the unit.

Psychiatric units also differ from other medical treatment centers because patients spend little time in their rooms, generally only at night to sleep. They eat in a common area, and some hospitals have open patient kitchens where they can prepare their own food. During the day, patients do crafts, watch television, and, in some better-equipped facilities, exercise in a gym or go on group outings. To some, crafts seem mindless and childish. Yet they can be helpful to medical staff in evaluating a patient and drawing up a treatment plan. What a patient does in crafts reveals something about concentration, coordination, interaction with others, and the ability to follow directions and thinking.

Most psychiatric units include some kind of therapy—individual, group, or both—as a regular activity. Group therapy can take many forms, depending on the size, who participates, and what's being accomplished. Groups may involve working toward specific goals, daily interaction and role playing, transitional activities for patients about to leave, accepting and stabilizing medication regimes, male or female social problems, family issues, or daily coping skills to prepare one for the outside.

Most hospitals try to offer regular individual therapy. Patients may work with psychiatrists or meet for counseling with social workers, psychologists, or patient self-help groups, such as Alcoholics Anonymous, Al-Anon, Narcotics Anonymous, or a Manic Depressive Association. Hospitals offering therapy also sometimes require family members to be part of the process.

Extensive group and individual therapy is the ideal, and unfortunately not all hospitals are equipped to offer them. Nevertheless, patients and families should know what's possible and push for the best care available.

The Emergency Room

For many with mental illness, the emergency room is the first point of contact with the medical establishment. The job of the emergency-room staff is to stabilize a patient and get some idea of the nature of the emergency. The most serious psychiatric emergency is the risk of suicide, and ER staff are trained to treat it with fast-acting medication, physical restraints, or isolation. Other kinds of emergencies, such as behavior disruptions, are sometimes accompanied by physical complaints. So ER personnel sort out the physical from the mental problem, and may even call the local police to help subdue an unruly patient.

The dual-diagnosis patient—someone with an alcohol or drug problem as well as other mental illness—presents a real dilemma for ER personnel. Some professionals feel that more than half the psychiatric patients between eighteen and thirty-four years old may also be alcoholics or drug abusers. In an emergency room, this patient may be perceived as "just" a substance abuser, and his other diagnosis may be given short shrift.

Many hospitals, especially those devoted to long-term care, do not have emergency units—their patients come from doctors' or a hospital's referral.

The Safety Question

Suicide is the number-one emergency in psychiatry, and suicide is the central focus of any place that treats the mentally ill. In psychiatric parlance, suicide is often obliquely referred to as the Safety Issue. When a psychiatrist talks about safety questions, he means the threat of self-destruction. Drugs that are not fatal if taken in excess are said to have "a good safety profile" and are given to patients who may attempt to kill themselves. Fear, and a desire to mask a terrifying reality, have produced these mild-sounding euphemisms.

As a routine matter, psychiatric hospitals put careful thought into being safe. Mirrors are not made of glass but reflecting metal; nurses dispense matches and cigarettes one at a time. Perhaps the most difficult screening job for a hospital is identifying patients likely to try suicide. When they do spot someone likely to try, they employ extra supervision and control. Patients are carefully monitored—if necessary, continuously by a staff member—and may be given strong medication to calm their anxiety. But even the threat of a possible suicide does not give hospitals unlimited control or abrogate patients' rights.

Patients' Rights

The issue of patient rights comes up when someone is placed in a hospital involuntarily. This involuntary admission is sometimes called "commitment." The voluntary patient can come and go as he likes, and refuse any treatment or medication; the involuntary do not have these rights all the time.

The patient-rights movement began, of course, in California in the 1960s, where laws of commitment were based on the need for treatment. A person could be committed against his will if others judged that he *needed* treatment. Now, commitment statutes reach beyond this concern to questions of civil rights and the rights of individuals. The revised commitment laws were written on the premise that basic civil rights preceded a patient's need for treatment. Now, even the need for treatment is being challenged. It's no longer a cause for involuntary commitment, and has been replaced by criteria related to dangerousness or inability to function.

Another branch of the patient-rights movement concerns what happens inside a hospital. In many states, patients have the right to refuse treatment, including medication. (The U.S. Supreme Court has never directly addressed the constitutional basis for a right to refuse treatment.) The reasons patients refuse—unwanted side effects or denial that they need drugs or that they're sick—do not matter. They can refuse to swallow the pills, which generally sets in motion a review process by the hospital of a person's treatment plan. Many refusers eventually accede to treatment. A study of patients who refused medication showed that 70 percent received treatment after their case had been reviewed.

Patients' rights go beyond being able to refuse medication. They also encompass standards for hospital conditions, daily activities, and a hospital staff's obligations to give patients as much freedom as is reasonable. Typically, these rights are very specific. What follows are the formal patient rights issued by the state of Washington.* Every psychiatric patient in the state receives these, and they offer a good model for what patients and families should expect from a hospital.

1. Unless released within 72 hours, all involuntary patients have a right to a judicial hearing not more than 72 hours after the initial detention to determine whether probable cause exists to detain such persons after 72 hours for a further period up to 14 days.

2. All involuntary patients have the right to communicate immediately with an attorney and, if indigent, they have the right to have an attorney appointed to represent them before and at such hearing and a right to be told the name and address of the attorney who has been designated.

3. All involuntary patients have the right to remain silent.

4. All involuntary patients have the right to be told that statements they make may be used against them.

* By permission.

5. All involuntary patients have the right to present evidence and to cross-examine the witnesses who may testify against them at the probable cause hearing.

6. All involuntary patients have the right to refuse medication beginning 24 hours prior to the probable cause hearing.

7. When taken into custody by public officers and then placed in a mental health facility, the involuntary patient shall receive within 12 hours a statement of specific fact alleged to have caused the present detention and possible future detention.

8. No patient shall be restricted from sending written communications of the fact of his detention; any such communication will be mailed to the person to whom addressed by the physician in charge of the patient and/or person in charge of the facility.

9. All patients shall have the right to adequate care and individualized treatment.

10. All patients have the right to wear their own clothes and keep and use their own personal possessions, except when deprivation of same is essential to the protection and safety of the resident or other persons.

11. All patients have the right to keep and be allowed to spend a reasonable sum of his or her own money for canteen expenses and for small purchases.

12. All patients have the right to access to individual storage space for his or her private use.

13. All patients have the right to have visitors at reasonable times.

14. All patients have the right to have reasonable access to a telephone both to make and receive calls.

15. All patients have the right to have ready access to letter writing material, including stamps, and to send and receive uncensored correspondence through the mails.

16. All patients have the right not to consent to the performance of shock treatment or surgery, except emergency life-saving surgery, and not to have shock treatment or nonemergency surgery in such circumstances unless ordered by a court pursuant to a judicial hearing in which he is present and represented by counsel, and the court shall appoint a psychiatrist,

psychologist, or physician designed by such person or his counsel to testify on behalf of such person.

17. All patients have the right to dispose of property and sign contracts unless they have been adjudicated an incompetent in a court proceeding directed to that particular issue.

18. All patients have the right not to have psycho-surgery performed under any circumstance.

19. All patients have the right to object to detention or request release, and such request shall be filed with the clerk of the Superior Court. If the patient is not released within two days, the clerk shall notify the judge, who will immediately appoint an attorney to represent such patient.

20. No person shall be presumed incompetent or lose any civil rights as a consequence of receiving evaluation or treatment for mental disorder.

Right to Privacy

Closely linked to a patient's civil rights is the right to privacy. No reputable hospital treating the mentally ill reveals whether an individual is a patient. Phone calls into a psychiatric unit are answered with a simple "Hello." Patient privacy also extends to medical staff, who must keep confidential anything learned through therapy.

Exceptions to confidentiality rules are professional, medical reasons. Hospitals using team treatment allow medical staff to share information about a patient with each other and sometimes family, but this information goes no further. Similarly, medical staff can go outside a hospital for a professional consultation. In rare cases, a hospital may cooperate with local authorities if a patient leaves the hospital grounds when he shouldn't.

It's very difficult for outsiders to find out if someone is a psychiatric patient. There are no names posted outside rooms or on any bulletin board. Patients who want their presence revealed have to put their request in writing.

The Adolescent Patient

More and more teenagers are filling psychiatric units. According to the National Center for Health Statistics, the number of people between ages ten and nineteen discharged from psychiatric units between 1980 and 1987 increased by 43 percent. In the same period, the number of these youth in the general population dropped by 11 percent. Most of these patients, say mental-health professionals, were not suffering from affective or psychotic disorders but from personality disorders, disorders of conduct, and drug abuse.

Hospitals accepting (some even say inviting) patients whose psychological problems are not considered serious have been described as greedy money machines. For most, this is an unfair characterization. Major mental illness often first appears in the late teens or early twenties, and only admission and evaluation can identify and begin to treat these lifelong illnesses.

Mental-health care providers are beginning to realize that adolescents do not necessarily need more facilities, but better programs. "The problem," states the director of a university rehabilitation program, "is not unmotivated clients, it is unappealing programs." Until recently, mental-health institutions have been populated largely by adults, and their programs were aimed at this age group. For adolescents to seek out and agree to treatment, they need to find programs tailored for them—programs that take into account their unique emotional and social needs.

These young patients can be hard to handle, especially when their mental disorders are mixed with the typical energy, quirks, and needs of adolescence, and so hospitals limit how many they treat. Generally, hospitals try to keep their adolescent patients to fewer than their adult patients. Otherwise, say observers, "mayhem may reign."

Often hospitals treat adolescents differently from adults the minute they walk through the door. An important difference is how they evaluate them. Knowing that normal adolescent behavior may be confused with psychotic behavior, doctors undertake one of four possible evaluation and treatment methods. These are:

1. Short-term evaluation and treatment
2. Extensive evaluation, then referral elsewhere
3. Crisis intervention and immediate hospitalization
4. Stabilization until extensive treatment can be started

Conditions are changing for teenagers as their numbers grow and their problems seize our attention. One noteworthy sign of progress is a program at the Center for Psychiatric Rehabilitation at Boston University. This is a continuing-education program for young adults with psychiatric difficulties, consisting of classes designed to help students learn and plan for meaningful work. Classes go for four semesters and give students a sense of mutual support and sharing. Although the program is expensive at $5,300 a semester, it addresses head-on two of the biggest problems for adolescents struck by mental illness—getting an education and getting a job.

Who Pays the Bills?

Psychiatric care, despite the absence of high-priced machines and elaborate laboratory tests, is enormously expensive. At a top-rated private hospital, daily room rates, excluding doctors' fees and diagnostic tests, can run between $500 and $1,400. Most of the cost is for staff. Caring for the mentally ill is labor intensive—patients must be constantly monitored and given therapy, activities that involve large cadres of professionals.

Health-care costs are regulated by state and federal law. Yet the regulations give hospitals a certain amount of freedom. In Massachusetts, for instance, the Rate Setting Commission determines how much income a hospital can generate. The hospital can adjust its fees for various services, as long as it does not exceed its state-mandated cap.

The issue of hospital costs inevitably leads to the controversial and rancorous issue of health insurance. Patients and families faced with psychiatric-hospital bills learn quickly that in the world of health insurance, mental illness is in a class by itself. Typically, they discover that their health insurance would cover an expensive organ transplant but not payment for a patient living in a psychiatric halfway house.

Most insurance policies provide less coverage for psychiatric expenses than for other "medical" expenses. That is, among insurers, psychiatric illness is considered something other than a physical ailment. Some states require insurance carriers to provide at least a minimum amount of coverage for psychiatric care. Yet these amounts are far less than payments for other kinds of illnesses.

Here's a comparison of the costs and coverage (for a federal employee plan and a private plan) for two kinds of illnesses:

Ischemic Heart Disease (Diagnosed at forty-five; cost of coronary bypass, balloon angioplasty; death at fifty-five). Costs:

Hospital: $82,750 Outpatient/drugs: $25,600
Total Cost: $108,350

Covered by federal employee plan: $99,210
Owed by patient: $9,140
Covered by private plan: $97,750
Owed by patient: $10,600

Chronic Schizophrenic   (Diagnosed at twenty; lives to sixty with hospitalization every three years). Costs:

Hospital: $135,000
Intensive Care: $6,000
Outpatient care: $66,200
Drugs: $87,600
Total Cost: $294,800
Covered by federal employee plan: $75,000
Owed by patient: $219,800
Covered by private plan: $50,000
Owed by patient: $244,800

Life's Blood and Mother's Milk: Public Assistance

Without publicly funded programs such as Social Security, Medicare, Medicaid, and state hospitals, many mentally ill would have no support or medical care. These programs are vital and, for a patient, maintaining eligibility is critical.

Mentally ill patients may qualify for financial help from either Social Security Disability Insurance (SSDI) or Social Security Supplemental Income (SSI). The caveat for either of these programs, of course, is qualifying. While Social Security officially regards mental illness as a disabling condition, not all mental-illness sufferers qualify for its benefits.

The SSDI program is for disabled workers, the key word here being "worker." A person has to have held a job and contributed to FICA, something which many young mentally ill people have not done. Under SSDI, the definition of disability is related to a person's ability to work. A severe mental or physical impairment that prevents work, *any* sort of work, for a year or more is required to qualify for SSDI.

The other Social Security program—supplemental security income or SSI—pays monthly to qualifying disabled people regardless of their work history. To be eligible, a person has to be at least eighteen years old and have a physical or mental disability to keep him from working for at least a year and have no resources over nineteen hundred dollars.

An adolescent manic-depressive who is going to school or college could qualify for this program. Unlike SSDI, which requires its applicants to wait five months before receiving benefits, SSI patients can begin receiving money as soon as their disability is established.

The basic SSI payment is $368 a month (as of 1990), but it may be less if a person has job income or more if he lives in a state that also pays benefits. Family income is not a consideration for SSI eligibility or the amount of benefits. While the government does allow a beneficiary to work, it does limit how much an eligible person can earn. There are extensive eligibility requirements, and either a patient, or someone else for him, can apply at any Social Security office.

Another government program, Medicaid (also called Title XIX) is administered by the states and helps pay for acute general hospital costs, nursing care, doctor's fees, and outpatient services. Usually, Medicaid does not cover inpatient treatment at private psychiatric hospitals. The eligibility rules for Medicaid are very complicated. So complicated, admits the government, that people should not try to figure out by themselves whether they qualify but go ahead and apply for present expenses as well as past or future costs.

Once a person is deemed eligible, the government gives him a medical card, which is shown to hospital and doctors. Medicaid pays directly to the service provider at rates the agency, not the hospital or doctor, determines.

Staying eligible is important for all recipients, and while a mentally ill person usually can't lose out for medical reasons (mental illness is for life), circumstances might put payments in jeopardy. An inheritance or large gift could disqualify someone because he would then exceed the earning cap. A person inheriting part of an estate from parents who died without wills, or wills that named him a beneficiary, could be rejected from the rolls of SSI or Medicaid. Wills, and trusts, have to be written carefully by attorneys familiar with state and federal eligibility laws.

Other grounds for disqualification include asset transfers—selling or giving away cash or property in order to become indigent and, presumably, qualify for these publicly funded programs. The government scrutinizes such transactions very carefully, and in particular whether they were made within twenty-four months. The rules for qualifying or not qualifying are complex, and families and patients should consult experts before making irrevocable financial moves. Also keep in mind that applying for any federal or state program requires complete financial disclosure, and the law carries stiff penalties for fraud.

For a middle-income family of someone with serious mental illness, disinheritance or financial alienation may be the only way to maintain the indigent status demanded by publicly funded programs. This process is emotionally traumatic and needs to be coordinated by experts in both the family's financial affairs and in the respective eligibility requirements of the public programs. Errors can be tragic.

Where Next? After the Hospital

Most psychiatric patients aren't in the hospital for long periods. Stays generally last from a couple of weeks to two or three months. Psychiatric hospitalization is usually short for two reasons: Once stabilized on a drug and therapy regime, patients do not need to be in a hospital, and the cost. With insurance companies imposing low ceilings on coverage for psychiatric hospitalization, patients keep close count of hospital days.

The question "Where next?" is a frightening prospect for many patients and families. Often the mentally ill can't live alone or go to work, and need help in daily living. But there is no ready, obvious institution to house these people. Thus, states and communities have weaved a patchwork quilt of group homes, halfway houses, supervised apartments, three-quarter-way houses, transitional-living quarters, and residential treatment centers. These places go by a variety of names, but their purpose is the same: to bridge the gap between the hospital and independent living.

As they vary in name, so too do they vary in cost. Some are non-profit, government subsidized, others private and for-profit. Regardless of who foots the bill, usually it won't be an insurance company. Most insurance policies do not cover nonhospital, residential care, and monthly fees can be as high as $2,500.

Money is not the only complication with residential treatment centers (for simplicity, we're using this term to refer to the whole spectrum of homes and facilities). Many do not accept patients with a history of violence or substance abuse. Also, someone with a recent suicide attempt or physical disability may be excluded. Most of these centers require a minimum stay, usually ninety days or more (some insist on commitments as long as two years).

Daily life in these places varies from very regimented and highly supervised to few required activities and no supervision. Patients living in most types of centers have to participate in part-time work, school, or volunteer activity. For the manic-depressive, as well as other mentally ill people, staying busy and learning self-discipline is a vital coping skill. Thus, patients are not allowed to sleep through the day or to spend their time watching television. Most patients continue personal psychotherapy and are under strict demands to be drug-free and stay off alcohol.

Another element of these homes is community living—residents learning how to interact with and help each other. Cooking is shared, housekeeping chores are rotated, and residents attend regular, sometimes daily, group meetings to talk about themselves and their problems.

Ideally, a residential treatment center is a microcosm of the outside work where the mentally ill can relearn how to take care of themselves, relate to others, and do a dependable day's work. They do this in a place that offers a safety net, and hopefully, a way to slide back into normal society.

Support Groups
If mental-health-care hospitals and treatment centers had all the staffing and programs described here, there would be no need for advocacy groups. But mental-health care still has miles to go, and much of this distance is being covered by private organizations of patients, families, and friends.

The National Alliance for the Mentally Ill (NAMI) is the most vocal, most organized, most effective such group. Created in 1979, it has spread to nine hundred affiliates located in all states and a membership topping seventy thousand. NAMI splits its efforts between insisting that mental-health issues be at the forefront of national and local political debate, and providing support for individuals. It has demanded attention and funding for such issues as health insurance for psychiatric care, drug research, and new product approval.

NAMI is not all protest and demands. It reviews potential state and federal legislation with an eye to its impact on the mentally ill. It also makes things happen. It's credited, for instance, with convincing the National Institute of Mental Health to reallocate $345 million from sociological studies to research into the cause and treatment of schizophrenia.

On a personal level, NAMI sponsors thousands of support groups throughout the country—groups for the mentally ill, friends of the mentally ill, parents and children of the mentally ill—any kind of group people need and want. Finally, NAMI has an elaborate public information effort that publishes newsletters and booklets, and national and local news affecting the mentally ill. (For more information, call or write NAMI, 2101 Wilson Boulevard, Suite 302, Arlington, VA 22201, 703/524-7600.)

Another national support organization is the National Depressive and Manic Depressive Association (NDMDA). This too is an educational group that organizes support groups. It publishes a newsletter, maintains an information clearinghouse, and holds an annual convention. (For more information, call or write NDMDA, Merchandise Mart, Box 3395, Chicago, IL 60654 312/939-2442.)

Chapter 9

AUTUMN REVELATIONS

September

"*I* can't live in the group home. It's dirty, smells like old food, bedspreads on sofas, full of psychos. I can't live there," Mark repeated on the telephone. "I want to come home," he pleaded in a soft voice full of yearning. Tears of relief rolled down my face as I choked on my words.

"I'll find a way to get you home," I promised.

I had left Mark behind in the hospital in Washington State, waiting for a group home. I felt as if I had deserted him. Chris and I went through the motions of Life as Normal, but Mark's shadow hung over us. My telephone conversations with him and the doctor gave me only superficial details about sleeping habits and days filled with piano music and craft classes. Chris and I were helpless.

"If Dr. Harp agrees, I can have you out of there tomorrow," I recklessly assured Mark before talking to the doctor, and started a checklist of things to do before he arrived. With a reacquisition of control, I felt a new energy. "Let me call the doctor and I'll call you back as soon as I can." After my leaving several messages, Dr. Harp called back.

"Mark is much better, but he has a long way to go. He has responded very well to the lithium, but needs more treatment. He seems to be adamant about not going to the group home. The only other choice would be to put him in the state hospital until we find a situation he'll accept. I guess he could go home," said Dr. Harp evenly. We could have been discussing a sick houseplant. I marveled that this colorful medical discipline attracted such gray personalities. Dr. Harp was a blue dot on a blue wall. After talking with him, I had no sense of Mark's health.

"The state hospital's out of the question," I blurted with finality. The state hospital, according to the local press, was a modern-day snake pit—an overcrowded dumping ground for homeless patients. If he refused a group home for food smells, how would he react to a state mental hospital? "I'll arrange for him to pick up tickets at the airport and fly straight home," I said.

"We have no objection to that," said Dr. Harp a shade too quickly. "I'll make arrangements with the hospital." His reaction reminded me of my two years doing social work after college. In that job, the real goal was to move welfare recipients to someone else's caseload. Movement was seen as progress, and that's how success was gauged. Now, Mark was being moved along.

The past spring taught me that chicken soup, clean sheets, and cookies were not going to reassemble Mark. He needed more than living at home with weekly visits to a wooden psychiatrist. My starting point was a *Hartford Courant* Sunday supplement article about the Institute for Living, a nearby psychiatric hospital. I called their main number.

"My son is being discharged from a hospital in Washington State, and I need to find out what you offer for after-hospital care," I began vaguely. Voice after voice passed me along until I found Anita, a cheerful, chatty voice describing herself as the residence treatment director.

"What exactly is residence treatment?" I had asked.

"Simply stated, it's supervised living for patients too well for inpatient hospitalization and not well enough to live alone. We have supervised living units near the hospital. Our residents work, go to school, see their doctors." Perfect for Mark.

"But," she added apologetically, "we won't have any openings for at least six months." I sank again.

"Let me ask you a rhetorical question," I began, after recovering from my disappointment. "If you were me, the mother of a nineteen-year-old manic-depressive, and had private insurance, where within, say, three hours of here would you go for the best treatment?"

"Hillview Hospital, Boston," she replied as rapidly as a game-show contestant. I had never heard of it, and asked her to tell me more.

"Hillview Hospital is a major teaching and research facility near Boston. They're doing really ground-breaking work in mental illness, and their staff roster reads like a *Who's Who* of mental health," she answered. "Give me your address and I'll send you some information about support groups and the programs we offer," she volunteered as an afterthought.

Except for its street number, the brownstone house on the sedate, tree-lined street in Boston's Back Bay was indistinguishable from the houses on either side. No sign indicated that it was a psychiatric residence. Mark and I studied the elaborate stone facade for a moment before going through the wrought-iron garden gate and ringing the doorbell.

"You sure this is it?" he asked with a frown.

"Pretty sure. It's the number they gave me." I wasn't sure at all. The doorway was framed with a large dogwood beginning to show hints of red. By the end of September, this street would be ablaze. For the moment, summer lingered in the fading asters and tired cottons of the passers-by. I punched the bell again and waited. A voice in a speaker box confirmed our identity, and the door buzzed us in.

Mark and I sat in the only two chairs in the darkened foyer. Its worn carpet and scratched-up mahogany furniture could not hide the beautiful proportions of an old house in the high-rent district of Boston. Like the dowager who wears her tattered furs to the grocery store, there was a shabby elegance and Yankee thriftiness to its use as a medical facility. The furniture could have been decorator discards from a well-heeled contributor. Piles of coats and hats from the past winter smothered a freestanding clothes rack in the corner. Despite distant sounds of slamming doors and telephones, we saw no one.

Sitting on a hard chair in a darkened hall, I felt as if I were on my first job interview. I shifted in my seat, reapplied my lipstick, and covertly examined Mark. He had shed the sushi-chef headband, but the yellow calico bracelets, now frayed and at odds with his new clothes and glasses, were still there. He leaned his chair back against the wall, eyes closed, outstretched legs crossed at the ankles, arms akimbo as if he were soaking up sun on a hot beach.

"How are you doing?" I whispered, feeling as though we were being watched by unseen eyes. The words were out before I could stifle them.

He half-opened his eyes and looked sideways at me without moving.

"Tired. It's too early for me," he yawned. I had roused him out at dawn for this appointment with the director of Covington Lodge, a residence treatment house associated with Hillview Hospital.

"Did you take your pills this morning?" I asked, not heeding my own rules on hounding him. He sleepily nodded.

"You were in the hospital in Washington?" asked the thirtyish director after we had seated ourselves in his office upstairs. He perched on the front of his desk. I picked up his card from the table. Ph.D. were the only initials I recognized.

"Mark was in the hospital for a month," I volunteered. His eyes flicked from me to Mark. "Mark, not you," they said. I sat back, quiet.

"They said I was manic-depressive," Mark recounted through another yawn.

"And you don't think so?" he asked in a neutral tone.

"I don't know what it means," Mark replied while trying to light a cigarette with shaking hands. The director pulled an ashtray from the drawer behind him.

"How do you feel about living here at Covington Lodge?" he asked, handing Mark the ashtray.

"I don't think I need to, and I don't want to. This whole thing is my mother's idea. I just want to go back to school," Mark declared, with tinges of hostility seeping to the surface.

Mark, I silently pleaded, just be cooperative, tell him you want to come to live here. Make the right noises.

Mark looked every inch the mental patient. Hair uncombed, rumpled clothes, the now almost-trademark mismatched socks. Mark's dress would have been totally unremarkable on a college campus, almost predictable, but on someone coming from a psychiatric hospitalization, the disorderly dress suggested disorderly thought.

"Who is your doctor here?" the director asked, finally turning to me.

"We don't have one yet. I'm still working on that," I replied in a reedy voice. I heard my voice as a listener would—thin, uncertain, unconvincing. My reply had a false, tin ring to it, as if I had made no effort to find a doctor for Mark. I didn't mention the dozens of calls to doctors who "weren't taking new patients now—call back in six months," and to secretaries who cut me off midsentence. Those explanations felt like excuses, so I omitted them.

"And you feel he is ready for Covington Lodge?" he asked with a let's-cut-through-the-crap directness.

"I don't know exactly. I'm just starting to look for the right place for Mark," I waffled, and tried to suppress the quaver in my voice. I wasn't prepared for these questions.

"Most of our residents stay here about two years. Mark, are you ready for a two-year commitment to this recovery process?" I looked at Mark, who had come awake at the mention of two years.

"Absolutely not. I'm going back to Colorado this spring for school. No way," he announced defiantly, loudly. Don't be a fool, Mark, I silently cried. Just tell him this is what you want to do, and we'll work out the details later.

"I don't think Covington Lodge is where you should be right now. You really are not suitable for our program," the director continued, with no hint of reaction to Mark's outburst. "I suggest you give the Hillview residence treatment director a call and see what else they have for you." I had bypassed this director in going directly to Covington Lodge. He was reminding me that without going through channels, there were no results.

I had already mentally moved Mark into one of the sunny upstairs rooms with a street view and had him going to a job twenty hours a week, maybe taking an art class, seeing a doctor. He and Chris and I would go out for dinner, and Mark would come home for occasional weekends. The vision evaporated like morning dew in the hot sun. Before I had time to think, we were out on the street. The interview had lasted ten minutes. Back to being two mice and a pumpkin after the ball.

The prospect of Mark's illness extending beyond the vanishing point on the horizon was eroding my strength. I was still waking up at 3:00 A.M., when all problems were unsurmountable. I'd slip out of bed so as not to wake Chris, crawl downstairs, and listen to Larry King on the radio while looking at whatever magazine was on the top of the pile on the coffee table. After a while, I would go back to bed and sleep dreamlessly. But as quickly as these thoughts appeared, I pushed them aside. Mark's disease was a major trek, not a day hike.

"What now?" Mark asked without interest. I gave him a critical look.

"Do you have any winter clothes left from Colorado?" I asked. The sky was darkening with a late-summer storm. I could feel the telltale chill in the air that marked the coming season.

"No," he said shortly, not looking at me as we stood in front of the house.

"We could go to Filene's Basement and look at the winter things. What about that?"

He shrugged with indifference. "Whatever," he said, following me as I headed for the nearest subway.

"These don't look too bad," I proposed, tentatively fingering a slag heap of blue oxford-cloth shirts in Filene's Basement. Heavy women with large shopping bags nudged us toward the men's jackets in the far end of the store. Hands reached in front of me to extract an item from the mountained merchandise; customers dumped sweaters and purses on the floor while trying on clothes.

I believed in the American dictum that you were what you wore. Clothes were protective coloration, sometimes even camouflage. I took it for granted that style was something you purchased. Not Mark. For him, what he wore was an extension of his self. His garments were worn over and over, the fading of the fabric and the loosening of the seams making his things uniquely his. Even his mismatched socks, always green and blue, were by design. Like his childhood blanket, his shirts and jackets were prized possessions that gave him comfort and a sense of identity. His purchases were serious affairs, not flirtations or infatuations. I flipped through the blue shirts, covertly glancing at Mark. He was impatiently looking around. I was going to lose him if I didn't move along.

"We could check out the blazers," I suggested casually. He shot me a hard glare. This was an old dispute. The button-down-shirt-navy-blazer-gray-slacks-Bass-loafer look was what I resorted to for adolescent male dress. Only with all my bargaining chips could I prevail on him to wear such a uniform. Seeing Mark fitted out in predictable dress always made me feel back in control. Maybe we would have had more success at Covington Lodge if he had looked better, less chaotic.

"I want one of those wool jackets with little colored threads in the material, like this one," he said, tugging at the sleeve of a sport coat.

"Tweed," I said over the head of a short woman inching between us to inspect the tags of the 42 regulars. "This looks like your size," I pointed out, rounding the corner to the next rack. Mark lingered, still holding the jacket sleeve. "That's not your size," I told him over my shoulder.

"I don't care," he replied furiously, his voice rising above the din of the basement shoppers. "I like this one."

"Mark, you'll swim in it. It's much too big."

He ignored me, pulled on the jacket, and marched with determination to the nearest mirror.

"Even here, this is expensive," I said, looking at the price tag. "I don't want to buy something that is clearly the wrong size."

"Look," he shouted, "I don't need you here at all! Just give me the money, and I'll buy my own things." While this argument was familiar territory, Mark's rage was not. He glowered at my tepid responses, and reluctantly I decided that there was nothing for me to do but leave.

"You're right," I snapped, digging into my wallet for cash. "I don't need this either. Buy your own jacket. I'll be at the car reading my book." I slapped the cash into his hand and wheeled around and headed up the escalator, leaving him rummaging the racks for tweed.

I drifted off the escalator to the lingerie department, thinking I'd poke around for a while and then go back downstairs to see how he was doing. I found the nightgowns among a forest of tightly packed racks in a remote corner. Women in various stages of undress were slipping on clothes on the lee side of the display racks. I leafed through the "smalls" indecisively. Idly, I looked at the shopworn gowns with the Saks and Neiman-Marcus tags and selected one. I stood in line for the nearest register, still mulling over my alternatives. At some point, Mark had to go it alone.

"Screw it," I said aloud, surprising the clerk taking my money. "Sorry," I mumbled, seeing her suddenly lift her head from the register. Mark could handle this one alone. Now was the time to start cutting mooring lines. I picked up my bag and went out the basement doors, heading for the subway back uptown.

Sitting on the "T" rattling under the Boston Common, I reworked our session at Covington Lodge. It wasn't Mark's appearance or words that had slammed shut the doors of Covington Lodge. It was Mark. The erratic conversation barely tempered by lithium, the fireworks temper flashing sparks one instant, black silence the next, and the momentary glimpses of his wild, untamed thoughts brought a look of his eye.

I wanted to repackage him to drop perfectly between being sick enough to treat but well enough not to lock up. If I allowed myself, I could panic about what was going to happen to Mark. Hillview Hospital was my next shot in the dark.

I didn't know any medical people in Boston—no family doctor or friend of a friend. All I had was a telephone number. Getting into a private hospital can be like winning admittance to an exclusive private college. They can be very picky about whom they take. You don't apply unless you have the insurance or other resources; patients have to meet certain criteria; and personal interviews can make the difference.

To crack this institution—to get into the admitting process, to get an interview—I became a persistent pest. For more than a week, every day, sometimes twice or three times, I telephoned the woman who headed up the treatment programs. I was on a first-name basis with the office staff, and recounted my story to any willing ear. I don't think the administrator was dodging me. She had a full schedule with wall-to-wall meetings. I had to get lucky and be ready when she had a few minutes to talk.

"I have an hour this afternoon. Can you be here?" Her call came in the middle of the morning as I was doing desk work. I had spoken with her office just thirty minutes earlier. I shot back with "yes" before she could reconsider, hung up, and prodded Mark out of bed. As usual, he was indifferent.

Hillview Hospital is in a suburb of Boston. After many U-turns, we found the main gate marked with an impressive granite sign: ESTABLISHED 1811. It could have been an Ivy League campus. Large brick buildings with mullioned windows and steep gabled roofs with aged slate and green copper flashings were widely spread among gently sloped lawns anchored with oaks and maples. I found the admissions building and went inside for directions to the building where our appointment was.

The admissions building sat on the highest point in the hospital complex. Built of yellow brick with a columned portico and marble steps, it opened to a panoramic vista of acres of rolling hills and woods. The foyer of the building was lined in dark paneling and softly patterned bottle-green carpet. It smelled faintly of lemon-oil polish, and money.

For weeks I had been anticipating the bill from Holy Cross in Spokane. I had taken to opening the mailbox as if a coiled snake waited inside. Some days I didn't pick the mail up at all. I would tell Chris that it was just bills and junk mail, nothing important. Chris had just started a new job with a small start-up company, and we had no extra money.

When the fat, windowed envelope arrived, it was no surprise, but it shook me. It ran to ten pages and totaled more than $13,000. Rubber-stamped on it was a notice that our insurance company was being billed, and this was for information only. I threw away the bill and didn't tell Chris about it. He might insist we look for more afford-able care for Mark closer to home, and I didn't want to do that. In a world where mediocre medical care is expensive, why not get the best? I picked up a hospital map and went back out to the car.

The hospital grounds, acres of rolling grass and trees, had a feel of luxury and old endowment about them. Not the glossy magazine lux-ury of manicured plantings and shiny buildings but the ultimate luxury of space and quiet in a suburban setting. The early fall light through the just-turning trees enhanced the campus feeling. But unlike a campus with students everywhere, the only people were groups of twos and threes, file folders and briefcases in hand, walking on the grass paths between the buildings. No one looked like a mental patient. Trucks rumbled up and down the narrow roads crisscrossing the grounds to the various construction projects identified with "future home of" signs.

The long drive to Boston from Connecticut had given me time to think about what Mark needed. It was someone who would involve him in the healing and rehab process. He didn't feel he needed help. So far he had been an outsider to the process of his care, like watching a doctor repairing a wound treated with a local anesthetic. Mark knew none of the whats, whys, and hows of manic depression. His only certainty was that his life had disintegrated under his feet. He was just a passenger on someone else's boat.

"What you need is a good doctor," said the residence treatment director after talking to Mark and me separately for thirty minutes each. The mature woman's voice from the telephone call turned out to go with a young woman anywhere between twenty and thirty-five years old, no makeup, Laura Ashley print dress, and large glasses with pale pink frames. Just a few minutes with her and I felt I was in a different league from the Spokane social worker or Dr. Anderson. She spoke with authority, compassion, common sense, and without jargon. My relief was palpable. "I know just the doctor if he will take Mark as a patient. Dr. Rostov. I'll find out as soon as I can and let you know. Can I call you tomorrow?"

She continued, "We'll need to do a complete assessment and for-mulate a treatment plan." These were new terms to me. Almost one year into manic depression and this was the first time anything of this sort had even been hinted at, let alone articulated. Maybe there was a bread-crumb trail out of these woods after all.

Mark and I rode back to Connecticut without conversation. He silently watched the scenery fly past the windows while I listened to the afternoon news on the radio.

"Doctor Rostov's office is around the corner, last door," directed the secretary. We were back at Hillview on the third floor of one of the older buildings. The elegance of the admissions building was nowhere evident. This was work space. Old, dim hallways, exposed pipes in the ceilings, scuffed yellow linoleum-tile floors, plastic chairs pushed against walls outside double-door offices. Mark knocked on a door with Dr. Rostov's name on it and disappeared inside, while I sat stiffly on one of the plastic chairs and paged through a stack of old *Bon Appétits* with the recipes cut out.

Dr. Rostov would be psychiatrist number five in ten months. The residence treatment director had described him as a psychopharmacologist. "He's a wizard at drug therapy and has extensive experience with bipolar patients," she had said. "Plus," she had added, smiling as an afterthought, "you'll like him." That'll be a new experience, I thought wryly.

I had been afraid that Mark would resist my marshaling him up here for treatment, but he hadn't. He had arrived from Holy Cross with a week's worth of lithium and Thorazine, which he seemed to still be taking regularly. He was quiet, subdued, almost as if he had a secret. He had bought a tweed jacket that day, a better-fitting one than the first selection, and showed up at the car an hour later wearing his new purchase. We pretended our argument had never happened, but his extreme anger niggled at me. I worried that the medicine wasn't working or he was skipping doses.

"Come on in, Mrs. Wakefield," a voice from around the corner of the office said.

"I'm Dr. Rostov," said a blond man in a good business suit, energetically hopping up from his chair to shake hands. Another under-forty professional. This was the New Guard in psychiatry. "Welcome. Please have a seat. Just move those books to the floor." The small third-floor office was tucked under the eaves. The triangular, leaded-glass window overlooked the back of the building. Books and dog-eared journals were piled on every flat surface, and against the wall was a full-sized chalkboard with half-erased numbers and arrows. There was a comfortable, nonthreatening academic feel to the office. Mark was seated in a chair beside the desk, looking alert.

"Duck tape," he said, pointing to a transparent tape dispenser shaped like a Mallard with the cutting bar on the tail. He smiled cheerfully at his pun.

"Mark's been giving me a rundown on the past year. You certainly have been all over the map. But," Dr. Rostov continued quickly, not lingering over that thought, "we need to get an assessment on Mark and get him back to being functional as soon as possible." He had a non-aggressive urgency about him. He spoke rapidly, and made eye contact with each of us as he proceeded. "First, we need to check the lithium level, and, Mark," he said, focusing intently on Mark and leaning forward in his chair, "you can stop the Thorazine. We don't use it much anymore. Let me tell you a little how we do things here." He spoke rapidly.

"Each patient has two doctors—an M.D. like myself who's responsible for the drugs, and a therapist, who's sometimes a Ph.D., sometimes not, who helps the patient with the psychological and emotional problems of chronic illness, which is what the affective disorders are. The therapists do not delve into your dreams or childhood, but concentrate on how you're doing with the here and now. Couch therapy is not done for your sort of problem.

"We feel this system works well. When one person does both drugs and therapy, he has a powerful hold on a patient. Therapy can be painful, and arguments with the therapist are not unheard of. We don't want patients interrupting their drug program because they change therapists. So we split that part up. Once Mark is stabilized, he will see his therapist much more than me. The added benefit is that the hourly cost to the patient is less with this approach. M.D.'s all have those huge student loans to pay back. At least here they do." I glanced over my shoulder at the MIT and Harvard diplomas on the wall.

"Has Mark had a complete medical workup?" he asked.

"I'm not sure. Maybe. His doctor in Spokane would know. They never told me anything about it, and Mark was in no condition to notice." And, I didn't mention, it's probably on the bill I threw away.

"I'll contact him. We don't want to duplicate tests," he said, writing with fast, short strokes in a file. "What I feel Mark needs is an inpatient evaluation," he said as he wrote. "Mark, I see some psychotic thinking in you. How would you feel about checking into Hillview so we can see where we are?" I froze and slowly turned to look at Mark. Dr. Rostov's frankness was a surprise, and I didn't know how Mark would react. Psychotic was a powerful word.

"I don't know," he replied tentatively. Until now, all his hospitalizations were involuntary.

"This would not be like your other hospitalizations. You would be in the Terrace, an open unit," he said, reading my thoughts. "It's up to you. I want this to be voluntary." He paused expectantly.

"I could try it," said Mark hesitantly. I sat back and exhaled. I had been holding my breath throughout their exchange.

"Good, good," the doctor said, picking up the telephone and writing some notes on a pad. "Here's who to call to set up the admission, I'm going to check on a bed. You'll have to talk to your insurance company." Doctors did not handle money matters. He handed me a list of names on a prescription slip.

I stayed serious and calm, but felt like skipping and grinning. Mark was in.

The early October rain pelted the car with such force that conversation was impossible. The headlights of the cars behind us freckled our faces with the raindrop shadows. The wipers battled buckets of water thrown up by passing cars. I had asked three times about the time of the admission interview. "Eight o'clock *in the evening?*" Yes, the admissions people had said. That's the time. Chris wanted to come along to the interview at Hillview, but had been weather-delayed in Chicago. So it was the usual team, Mark and me.

The Terrace Unit was located in a new building. Its stone marker said "1986". Three stories with high, peaked gables, this new building was designed to mesh with the older mock-gothic campus style of the hospital grounds. No prefab architecture here—this was custom stuff. We sloshed through the parking lot to the main entrance, leaving our wet, open umbrella drying by the door. Mark had been inscrutable in his feelings about going into the hospital again. But for the force of Dr. Rostov's personality, I don't think he would've acquiesced so quietly.

He lugged his wet, well-traveled duffel inside, and we took the elevator upstairs. I noticed that the second floor required a key into the control panel for a stop. The elevator clicked over the floor number and opened on three.

Soft peach walls, jade carpeting, framed posters, pale wood-trimmed furniture, were what we saw as the doors opened on the third floor. On an opposite wall was a large lined chalkboard with names, times, and destinations around the area. Around the corner was a hand-lettered sign that said in large letters, REMEMBER NOT TO EAT THE

FOLLOWING FOODS WITH MAO INHIBITORS, and a list of foods and a drawing of a pizza with a red line across it. An MAO inhibitor sounded like a car part.

A young man Mark's age spotted us and said we were expected. He took Mark's bag and chattily explained that this was a between-semesters job for him, and he was the first rung on the chain of medical help here. He had a relaxed, easy manner, and I could see Mark hesitantly responding to what had to be the first conversation with a peer in some time.

"Here's your room," he said, showing us a two-bed room with built-in furniture in the same style as the rest of the floor. "You're by yourself for the time being. The doctors will be here shortly. You can unpack," he said, opening the closet for emphasis.

Mark tossed his clothes into drawers and into the closet. I sat on my hands not to offer to hang things up. He carefully laid out his Walkman and tapes, and from the bottom of the bag produced a trio of sanguine ceramic-class angels, which he ranked carefully on the bedside table. They sat like guardians, angelic faces turned skyward, eyes closed, holding hymnals, mouths small o's, wings spread tidily behind them. Mark had painted them a base of yellow ocher and dribbled blood red cadmium down their faces and over their wings.

Eight in the evening was quiet but for the rain outside. The carpeting swallowed up footfalls, and voices were subdued. The Terrace Unit had a fine-hotel feel to it. Literally and figuratively, no sharp edges. Mark and I sat in silence on the bed, waiting for the curtain to rise.

A young man and woman a bit older than Mark dressed in chinos, tennis shoes, and white coats arrived just after eight. Stethoscopes and penlights poked out of pockets, and they each had a clipboard. They identified themselves as the admitting doctors, said we might not see them again, but they wanted to take a complete history. This was a medical-school teaching hospital.

I told them about how we came to be here today, and they carefully wrote everything down. I caught one of the doctors glancing over at Mark's angels with a clinical eye, but generally they had a youthful, easy manner. We could have been talking over coffee.

"Did you hear voices or see strange things?" they asked Mark well into the interview.

"Yeah, a lot. Devils, angels, lots of things. They would talk to me." I don't think I even blinked, but this shocked me. I had no idea what had been going on in his mind all these months. Mark's replies were guarded, but his answers sounded truthful, honest.

"Scary stuff?" the young woman asked.

"Yeah," said Mark, "*Real* scary. *Rocky Horror Picture Show*." The three of them chuckled at the campy horror-movie allusion that might have escaped Doctors Anderson, Harp, and Lee.

"The voices tell you to do things?" they asked casually.

Mark paused and slowly replied, "Sometimes." The question slid by without follow-up, and they were on to other questions.

I kissed Mark good-bye as the doctors escorted him down the hall for a physical after his interview was over at nine-thirty. I collected the dry umbrella from beside the door downstairs and drove home alone.

I expected some anguish or at least sadness at leaving Mark in yet another hospital, but, to my surprise, I felt light and free. No pangs of guilt at turning him over to someone else. This problem was too big for me to handle alone. Now, my medical worries transformed into financial worries. This place was almost $600 a day, and the meter was running.

MARK

This isn't going to work. They don't understand me. My destiny. They're all older. But there's Sara. Ten years, in and out. Pregnant. She knows the pain. Contract group thinks I'm bullshitting. They want to see me spill blood. Okay, I tell them what they want to hear. Craziness, depression, drinking weed killer. But they don't believe me. Think I'm hiding something. If they only knew I'm trying to act healthy. Studying them playing Trivial Pursuit last night, watching, hearing what they said, how they acted, when not to yell, when to laugh. Copy them, be normal. It's so quiet here.

I had been holding through two rounds of *Moon River* and was well into *Twilight Time* for the second time when the health-insurance representative came on the line. Because Chris had changed jobs, I dealt with two companies on Mark's coverage.

"This diagnosis comes under the heading of 'Nervous-mental,' " she declared.

I called Chris's employers, the insurance company, the patient account's office at Hillview, and tried to coordinate Mark's admission and coverage. In the end, all I received were uncertainties. No one would commit in writing to pay anything. As I later discovered when a dispute arose over the bill, the best thing I did was to take names and keep a log of all conversations. My ostrich complex about the bills was disappearing under the biweekly billings. It was impossible to ignore the money side of Mark's problems, and manic depression was proving to be a very expensive illness.

"I feel as if I'm living underwater. Shafts of light slant down on me but the real world is way above me, distorted. I'm floating and I can only move slowly. My mind has slowed to a crawl. My thoughts come out like cold syrup," began Mark.

He kicked at the fallen leaves, looking like bran flakes under our feet, and reached down to pick up a twig in the path as we walked along on the Hillview Hospital grounds. He had just changed medications for the third time, and had been at Hillview a month.

"Can you remember the past year?" I asked him tentatively.

"Of course I can," he replied evenly to what he obviously thought was a foolish question. I was full of questions. Why had he thrown the microwave through the window in Colorado? What was he thinking when he was home last spring? What had really happened in Arizona? But I couldn't grill him, only slip in the occasional query. He had a therapist for that.

"I look back on the past year as if it were happening to someone else. Not me. I saw things, crazy things. I had fantastic thoughts. You know, God spoke to me. I saw devils, demons, angels. Heaven and hell. I lived with them every day. They told me to do things. I hung charms in the trees behind the house and tried to do a pentagram to scare the devil away, but nothing worked. I would lie in my bed at night and see red eyes glowing at me in the dark and feel spiders crawling all over my body. I couldn't make them stop.

"Go down to the large ash tree behind the vegetable garden. I hung a charm on a branch. Do you know I even went to a Christian bookstore to ask if they could do an exorcism for me?" he went on conversationally. I wondered if this was the Mark who saw the angels or the one who knew they weren't real.

"Do you still hear things?" I asked, half-afraid of his answer.

"Not anymore. A voice said 'God bless you' when I sneezed just after coming here. That was the last time."

"Maybe it really was just someone else nearby?" I suggested.

"Couldn't be. I was alone in my room at night. I clearly heard it. It's the religious stuff that has me confused," he continued. "It was so real. Biblical, almost."

He paused over his next words as we sat on a bench at the top of the hill overlooking the hospital grounds. The far hills were flame red in the late afternoon sun. He was weaving his twig in and out of his fingers as he talked. He studied the twig momentarily between sentences.

"God told me I was special, that I was anointed to go on a special mission. That's what I was doing in Colorado, getting ready for my mission. It was my destiny. I knew that only I spoke to Him and that I was special. Until now, I have been afraid to tell that to anyone. That was my secret."

"What do you think about all that now?" I asked. Evangelical Christianity had played no part in Mark's upbringing. If forced to declare, we were lapsed Episcopalians.

"Part of me *knows* it's the illness. But there's another part of me that can remember with vivid detail what I saw and heard. It's hard to argue with your senses, even if you know they weren't working right." He frowned in concentration. These were thoughts he had gone over many times before.

"What I think now is that heaven and hell are really inside of us. Not somewhere else on a cloud or fiery pit. I feel as if I have been on a long journey and am now coming home."

Mark had emerged from the crucible of manic depression with the eyes of a very old man. The youthful openness of the boy who used to hop on to my kitchen counter with a funny story was gone. But gone also was the look of wild craftiness that had frightened me in the homeless man in New York last Christmas. He had a sober sadness, what the French call *tristesse,* about him. His ebullient self-confidence was shattered. The youthful conviction of being capable of anything was gone. He had seen the world turned inside out and couldn't forget it. But in spite of these dramatic changes, it was Mark, not some crazy stranger, sitting next to me on the bench, telling of his journey.

"They tell me that's what the therapist is for. To help sort out what I went through, to try to understand it. Dr. Rostov says I need to be stable on the meds before I really start therapy."

"Meds?" I asked.

"Medication, pills. Everyone is on pills. No one calls it medicine here," he explained patiently.

"Tell me about the hospital," I said, changing the subject.

"It's not like the other hospitals. No 'Weird Clyde and the Strappers' here," he said.

"Sounds like a rock group. What's Weird Clyde and the Strappers?" I asked, puzzled.

Mark laughed. A normal, ordinary, but wonderful laugh. "That's just my name for some of the other patients. The ones that had to be strapped down." I didn't remind him that he had been in that condition once.

"No, patients here seem normal, but with troubles. They don't seem crazy. Lots of depression. That seems to be the thing to have. They spend a lot of time talking about how to kill yourself. You know— methods, what works, what doesn't. It's topic number one on the unit." I winced. Going to jail to learn safecracking from the masters. Only here, the real experts were dead.

This last exchange sobered us. We sat in friendly silence, watching the sun, looking like a Sunkist orange, disappear behind the hills. "I have to get back," said Mark, rising, throwing his twig away as a pitcher hurls a fastball. "I'm only out for a while yet. Next week we can go out to dinner. Okay?" We ambled down the hill, leaves crunching under our feet.

MARK

Did you hear that? Jim says he can see a difference. No more zombie, no more lifeless mummy, no more sermons about religious symbols, no more emotional harangues. I wouldn't have used that word. It was just that I HAD TO EX-PLAIN. It feels so good being level, even-keeled. So good. Like an A on a test. Or some girl saying she'll go out with me. Way to go. My hands, they're relaxed, not shaky. I'm not pacing. Maybe it's the Trilafon. Anything's better than Haldol. What a brain killer. He's a good one to copy, college grad, smart but not sappy. Everybody likes him. He's easier to talk to than the Contract Group. I mean, how can you spill your guts to fifteen people? No more gut-wrenchers with the others.

The calico bag hung just out of reach on the lower limb of the ash tree. I scrambled over copper-colored bittersweet vines studded with orange berries, careful not to engage the poison ivy that hung every-where, and with a leap retrieved the sack. It was made of brown calico cloth with a crudely woven yarn closure at the top. I recognized the fabric from the craft class at Holy Cross Hospital in Spokane. It started to come apart as I turned it over in my hands. I carefully carried it to the workbench in the garage and went to look for scissors to cut the knots at the top.

Chris witnessed my acrobatic retrieval and set his rake aside to follow me into the garage.

"Mark's," he figured. It was a statement, not a question. "Throw it away," he said flatly, eyeing the sack. "What do you think you are going to find there? Do you think you are going to solve the puzzle by going over this stuff? That's like an alien trying to discover if there is intel-ligent life on earth by listening to radio static. That's just Mark's static. You keep looking for meaning in things which, by definition, have no meaning at all. Don't even bother with looking at that junk." He hung up his rake and clumped out of the garage, heading back to the house.

He didn't wait for my reply because he knew that I would pore over everything of Mark's. He was right. I was looking for a Rosetta stone to Mark. Something to make some sense out of nonsense. Mark called almost every day from the hospital. He was pitching and yawing through the peaks and valleys of drug trials. Some things made him sleep twenty hours a day, and others kept him up all night. He would be pliant or irritable or morose or lively depending upon where in each trial he was. But throughout, the person who called was Mark.

The person had returned, but his capabilities did not. He said he couldn't read for any length of time and that his handwriting was that of a stranger. His shirttails were never tucked in, his cuffs hung un-buttoned at his wrists, and his laces were often untied. He had grown his hair long and tied it back into a ratty ponytail. I hated how he looked, but tried not to nag him about it. Sometimes my resolve failed at the entrance of a restaurant or in a store. In spite of all this, Mark the child I had reared had come back.

The bag fell apart in my hands as I cut the yarn holding it together and the contents spilled out. There was a collection of small pouches of calico individually tied with yellow ribbon. Each contained some-thing different. One held seven used tea bags, another a folded piece of paper with red ink scribbles of an embracing couple. Another, a picture of a couple with a baby being embraced by an angel. There were three thin tooled-leather thongs with half-moons and stars worked into the smooth side. Finally, there was a straw plate with colored ribbon woven in and out of the face and a small plastic box containing smooth pebbles like those found on a riverbank.

I remembered the story of the Littlest Angel and his offering of a bird's egg and stones to God in place of the grand golden offerings of the other angels. Those things, however humble, were treasures to him, if not others. Finally, I bundled everything up again into the sack and shoved it into the back of the garden storage cabinet. I couldn't bring myself to throw them into the trash. If they were static or meaningful items, I couldn't tell, but they were Mark's, so like the grammar-school pictures and the clay ashtrays no one ever uses, I held on to them as mothers always have.

"Mark will be right with you. Have a seat," said the unit nurse when I came by to pick him up for an early pizza dinner in Cambridge. Chris was meeting us later after a downtown meeting. I thumbed through a day-old *Globe* while waiting for him to shower. He had been asleep, and they had had to get him up to go out.

"I'm Alicia Adams," said a beautifully modulated voice at my elbow. I looked up at a pretty woman about my age, forty-to-fifty range, in perfectly tailored slacks, cashmere pullover, And pale blond hair neatly turned under. Another mother. She seated herself next to me and reached for a section of the newspaper. "You're visiting someone here?" she asked politely.

"Yes, my son Mark." She nodded as if she knew him.

"The care here is quite good," she offered. I nodded at her remarks, and we chatted idly about the weather, the traffic, and how hard it is to stay thin after forty. We could have been mothers in bleachers watching our sons play football. Mark finally rounded the corner, hair wet but neatly combed.

"Hi, Alicia," he said offhandedly, as if to a school friend. I swiveled toward Alicia, still sitting next to me. We're in the same therapy group," he added. Just like, "We have biology together."

"I've enjoyed our talk," she said, rising, not noticing my double take. It was then that I saw her feet. Slippers. I mumbled courtesy words to her, embarrassed at my clumsiness, and Mark and I hastily left for dinner.

Chris, Mark, and I crowded into the last open booth at the back of the raucous Cambridge pizza restaurant. The wooden tabletop was carved with initials of long-forgotten patrons, loud rock music flooded the air, and we had to shout over the noise to the girl taking our order. She had long red hair, which she unsuccessfully tried to flip out of her eyes with small jerks of her head as she wrote our order on a pad.

When she came to Mark, she teasingly asked him if he wanted more cheese and why he didn't like olives. He stumbled through his order, refusing to catch her eye, all bantering skills gone. After scribbling our order, she snapped her pad shut with a flourish and moved to the next table. Mark slumped back into the shadow of the booth. Chris and I pretended not to notice.

"Robert's coming home for Thanksgiving. He got one of those discount tickets from a friend," ventured Chris. "You should be out of the hospital by then. It will be the first time all of us have been together for a long time." He tried to inject into his words an enthusiasm he didn't feel.

Mark listened while playing with the sugar packets on the table. He was stacking them into a house shape, complete with peaked roof. "There are some good movies coming out soon. And we should have some good ball games on television," Chris lamely went on. He was no good at these conversations and knew it. I could see the frustration in his face as he tried to capture Mark's attention.

Mark had shoved the sugar packets aside and was gazing off to the far end of the restaurant. I followed his eyes to a table of two girls and two boys, books dumped on the floor, laughing over a pizza. One of the boys was feeding a piece of pizza to the girl next to him, who, cheese string stretching to a thread from her mouth, was trying to eat without using her hands. Mark's eyes soaked up their gaiety. He had a sad, wistful expression.

"I think I'll do the big bird this Thanksgiving, the works. It's been a while. How does that sound?" I asked Mark as if the idea just occurred to me.

"Sounds fine, Mom," he said without interest, eyes still riveted on the foursome across the room. Our order finally arrived, and we were spared conversation as we picked up our slices and ate.

"Look," started Mark after only a bite. "I'm sorry I'm lousy company today, but I just feel down. I can't shake it. I'm fighting with the nurses on the unit. They're after me to get up every morning early, and I have nothing to get up for. I don't see why I just can't be left alone to sleep. I don't like my new roommate, who can only talk about suicide and how rotten the food is. I just want to be anywhere else. It's hard to care about anything anymore. My life is running through my fingers. I'm being left in the dust as everyone else my age gets on with their life."

"What does Dr. Rostov say?" I asked.

"He says I have to give it time. But I don't have time. Everything is passing me by. I don't want this pizza. Let's go. I'm tired." We gathered our jackets, paid the bill, and left our barely eaten pizza on the table.

"Mark can be discharged next week if all goes well," reported Dr. Rostov over the telephone. "We would like to see him in a residence treatment house, but he's not sure that is what he wants. He needs a structured environment coupled with therapy."

"I thought therapy wasn't done for patients such as Mark," I asked.

"Not the couch therapy of Freud, but what we call 'reality therapy.' Mark needs help dealing with the everyday aspects of his life, putting everything back together, learning how to live with a chronic illness that needs constant attention at least in the form of medication. Call it coping skills. That's what a good therapist does."

"He seems fragile, shaky. Is he really ready to go home?" I asked.

"He's all of those things, but he no longer needs hospitalization. We feel he is stable on his medication, and most important, the manic symptoms have subsided. His thinking is much clearer. It's his social functioning that still needs help, but that is not an inpatient problem. I'll continue to see Mark, first weekly, then monthly. Eventually, it's his therapist that he will see regularly."

Mark was sitting on his duffel in front of his building, discharge papers in hand, when I arrived at Hillview Hospital to take him home.

"We need to stop at the drugstore to fill these prescriptions before we go to Connecticut," he said as he tossed the bag in the backseat. "I only have a few days' supply."

We came out of the drugstore four prescriptions and $150 later. Mark settled into his Walkman headphones as I drove.

Thanksgiving morning was bright and cold. The last of the leaves had dropped, and everything seemed light and open, without the shady foliage. Robert had arrived late the night before, and the boys were still asleep at ten in the morning when I put the turkey into the oven.

I poured another cup of coffee and sat at the kitchen table. I gazed at the watercolor-wash November sky bisected by a wedge of Canada geese. The kitchen smelled like simmering cranberries.

"Not pumpkin, I hope," said Chris, looking at the empty pie shell as he nibbled extra stuffing.

"Pecan," I told him, still following the birds' flight south.

"It's good having us all home together. You know, it's been almost two years. What do you think Mark'll do after the holidays? He's made up his mind—he won't go into a halfway house?" He sat across from me with a steaming mug.

"I guess so. I'm not going to turn myself inside out over his plans. I'm all played out. I can't do that anymore," I answered with a firmness neither of us expected.

"That's a change. What's different now?" Chris asked carefully.

"Immolating myself is not going to make Mark better. My life's too good to throw it away because it isn't perfect. Agonizing over Mark destroyed the small everyday pleasures that made me happy. Mark wasn't making me miserable, I was. What if this is as good as he's ever going to be? I have a choice: I can either live the rest of my life in a permanent state of misery or get on with the good parts of my life. Like you, my friends, my work, our family. Mark's future won't be affected one whit by my decision. Sounds cold, doesn't it?"

"Not really," Chris replied. "I guess it's the way I've felt all along. Our son has a mental illness. That's fact. We need to accept it and move on. Mark's my son too, but I can do little for him. That's the nasty reality. This must be the reality of most families with handicapped relatives. I always wondered how they coped. Now, I know."

I continued, "He says he wants to live at home, work part time, and take a class. He'll still see Dr. Rostov for his meds, and we've found a therapist here for weekly visits. It's back to cut-and-paste, I know, but it's what he wants. And I've decided to put more energy into real estate—that's what I want."

"You know," Chris began tentatively, "it'll probably happen again. Mark's craziness."

"I know. But it'll be different this time. I'll know that he can come back and isn't lost forever. And I know where there's good medical help. I'm keeping a list," I assured him and myself.

"He seems much better," Chris offered. "All that craftclass crap has disappeared. Even those awful angels."

"I asked him about those last night when he was unpacking. 'Threw that shit away' is what he said." I smiled slightly. "One step at a time."

Chris rose. He had enough of psychology for the day. "Send the boys outside after breakfast. I need help putting up snow fences." He pulled on his boots and clunked outside. I poured another cup of coffee and went back to fixing dinner.

Late in the morning, long after Robert had jogged down the driveway and Chris had installed the snow fences alone, Mark appeared. I watched covertly from the stove as he lined up his five bottles of medication and methodically picked one pill from the first, two from the second, and one from each of the other bottles, then swallowed them all in a large gulp of orange juice.

"I'm going to take Jake for a walk," he announced, rinsing off his cereal bowl.

I stood at the sink, watching the pair walk down the stone path toward the garage, Mark waving a stick high above Jake's head. The dog danced about, tail high and wagging.

MARK

So, Jake, here we are again. Different now, huh? It's so hard sometimes, with the Voice gone, angels gone. No more Destiny. Like losing close friends. I always had someone to talk to , someone who knew everything. Sometimes I wish I had them back, but I know that's crazy. Back to atheism even if it is lonely. At the end, the Voice was awful, scary. I don't want that anymore. But I don't know what I do want. What should I fill the space with?

The late November afternoon was cold enough that we lit a fire in the dining room. Our dinner was like millions of others Thanksgiving Day. Everyone claimed a favorite cut of the bird, stuffing and gravy vanished first, and heaps of squash went uneaten. It was garden variety, ordinary and wonderful. It was our best ever.

"I didn't know Mark was so sick," Robert said quietly as he helped me clear off the plates. Chris and Mark were in the living room discussing the future of the L.A. Rams. "He told me about the Voice and the angels. He said he burned fires at the cemetery down the street."

I nodded. "Mental illness is a terrible thing. He really lost himself in his mania. You know, Robert, you will someday be responsible for what happens to Mark." I meant to tell him some other time that Chris and I had changed our wills to leave Mark's share of any inheritance in trust with Robert, but this was as good a time as any. He listened as I explained that he'd be Mark's trustee.

"Sounds fine, Mom," he said easily. He was twenty-two, an age when the future is next spring.

Although dinner was barely thirty minutes old, Mark wandered into the kitchen to pick at the bird.

"Take this out to Jake, will you," I asked him, pointing at a large hambone in the sink. "He's been eyeing it all afternoon."

"Sure Mom. *Jake!*" he yelled, and rattled the door handle to summon the dog. Jake slid into the kitchen just as Mark was opening the door, and they headed down the path toward the garage. But unlike earlier, Mark wasn't tantalizing Jake with the bone by waving it over his head. Instead, he purposely marched up to a maple tree and wedged the bone between two branches, out of Jake's reach.

Mark stood still for a moment, studying the bone, ignoring the dog. Watching Mark's back, not knowing what I was witnessing, my breathing grew short. I thought of sacks in trees, mysterious fires at night, and witchcraft rituals. I couldn't believe Mark's demons could return so soon.

I studied his face as he walked back to the house. It revealed nothing. No smile, no anger. He stepped through the back door, saw me staring at him, at the bone in the tree, and back at him.

"You think . . ." He smiled briefly. "No, Mom, I'm not crazy. I just didn't think Jake should have the bone now."

TWISTS AND TURNS

Manic depression is unique. While it shares some features with schizophrenia and unipolar depression, it has special quirks that are frightening and fascinating, mysterious and inexplicable. Some of these surround the myth of mania and the link between madness and genius. Another compelling quality is the illness's complex relationship with suicide. And questions about environmental influences on the disorder—weather and seasons, for instance—continue to crop up. The illness takes unexpected twists and turns when it hits teenagers or the elderly, and these are highlighted here. Last, this chapter offers the hope of success and normalcy in the stories of four manic-depressives who have controlled and triumphed over their illness.

The Demon in the Shadows—Suicide

Suicide is the demon that haunts the shadows of affective illness. It's always there, and especially threatening for bipolar patients whose illness leans toward depression. While less than 1 percent of the general population dies from suicide, 9 to 15 percent of patients with affective illness kill themselves. In one study, 58 percent of the manic-depressive patients tried suicide at least once.

Suicide has been studied from every angle, and medical professionals know many of its dark secrets. While collecting data and patient profiles may not ease the pain and devastation, it helps doctors pinpoint patients most likely to commit it and, they hope, prevent it. Researchers hover over two questions about suicide: What causes it? Who's most likely to commit it? So far, they've found partial answers.

In searching for causes, researchers have noticed that suicide runs in families, and these are often the same families stricken by affective illnesses. This connection points to a genetic ingredient in suicide. Again, the Old Order Amish in southeastern Pennsylvania contribute illuminating genetic evidence.

The Amish are a treasure for genetic studies. The closely knit agrarian society forbids alcohol and drugs, which complicate behavioral and genetic strains. Stresses common in modern society that can push a person toward suicide—unemployment, divorce, solitary living, social isolation—do not exist among the Amish. Everyone works, multi-generational families live together, and marriage is for life. Furthermore, marriage outside the community is forbidden, so over the generations families have intermingled. Thus, hereditary diseases stand out.

Janice Egeland, a researcher from the University of Miami School of Medicine, has studied suicides spanning a hundred-year period among the Amish. Crime is unknown in this deeply religious society, and suicide is taboo. Nevertheless, Egeland uncovered twenty-six suicides.

Most of these suicides—more than 90 percent—were committed by people diagnosed with an affective illness. While this discovery was not unexpected, the family connection among the suicides was remarkable. Almost three quarters of the suicides clustered within four families. In a family reaching back six generations to a nineteenth-century pioneer, five people committed suicide, and two more were suspected of killing themselves (nineteen family members had an affective illness).

Four generations of another Amish family produced seven suicides (twenty-two family members had some type of affective illness). Amish family trees extend far and wide, and the community has grown to 12,500 people, comprising hundreds of families. Thus, these suicide clusters among just two families are extraordinary. Suicide clearly contains a genetic connection, although no one knows yet which gene or how it is passed along.

While the Amish study raises ample evidence for this conclusion, it doesn't solve the entire mystery. For instance, researchers cannot explain why some Amish families with generations of affective illness show no evidence of suicide. Egelands suggests looking at personality traits on top of genetics as a possible reason.

Her research did produce other pieces that fit the suicide puzzle. Men killed themselves four times more often than women. The average age of the suicidal men was forty-one years, and for women fifty-five years. The deaths showed strong seasonal patterns, peaking in the spring, May, and fall, November. Egeland reminds us that in early European literature, November was known as the "hanging month."

But it's the stark evidence of the inheritability of suicide and its partnership with mental illness that distinguishes the Amish study. The possible genetic link in suicide removes this painful subject from the realm of family guilt and psychology, and lodges it squarely in the laboratory.

The family connection in suicide has been verified in different ways. Experts by and large acknowledge the importance of family history of suicide—having a close relative (parent, sibling, grandparent, grandchild, aunt, uncle, niece, or nephew) who commits suicide raises the odds that someone will kill himself. Patients of families with histories of violent suicide, as opposed to nonviolent suicide, are more prone to this method.

One study compared the rate of death by suicide between affectively ill patients with a family history of suicide and those without a family history, discovering a difference of 49 percent versus 22 percent. Other studies comparing identical twins and fraternal twins again highlight the genetic, family connection. So too do adoption studies. These looked at suicide among biological and adopted families and confirmed the suicide link through the biological relatives.

All this evidence leads researchers to three possible explanations for why suicide clings to families: Relatives may be identifying with each other; the genetic vulnerability carried by the affective disorders may also run in suicide-prone families; and a genetic vulnerability may be inherent in suicidal behavior—that is, a biological condition may appear in times of stress. This is as close as researchers have come to solving the mystery of the origins of suicide.

Researchers have columns of figures and lengthy details on the kinds of people, in addition to those with a family history, most likely to try suicide.

While suicide is not uncommon among manic-depressives, it also surfaces among people deeply depressed with unipolar affective illness. This sounds obvious, but this depression is unlike what most people experience even in their darkest moments. Typically, it is a persistent feeling of hopelessness. Patients say their future looks unremittingly bleak, and they see no end to their pain. Temporary despair may be bearable, but a never-ending, barren life is not. This presuicide depression is also characterized by guilt, emptiness, hostility, and an inability to feel pleasure.

The patient with the highest risk of suicide is probably the psychotically depressed patient certain that he needs to die to complete a delusional circle. In fact, even manic psychosis is clearly linked to suicidal behavior, as is the nonaffective psychosis of the schizophrenic.

Aside from the special characteristics of a person's mental illness, researchers have noticed that certain conditions in a person's life can add to the risk of suicide. These include being unmarried, unemployed, and living alone. Patients from broken homes seem to be more susceptible, as do patients with drug or alcohol problems.

The lives of people who have attempted suicide, according to researchers, contain four times as many stressful events as nonattempters'. These stresses are typically a personal loss, like the end of a relationship. This loss may well stoke a patient's feelings of hopelessness.

The way a person thinks of or deals with problems can also signal a propensity toward suicide. One doctor divides suicide patients into two categories. There is the "risk-taker" who acts recklessly and frequently mixes alcohol and drugs. The other could be called the "obsessional" because he is painfully conscious of his feelings of hopelessness and is preoccupied with thoughts of suicide. This person may consciously want to die. Sometimes he may angrily push family and doctors into rejecting him or giving up, and so make suicide an extension of that rejection.

Certain times of the year or situations appear to make a person vulnerable. Research shows a high percentage of suicides within a year after a person has been discharged from the hospital.

Researchers quickly acknowledge that the "typical" suicide doesn't exist, and that profiles of high-risk people are a hodgepodge of qualities. There is no one formula for predicting suicide, and no one set of circumstances that brings it about.

The Sway of Night and Day

Manic depression is a wildly cyclical disease, and researchers are now discovering that its cycles can include a person's daily sleeping and waking habits, the so-called circadian rhythms (the word "circadian" was coined in 1959 to mean "about twenty-four hours"). Circadian rhythms refer to a person's entire biological clock, and encompass body temperature, blood pressure, heartbeat, and hormone and enzyme levels. All these rise and fall every twenty-four hours, and these ups and downs affect how people act and feel.

A shift in how long a person sleeps each day, or doesn't sleep, has long been recognized as a telltale symptom of manic depression. Depressed patients have a hard time falling asleep, then have disjointed dream sleep and deep sleep and may wake abruptly (this early waking is common and referred to as "terminal insomnia"). Yet by and large, depressed patients sleep more, not less, than normal, but at irregular times.

Patients in the middle of mania are notorious for going for days without sleep. Now, researchers are reversing the equation, and instead of regarding sleeping patterns as a symptom of the illness, examining sleeping habits to see whether they may be part of the cause.

Their studies focus on the quality and character of sleep itself, as well as the effects of sleeplessness on hormone levels and the release of certain neurotransmitters. Researchers theorize that a manic-depressive's circadian rhythms may be out of sync with either the natural twenty-four hour, night-and-day pattern, or with each other.

Researchers know, for instance, that hormones such as estrogen and testosterone shorten circadian rhythms. This may help to explain why fluctuations in estrogen levels are associated with premenstrual depression and postpartum depression.

Bipolar patients do not sleep like healthy people. Studies show that they generally take longer to fall asleep, sleep less deeply, wake more frequently during the night, and wake earlier in the morning.

Their dreams are different too. Their REM (rapid eye movement) periods—the time when all sleepers dream—are disjointed and jumbled. The normal REM pattern is a series of increasingly longer REMS, culminating in the longest REM at the end of the night, when we have our deepest dreams.

When someone's depressed, REMs are reversed. The REM sleep sets in early, and the longest REM, which lasts up to an hour, occurs first. In short, a depressed patient is quickly sent into a dream sleep. Research on the quality of manic sleep is sparse but remarkably similar in nature.

A manic's sleep reveals other clues about the illness. For example, a long stretch of sleeplessness often signals the beginning of a manic episode. Researchers have found that this sleepless period is not a random amount of time but represents two circadian sleep/waking cycles—that is, forty-eight hours.

Researchers conclude from all this that a bipolar patient's pattern of dream sleep is skewed compared with his sleeping patterns, and this imbalance could be feeding his illness. Knowing that bipolar patients experience either shortened or extended circadian cycles, doctors have been focusing on medication to restore sleeping patterns to normal. They have found that some antidepressants help regulate circadian rhythms, and they continue to experiment with new drugs.

The Power of the Seasons

A group of manic-depressives suffer from a distinctive type of depression. These patients, sometime around November, start going to bed earlier, rising later, and sleeping less soundly. Yet they sleep a lot more than usual. Twelve hours a night is typical. Their appetites increase, and they acquire a craving for carbohydrates, putting on weight. Their depression spreads from a mood of sadness and listlessness to irritability and loss of interest in work. Then, come April and springtime, their spirits lift. They go to bed later, get up earlier, and lose their great appetite.

Seasonal depression is usually linked to the short, sunless days of winter and has been successfully treated with daily exposure to strong artificial light. Less well known is summer depression, caused, scientists believe, by warm weather. As temperatures rise, some people grow more depressed. A lesser-known corollary to these theories is the idea that where a person lives—that is, the latitude—may affect depression. Living where there is more or less sunlight may well color the severity of a person's depression.

These depressions, clearly influenced by the seasons, climate, and sunlight, are called seasonal affective disorders (SADs). Researchers have discovered that its sufferers are often bipolar II—as high as 85 percent. A newspaper story about SADs research at the National Institutes of Health asking for volunteers produced more than two thousand responses from readers.

Scientists have known for centuries that the seasons can shift a person's moods and behavior. Weather patterns, hours and strength of sunlight, and air temperature are powerful forces. Some people are much more sensitive than others to seasonal patterns—so much so that their seasonal lows upset their daily lives. For the manic-depressive, whose life is already whipsawed by mood changes, the seasons may deepen their emotions.

Seasonal variations for certain types of manic-depressive behavior have been extensively documented. As already described, suicide rates follow the seasons, peaking in spring and fall. Doctors say that these times are not necessarily coincidental, but culminate at the end of months of winter depression or summer depression, and may also be associated with periodic incidence of mania.

Spring and fall are the seasons when manic episodes begin, when patients first seek out medical help, and when patients are first admitted to hospitals.

Not all medical professionals subscribe to the strong influence of seasons on moods and behavior. SAD experts at the National Institute of Mental Health note that clinical psychiatrists especially seem uninterested in assigning much importance to season mood swings. Some psychiatrists believe that theories of seasonal disorders are akin to the ancient theory of "humors" (vital body fluids that swayed behavior and were influenced by the seasons) and are as credible as alchemy. Many psychiatrists prefer theories based on psychology. These psychiatrists attribute seasonal variations to unique events or anniversaries of traumas instead of more biologically based yearly cycles.

Creativity and Madness: Myth and Fact
Creativity and mental illness are reluctant siblings. Creativity in various expressions—writing, poetry, musical composition, and painting, as well as nonartistic endeavors such as scientific research, entrepreneurship, or entertainment—is usually associated with extraordinary mental capacity. At times, this mental capacity, with all its energy and originality, resembles a kind of madness.

This kinship has been painfully apparent through the writings and works of artists across the centuries. Aristotle and Shakespeare referred to this grotesque pairing in their writings. The Romantic poets of the eighteenth century tied them even closer, suggesting that insanity was a source of inspiration for their brooding art. Poets and writers such as Goethe, Coleridge, Wordsworth, and Blake declared that melancholia was a necessary foundation for much of their work. In the nineteenth century, mental illness struck many outstanding writers, poets, and composers, like Gerard Manley Hopkins, Herman Melville, Edgar Allan Poe, Robert Schumann, Hector Berlioz, and Hugo Wolf.

Historical diagnoses—applying modern criteria to historical figures and concluding they were mentally ill—is obviously inexact and not a hindsight that is always 20/20. Inevitably, medical and personal records are incomplete, and the medical knowledge of one era shades interpretations of earlier times. Undoubtedly, not all the mad geniuses of yesterday were mentally ill. Their dramatic mood swings may have had an environmental or physiological basis. But even the possibility of misdiagnosis of some famous people cannot obscure the startling correlation between creativity and mental illness in modern artists. So even allowing for historical hyperbole and exaggeration, the link between creative genius and mental illness is startling. A survey of more recent creative talents reinforces the connection.

Literally legions of contemporary artists, whose medical histories are verifiable, suffer from some type of mental illness. Affective illnesses have struck numerous famous writers, poets, artists, and composers: Theodore Roethke, Robert Lowell, Ernest Hemingway, William Styron, Sylvia Plath, John Berryman, and many more. Almost daily, new names are added to the list of the productive creative people who suffer from some type of mental illness. Although doctors do not know why or how, they acknowledge that mental illness, particularly affective illness, seems to strike the exceptionally creative more than other classes of people.

Scientists first studied the connection between madness and genius in the late nineteenth century. Only recently have researchers delved into the subject scientifically, applying rigorous diagnostic criteria as well as clear standards for judging creativity. Their discoveries shed new light on the connection and raise more unanswered questions.

For a long time, researchers assumed that schizophrenia, as opposed to other kinds of mental illness, was most closely allied with creativity. Historians pointed to such reputed schizophrenics as Nietzsche, Nijinsky, and James Joyce. But current studies have revealed artistic genius to be more closely tied to affective illness—that is, manic depression and depression. In retrospect, the famous schizophrenics may have suffered from affective illness.

While doctors find less than 10 percent of the general population suffers from this disease, researchers have discovered that among groups of proven creative people, affective illness strikes upward of 80 percent. Another small piece of the mystery, maybe even a clue, is the fascination manic-depressives sometimes have with excessive writing (hypergraphia) and playing musical instruments. These traits are documented, but no one knows what they mean.

The affective-illness/creativity junction has been most dramatically unearthed by Nancy Andreasen, a researcher and psychiatrist who has studied the participants in the Iowa Writers' Workshop.

The University of Iowa Writers' Workshop is a creative writing school renowned for the accomplishments of its faculty and students. Its writers have included Robert Lowell, Kurt Vonnegut, John Irving, Philip Roth, Flannery O'Connor, and John Cheever. In her most recent study, Andreasen interviewed thirty writers and thirty nonwriters.

Among the writers, she found that 80 percent had had an episode of affective illness at some point in their lives. (Thirty percent of the nonwriters had had such an episode. Compared with the general population, this is still a very high percentage, and may be explained by knowing that these people were similar in economic, social, and intellectual accomplishment to the writers, and thus perhaps part of the "high risk" group for affective illness.)

Of the affectively ill writers, 43 percent suffered specifically from manic depression (10 percent of the nonwriters did). None of the people in either group was schizophrenic. These findings are similar to an earlier Andreasen study of Iowa Workshop writers. That probe of fifteen writers found 67 percent with affective disorders.

Other researchers have detected this remarkable tie between artists and affective illness. Another pioneer in the field, Kay Jamison, interviewed forty-seven British writers, poets, biographers, and artists. She discovered that 38 percent had been treated for an affective illness, mostly depression.

Remarkably, Jamison was able to distinguish among different types of creative people and learned that artists in nonverbal fields, like painting or sculpting, were much less likely to seek treatment for affective illness. Whether this means they suffer less affective illness or merely have a higher threshold for seeking treatment, no one knows. But she seems to suggest that writers, particularly novelists and poets, are more susceptible to mental illness.

Where exactly does the creative process intersect with mental illness? Again, researchers have been exploring the common qualities. The intense creativity that Jamison's writers describe closely resembles shades of mania, or what's called hypomania. They report increases in enthusiasm, energy, self-confidence, mental quickness, rapid ideas, and an elevated mood.

The feelings most useful to a creative hypomanic are heightened emotional sensitivity, absence of inhibitions, and prolonged concentration or intensity. Many say they need much less sleep during these times, and some awake at three or four o'clock in the morning, unable to sleep and ready to work. All the evidence points to hypomania as most resembling creative fervor. But mania doesn't always produce novels (Balzac's *Cousin Bette* was purportedly written in six weeks in a burst of mania) or musical masterpieces.

When hypomania crosses the line to full-blown mania, with flights of ideas rushing through the mind, delusions of grandiosity and invincibility, and distorted judgment, creativity halts. Manic-depressives say that what they produce during the height of mania—drawings, writings, musical scores—usually has little artistic merit. Similarly, the dark side of mania—thick depression—stifles creativity. Black depression can be so incapacitating that it is hard enough getting out of bed, let alone producing an artistic creation.

The similarity between early stages of mania and creative fervor has led to research on the link between cyclothymia (mild manic depression) and creativity. Unlike previous research that first identified creative people, then examined their mental history, researcher Ruth Richards started with a group of seventeen manic-depressives and sixteen cyclothymics, then examined their creative accomplishments. According to her Lifetime Creativity Scale, cyclothymics showed the second highest level of creativity.

On this scale, the most creative accomplishments were by immediate relatives of manic-depressives. Most of the research on mental illness and creativity has included the creative accomplishments of direct relatives of the mentally ill. And consistently, the siblings, parents, and children of manic-depressives have exhibited unusually high levels of creativity. (Not surprisingly, relatives of writers also produced many more cases of psychiatric illness than nonwriters' relatives.)

Andreasen's survey of the Iowa writers confirms the creative spillover to family members. She found 41 percent of writers' siblings showed creativity versus 18 percent of nonwriters' relatives. Interestingly, relatives' creative activities extended beyond writing to art, music, dance, and even math. She concluded, "Families of writers were riddled with both creativity and mental illness."

Thus, creativity and mental illness not only appear in the same people but in the same families. While this obviously suggests a genetic connection, no proof of this has been found yet. Mental illness and creativity seem to be irrefutably, mysteriously, tied together. Nevertheless, this connection is a dangerous one because it can distort the true nature of each. This partnership can paint an attractive picture of mental illness by suggesting it carries special talents and the seeds of extraordinary artistic creation. On the other hand, creativity may appear to be a product of sickness and chaos, with fabulous works of art composed by unhinged minds. So this partnership has to be kept in perspective. We have to be wary of generalizations about either madness or genius, recognizing that often they do not intersect and are usually at war with each other.

When It Strikes Early

While devastating at any time of life, manic depression early in life—before educations are complete, jobs established, lifestyles created—can be especially destructive. Manic depression in childhood or adolescence undermines formative self-images and destroys fragile and newfound relationships with friends and family.

Affective illness can surface incredibly early. Researchers have detected it in children as young as six years old. Recent reports estimate that 10 to 30 percent of adult manic-depressives get sick before they're eighteen years old.

Given children's limited communications skills and teenagers' natural moodiness, affective illness can fester undiagnosed and untreated for years. No foolproof test exists to prove the presence of manic depression, and some experts believe that full-blown bipolar disorder doesn't materialize at least until the teens. But others have seen telltale signs of the illness in young children, and very much want to hone their detective work.

When undiagnosed, manic depression in children or adolescents can hatch a host of other problems, from serious difficulties in school to drug abuse to tangles with the law. Thus, researchers are devoting extra drive and intensity to identifying early warning signs so that treatment can be started immediately.

Typically, troubled children and adolescents are first spotted by teachers, school counselors, social workers, or even a school psychologist or psychiatrist. Early warning signs of psychiatric illness may look like emotional problems with family or friends, discipline problems, attention-deficit disorder, even mental retardation. Sometimes a child or teenager shows so-called neurotic symptoms—that is, overanxiousness or inexplicable dislike or fear of school. A child may have delusions, feeling other children are always talking about her, or that teachers are conspiring against her. Another sign is hallucinations—for instance, envisioning a dead grandparent or hearing voices. Often these symptoms are labeled as adjustment or discipline problems.

Doctors diagnose children by talking to parents, teachers, and the child. They generally start with so-called secondary sources, because children's own description of feelings may be limited by an incomplete vocabulary or sense of self. One technique with children is the "play" interview—asking a child to act out experiences or feelings. Some doctors actually interview a child, asking whether she has felt certain symptoms and listening to how the child describes her feelings to decide their severity.

Experts believe that true manic depression does not appear at least until age thirteen, and that the average age for the onset of adolescent manic depression is around sixteen years. In younger children, the mania is milder and the depression is somewhat amorphous—a constant, vague "down-in-the-dumps" feeling or irritability.

In teenagers, the illness occasionally strikes quickly and dramatically and then flip-flops rapidly between mania and depression. But in most cases, it starts gradually. Affective illness can be disguised during adolescence by the moodiness and introspective "blues" that most kids go through.

However, while researchers are learning that hypomania is more prevalent among teenagers than parents report, the teenagers themselves know which feelings are out of the ordinary. In testing adolescents, doctors pose three key questions that help separate moodiness from mood disorder. These screening questions are:

1. Have you ever gone through a period when you became unusually excited?
2. Have you ever gone through a time when your mood went up and down quickly?
3. Have you ever gone through a period when you couldn't sleep at night because of so much energy?

If a child answers yes to these questions, she's asked another seven questions. These follow-up questions explore how a child felt during a "high" period. Doctors believe that positive answers to at least four of these point to hypomania. (These questions are part of the Diagnostic Interview for Children and Adolescents.) They ask:

1. Were you much more active than usual?
2. Did you talk faster or a lot more than usual?
3. Did you feel your thoughts were coming too fast?

4. Did you think you had a special ability?
5. Did you sleep a lot less without feeling tired?
6. Did you have a hard time paying attention?
7. Did you do things you wished you hadn't?

Manic depression does not reveal itself in any single behavior, regardless of how bizarre. It creeps up over time. In fact, one requirement for a manic-depressive diagnosis is recurring episodes—cycles over days and weeks, even months. Behavior that may alert a parent, teacher, or doctor are such activities as being seclusive, odd communication such as using unusual sounds or words, aimless wandering, fighting, drug problems, constant moodiness, impulsiveness, unpredictability, heightened sensitivity, attempted suicide, and failure in school. Physical symptoms such as stomach pains, nausea, insomnia, or headaches may signal mental illness. These symptoms may be elusive, appearing, then disappearing completely for days or weeks, finally reappearing.

Drug or alcohol abuse in teenagers may mask serious psychiatric illness. Unfortunately, substance abuse is widespread among people with affective illnesses. The usual pattern with manic-depressive teens is to use a variety of substances such as marijuana, LSD, cocaine, speed, and alcohol. No single drug seems to create the right feeling every time. One theory behind this combination approach is that the teenager is unconsciously trying to regulate her depression or mania.

Manic depression coupled with a substance abuse problem is called "dual diagnosis." It's a complicated diagnosis because it immediately raises the question of which trouble came first and whether one problem is fueling the other. While this may sound like a chicken-and-egg inquiry with no definitive answer, researchers have recently collected new information about young dual-diagnosis patients.

In a study of more than four hundred high school and college students, researchers discovered that contrary to first reports, psychiatric symptoms, particularly depression, prefaced substance abuse, not the other way around. This study and others like it reinforce the self-medication theory behind substance abuse and affective illness.

Once alcohol or drugs combine with psychiatric illness, they feed on each other. Chronic drinking accents a person's mania and depression. And substance abuse highlights psychiatric symptoms and adds behavior problems. On the other side, constant, debilitating depression aggravates drinking. Sometimes drugs can trigger depression, mania, or even psychotic thoughts in a person who is otherwise healthy. Cocaine and the hallucinogens (LSD, PCP), as well as steroids, are suspected of affecting some people this way. The recently popular designer drug "ecstasy" (MDMA), may be especially insidious, causing permanent brain damage in some people after repeated use.

Misdiagnosis of children and adolescents with affective disorders happens regularly. Doctors unfamiliar with manic depression or working from an incomplete picture of symptoms may conclude a child has a conduct disorder predicting a risk of adult personality order, schizophrenia, or attention-deficit disorder (ADD). A child showing psychotic behavior such as delusions or hallucinations may well be considered schizophrenic. On closer examination over the longer term, doctors might discover the disorder is more of mood, with cycles of mania and depression, than solely distorted thought as with schizophrenia.

Treating children and adolescents is similar, with certain caveats, to treating adults. While lithium has proved to be helpful, other drugs, such as antipsychotics, have long-term effects that doctors may not want to inflict on young people. Nevertheless, doctors do prescribe antidepressants, antianxiety drugs, and antipsychotic medication, and the children are watched carefully. They also recommend psychotherapy, especially with depressed children.

Late in Life
Spotting and treating mental illness in the elderly is tricky because of the natural changes aging brings. Everything shifts as we get older—physical health, emotions and hormones, personal psychology and thinking habits, even personal relationships may be in flux.

Mental illness, especially mood changes, can get scrambled with and hidden by all sorts of other ailments, conditions, and even natural events. For instance, grief, mourning, persistent feelings of loss, plus physical deterioration, are a constant in the lives of some elderly. Just as moodiness is a part of adolescence, depression is popularly seen as an ever-present part of growing old. And just as teenagers are commonly misdiagnosed as schizophrenic, so too are the elderly typically misdiagnosed as suffering from dementia—Alzheimer's disease.

Depression is more common in the elderly, though not as much as the stereotype might have us believe. Mania, however, is pretty rare, and found in about 10 percent of elderly patients with affective illness. Most manic depression reveals itself by the time a person is middle-aged. Studies indicate that 90 percent of all bipolar patients get ill by the time they're fifty years old.

Nevertheless, a few people are struck late in life. One study of sixty-seven patients over sixty years old found a number of instances of mania. More women than men were afflicted, and the first episode surfaced around age sixty, a couple years after depression appeared. Another study discovered mania besetting two people in their eighties—people with no history of the illness at all. A noticeable percentage of these patients had an organic brain disorder, indicating mania was a result of illness, not the cause.

In a study of 217 psychiatric geriatric patients, doctors found 10 to be bipolar, and the mean age for the first manic experience was about seventy-one years. None of the ten had a family history of mania, but some had histories of depression, alcoholism, and antisocial behavior.

Looking at what might have triggered these episodes, doctors discovered that seven of the patients had experienced a major traumatic event in their lives six months before mania struck. They had gone through separation, divorce, family arguments, family illness, death, financial loss, and in most of the cases, disrupted living arrangements. Researchers suspect that stress contributes to mania in younger patients, and now they are thinking it might play a role in the lives of elderly bipolars.

Mania in older people can also be brought about by illness—flu, fever, multiple sclerosis, neurosyphilis, encephalitis, central-nervous-system tumor, epilepsy—or drugs. This mania often is expressed by irritability, argumentativeness, agitation, paranoia, and litigiousness.

The ten bipolar elderly patients responded to neuroleptics and lithium, and experts believe their prognosis was good—their mania could be controlled.

A patient's ability to recover from the onslaught of manic depression depends on how severe the first attack of depression and mania (the appearance of delusions is considered very severe) and personal characteristics. An older person's physical and emotional health and what's happening in her life—whether it's filled with stress, grief, mourning, feelings of isolation, or with happier, positive feelings and experiences, all influence the impact and staying power of affective illness.

Researchers investigating why manic depression appears so late in some lives are focusing on changing brain chemistry. They speculate that the chemical changes that accompany old age might also invite affective illness. They raise similar theories about hormonal changes.

A New Beginning: The Successful Manic-Depressive

A manic depressive goes through stages—stages of self-awareness, knowledge, and maturity. At some point in this growth, a person's attention moves from preoccupation with the illness and its medical and clinical features, and back to daily living. The exact diagnosis a person has been given—whether it's manic-depressive, schizoaffective, bipolar II, or whatever—and the permutations of the symptoms fade slightly and become secondary. Concern about hospitals, doctors, and drugs take a backseat to a more compelling issue, one a patient and his family will wrestle with for the rest of their lives.

In medical jargon, this is called "level of functioning," and it encompasses questions about the quality and content of a manic depressive's life. The most compelling question is, "How has the illness changed a person's life and what kind of future does he or she have?"

Manic depression happens suddenly for many. Over a few months or a couple of years, a life is eviscerated, the substance and shape strewn about. Schooling, relationships with family and friends, jobs, interests in hobbies or sports, and leisure habits are all disfigured by manic depression. Yet once someone has come to grips with the illness, he wants his normal life back, to do the same things as before—to function at the same level of accomplishment and satisfaction.

Sadly, some manic-depressives never return to their earlier lives. The illness irrevocably changes their ability to think, to concentrate, to relate to others, and to handle conflict or stress. They lose some of the paper skills and people skills they had before. And the illness continues to whipsaw them between moods. This is especially true for the multitude of manic-depressives who at some point in their lives stop taking medication. Once medication is discontinued, the illness takes hold, and a person loses much of the normalcy he has achieved.

This is not the fate of all manic-depressives. Some people, through will, temperament, genes, or sheer luck, learn to control the illness and reclaim their lives. Finely attuned to their personal chemistry and psychology, they monitor and harness their mood swings. And they do this while performing highly demanding jobs, keeping hectic schedules, and maintaining complex personal relationships. In short, they lead normal lives.

What follows are profiles of four successful manic-depressives. Although they will never be "cured" of their illness, they have mastered it. Each person describes a couple of mental sleights-of-hand he or she uses to make sure the illness does not take over.

These are not composites or imaginary people. In truth, they are just a small sampling of thousands of functioning manic-depressives like them. We interviewed them through the Depression and Related Affective Disorders Association, a group that offers support and information and is affiliated with Johns Hopkins Hospital in Baltimore, Maryland. Although their lives in many ways are unremarkable, their perseverance and robust health offer hope for all manic-depressives.

Roy (Age: forty-one; Occupation: architect: married, two children)

It's taken Roy about ten years to understand and subdue his violent temper and black depressions. Growing up in Virginia, he was a "happy-go-lucky kid" up to his senior year in high school, when he was struck by a miserable, numbing depression that made him constantly think about suicide.

As with many manic-depressives, Roy was not diagnosed as bipolar until years after his moods had changed dramatically. He was thirty-one years old and in the middle of a second marriage marked by heated arguments when his wife persuaded him to see a psychiatrist. As he remembers it, the diagnosis required about three minutes. "My wife had told him all about me, so the minute he saw me, he said I was manic-depressive and, 'Have I got something for you!' meaning lithium." Roy had never heard of manic depression, let alone lithium.

Today, Roy lives in Utah, works as an architect designing homes and commercial buildings, and watches his moods very carefully. "I'm the kind of guy who has ups and downs every few weeks. My depression lasts for four to five days, then euphoria builds for two to three weeks, then depression comes back."

With the help of the psychiatrist who started him on lithium, Roy learned to listen to his body and detect signs of coming mania or depression. His mania is especially worrisome because it can show itself through violent reactions, confrontations, and arguments. "I'd get just short of slugging someone," Roy remembers. "I was verbally brutal with any provocation. I'd say anything, burn all my bridges. Even now, I sometimes let my tongue rip, but a lot less. I haven't completely shaken this confrontational style, especially when I get in a mean mood."

When Roy anticipates his temper rising, for instance if he is about to meet with a client who hasn't liked a design and refuses to pay, he'll head it off. He swallows a lithium tablet (he's on lithium and a very small dose of Haldol), and removes himself from the potential source of anger. He unplugs the phone, shuts his office door, or takes a walk. Then he waits for his body to calm down. "The hardest part of this illness," he concludes, "is getting past the anger."

He uses sports to fight depression. When a black mood looms, he'll go skiing, running, work out at a health club—anything to keep physically active.

Controlling manic depression entails more for Roy than anticipating and heading off destructive moods. He's also grappling with a drinking problem, which he's had since college but only recently admitted. "I never talked about it with any of the doctors, and they never seemed to notice that I was hung over every two or three days. It was always too much beer in front of the tube or too much wine over dinner. Now, I'm on the wagon. I slipped once, but I got back on."

Another handicap is drug side effects. Roy is always on a diet, fighting the twenty pounds that came with the lithium. He also finds his thinking fuzzy and his drive diminished. "I have a hard time reading, concentrating, remembering (that also could be the result of twenty years of heavy boozing). And I don't work as hard. Before, I was always energetic, pushing for more clients, more financing. Now, I'm much more laid back."

Alison (Age: thirty-six; Occupation: computer programmer; single, one boyfriend)

When Alison had her first experience with mania at age twenty-two, doctors told her she was schizophrenic. Three episodes and two years later, they declared her catatonic schizophrenic. Yet none of the prescribed medication restored her. The drugs dulled her mind, but didn't halt the frenzy. Only after the mania persisted for three months, when she was twenty-eight years old, did psychiatrists apply lithium and figure out Alison was really manic-depressive.

But the right diagnosis and right drugs still did not quell the illness. "After I was diagnosed, for three or four years I went on and off the medication," Alison explains. "It took a long time for me to accept the illness. I was hospitalized for a year—that brought the realization."

Alison has been faithful to her meds now for almost five years. Her daily regime of lithium, Haldol, and Tegretol is tedious, but it keeps her "destructive" mania under wraps. She has also learned how to check the manic thinking that creeps into her mind every two or three months.

"Sometimes an irrational thought pops out, and I start to wonder and worry if I'm getting manic. Like I'll see a street person and think he's Christ. Once the thought passes, I know it's irrational, but I'm on the lookout for more. If they do become more bizarre, I'll take more medication or see the doctor. Sometimes I'll call my mother and tell her about them and ask her if she thinks they're out of line."

Alison's incipient mania has never interfered with her work, even though the medication scrambles her memory. "I can focus on individual problems, like at the computer, but bigger questions are hard to remember. My mind's fuzzy sometimes. Ask me what I did yesterday and I can't focus. It's like a blockage."

Only the personnel department at Alison's company knows she's manic-depressive. When she first started there, she had to submit to a urinalysis for a drug screen, and so told her new employer about the medication they would find. Her employer confirmed that she was under medical care, and that's all that has ever been said about her illness. While she leaves work early once a week for therapy and once a month to visit a psychopharmacologist, her supervisor presumably does not know the reason for her early exits. "The computer world's been good to me," she declares.

Alison avoids the stigma of mental illness by letting few people in on her secret. "I have a couple good friends who I've known for years, and they know, but I wouldn't tell anyone else. At one time, I had a tendency to blurt it out. But my therapist coached me out of that habit."

"I'm pretty antisocial," she confesses. "I feel funny among people, like an alien, a freak. I know it's what I do to myself, but it's still there. I've had a lot of pain with people—married, divorced. I'm excruciatingly shy, now more than ever. Before, I tried to fight it. I don't fight it anymore."

In her few special relationships, she has discerned how to keep her illness at bay. "I had a tendency to talk about it a lot. I did that with my husband," Alison relates. "Now, I watch myself. You can't do that with someone who isn't sick. So I don't talk about it much with my boyfriend."

Though a loner, Alison considers her illness more of a challenge than a handicap. "It's made me very compassionate," she says. "And it gives structure and meaning to my life—I'm fighting a battle."

Paul (Age: fifty-two; Occupation: civil servant; married, three children)

When a psychiatrist told Paul at age forty-four that he was manic-depressive, he refused to believe it. "I told him he was full of shit. I didn't think much of psychiatrists, and had already diagnosed myself as neurotic," he recounts. His bursts of energy and debilitating depressions, he assumed, were simply part of his personality.

Spells of depression had plagued Paul since his early thirties. But when he sought help, the medical experts repeatedly alienated him. A psychiatrist where he worked, a government intelligence agency, voiced the opinion that the source of his trouble was "not enough love from my mother."

A correct diagnosis helped explain his erratic moods and gave him the knowledge to manage them at work. He's been with the same government agency for more than ten years, and his coworkers, bosses, and employees heard about the illness from Paul.

"A woman who worked for me, a good friend, came into my office and told me I was riding people too hard," he recounts. "Asking too much work from them, leaving stacks of work on their desks every morning. People were trying to do it all because they liked me, but they were overwhelmed. So, I called a meeting of twenty-two employees and told them I was manic-depressive, and that's why I would get charged up or disappear into my office and not want to see anyone."

While Paul has been promoted and supported by his government employer, there is a limit. His supervisor has told him that if he ever leaves the agency, he would not be rehired if he wanted to return. Mental illness is grounds for disqualification for a federal job. "It's definitely put a cap on my career," Paul says, "but it's not a problem because I'm fifty-two now and will retire at fifty-five."

Outside work, Paul struggles with depression that, at times, makes it hard for him to get out of bed and sends him into drinking spells. His medication, the antidepressant fluoxetine (Prozac), picks him up, but he still has days when he doesn't want to move. "The most difficult part is the depression in the morning, getting up and going when all you want to do is sleep forever and never get up. You have to kick yourself in the ass," he says.

Experience has shown him that structure and demands from others combat the depression. "Must-do situations," he calls them, whether it's an 8:00 A.M. meeting or a firm deadline, propel him through the bleak periods. The very worst times are weekends and vacations, when no one expects him to do anything. "The best medicine for depression is to keep active," he advises, "even though you feel you're functioning at only 40 percent."

Paul's relationships with his family also call for coping strategies. Understanding from his wife, plus a little Prozac, has quelled his erratic moods ("I'd get irritable at a dinner party and insist that we leave *now!*"). He's especially tuned into his children, watching and waiting for this genetic disease to appear. His heart-to-heart talks with them about symptoms and problems with alcohol have no doubt eased their fears and kept channels of communication wide open. Paul notes that all his children are teetotalers and devoutly religious.

Though in control of his life and never tempted to go off his meds, Paul enjoys facets of the illness. "It gives you that extra spark, a panache about the way you feel," he insists with a sparkle of enthusiasm. "It's another dimension of emotion, feeling, and experience. Life becomes a bit more vivid."

Ruth (Age: sixty-three; Occupation: community volunteer, student; married, six children)

A military wife, Ruth has consumed entire decades with relocating and moving her home and six children. She's sure that the stress of this constant disruption aggravated her first attack of manic depression at age forty-three. Like so many others, she was first diagnosed as schizophrenic, then shoved into the category of "involutional melancholia." Five years after her first attack, she was spotted as manic-depressive and is now on lithium for life.

Ruth's demon is mania, a flurry of hyperactivity that prevents her sleeping, compels her to spend hours cleaning house, and launches her into dawn-to-dusk meetings, classes, and community activities.

In her normal state, Ruth is remarkably busy. She ministers to the sick through a program created by a hospital chaplain; she's a leader for a group of manic-depressives that meets regularly; she joins organizations; and she's taking math classes toward earning a master's degree in social work. Given this regular flurry of motion, Ruth has learned to detect when everyday eagerness slips into mania.

An early sign is loss of sleep. "About once a month, I have a sleepless night. Then the next nights, I'll crash for eight to ten hours. If I don't, if I have two sleepless nights, I immediately call my psychiatrist and get sleeping pills," she says, and adds, "I listen to my body."

Stress also incites her mania, so she tracks her internal reactions carefully. Through a class at the University of Maryland on coping, she learned techniques for relaxation and medication. Ruth meditates twice daily, twenty minutes in the morning and twenty minutes in the evening. When she feels herself becoming anxious, she does breathing exercises and immediately gets away from the source of the anxiety—she'll cook, read, go to the movies, or simply be alone.

Anxiety sometimes fogs her memory—she becomes confused and forgetful. Knowing this is a temporary symptom of the illness, she's devised small tricks for keeping it in check. "I'll never say to someone, 'I forgot,'" she explains. "That just reinforces the bad memory. I say, 'It slipped my mind.' And I write things down and talk to myself, explaining why I'm writing them down."

"Another thing that helps with stress is making plans and schedules. I manage my time carefully, and always arrive early for appointments—never being late saves me from a lot of anxiety."

Lithium, plus acute sensitivity to the signals from her body, enables Ruth to enjoy the benefits of her illness. "I get lots done—I'm cheerful, happy, free to think creatively. I don't worry much, and if I have negative thoughts, it's usually because I'm tired, so I rest."

As to the stigma of mental illness, Ruth brushes it aside. "If I'm in a situation where the subject comes up, I'll tell people. It's no big deal. Everybody's got some ailment."

11

HOPE

March

I didn't want to take down the Christmas wreaths. They hung, withered, red bows drooping, until March. I liked being reminded of our magic Christmas. But holiday memories couldn't buoy Mark.

Determined to work his way back into being a student, he had signed up for two classes at the local college. He chose speech and history. "No papers or reading in speech, and interesting reading in history," he declared. "I should have no problem with this stuff."

But he would sit at the kitchen table for hours, idly turning pages in the history text. I would try to help him review material, but like a six-year-old impatient with a slow story, he would fidget and eventually wander off. His notes, left scattered on the floor, contained barely legible half-finished sentences.

He kept postponing his first speech. "I have a cold," he said. Or, "My speech isn't finished yet."

In the end, he never gave that or any other speech. He never took the first history exam, and stopped going to classes altogether. Chris and I said nothing.

He found a job busing dishes at a small restaurant on the town green. In his work uniform of black pants, tie, and white shirt, he looked tidy for the first time since Colorado. I was pleased he finally found something to do.

But by the second day, he was in turmoil. "My hands shake so much that I keep dropping glasses," he lamented. We talked about whether to tell his employer that he was taking medication that produced tremors.

"They think I'm on drugs. I can see it on their faces. What do I tell them? If I tell them about the illness, they'll fire me. If I don't, they'll fire me anyway because of all the things I'm dropping and because I'm so slow." He hated this dotty, shuffling person and saw himself as others did—a bumbling druggie.

We talked with Dr. Rostov about whether to tell his employer. "My patients do it both ways," he said. "Some are quite open and some are not. If you're not sure, probably it's best to be quiet." Mark said nothing and was fired.

We visited Dr. Rostov twice a month. Sometimes Mark and I went in together, sometimes just him. In one of our visits to Dr. Rostov, he suggested Mark move into a halfway house. Mark scowled, crossed his arms, and refused to move.

"Mark, your sense of hopelessness, the inability to read and concentrate, the persistent feeling that life has nothing for you—all this is depression. You need to understand this," he explained.

Dr. Rostov offered hope by putting Mark on the antidepressant Prozac. "This is a highly effective drug for depression," he said. "Let's give it a chance to work, but be patient, it takes time to work into your brain chemistry and do some good."

But Mark's gloom persisted. "I think of suicide sometimes," he admitted during a visit. "The thought won't go away. I see that paint scraper in the kitchen drawer, and I can't stop looking at it."

Dr. Rostov increased the Prozac dosage, but Mark continued to slide into a black hole. He slept most of the day, ate little, and stayed up into the small hours of the morning. Chris discovered that he was secretly drinking at night.

When we confronted Mark, no one shouted or became upset. We told him it was not healthy and that he had to tell his therapist and Dr. Rostov because the alcohol could be affecting his meds. The drinking seemed to stop.

Chris and I floundered over how to help Mark. We knew that his living at home was not good for any of us. But he refused to consider moving, and we didn't push. We put off making a decision, waiting for the distant future when he would get better and answers would be clearer.

"When the weather warms up, he'll be better," I declared.

"When he gets a job, he'll feel better about himself," Chris declared. So we waited, believing in the self-fulfilling prophecy that if we expected Mark to improve, he would.

Our fragile tranquillity ended on a hot Friday night in July about ten-thirty.

"Mom, I think you should see this," Mark called from the bathroom. His voice was flat, emotionless and chilling. Chris bolted out of bed. He found Mark sitting on the edge of the bathtub, blood pumping from his wrist. Chris wrapped a washrag around the gash and held Mark's hand over his head to stop the flow. I gasped, feeling breathless, as if the air had been sucked out of the room.

"Turn on the hall light!" Chris shouted, stumbling down the dark stairs, supporting Mark on one arm and holding his wrist over his head with the other. I couldn't remember where the switch was.

We raced to the hospital emergency room in Torrington, and delivered Mark to a nurse in tennis shoes and a young doctor. We followed them into a cubicle and stood in the corner watching Mark being repaired. The very neat stitching reminded me of a baseball. No one spoke. Chris held my hand, and Mark, even paler under the fluorescent lights, stared at his wrist.

The doctor said he was going to be all right. No tendons had been severed. Nevertheless, Mark would stay overnight in the hospital so they could monitor him. They gave him a shot as he lay down on a gurney, and we stood beside him as he dozed off. Just before sleep came, Mark spoke.

"I'm sorry, but I could think of no reason not to do it." His voice was a helpless whisper. "I planned everything. Bought the razor blades at the hardware store, planned it for Friday night. But when I saw all the blood, I guess I fainted."

Although it was after midnight, I called Dr. Rostov, and he arranged for Mark to be admitted back into Hillview Hospital. The next morning, Chris and I picked Mark up at the emergency room, and we drove into Boston.

Our decision seemed clear and obvious now. We didn't hesitate over checking Mark into Hillview indefinitely. He needed help, and we could not give it to him at home. All the details had bogged us down— cost of the treatment, Mark getting a job, Mark's progress in school— were inconsequential compared with the enormity of almost losing him. The experience of brushing up against our worst nightmare liberated Chris and me. Mark's life was all that was important.

Mark's room this time was on the second, not the third, floor, on the locked unit where staff looked in on him every five minutes. We all worried that he would try it again, until around the second week.

He told me something that eased my fears. "In the emergency room, when I saw your faces, yours and Dad's, I knew for the first time that you really loved me and you wouldn't let go. I don't know why I didn't know that before, but I didn't. Somehow I thought that if I killed myself, you'd be grateful after the shock wore off. It'd be a lot easier for you. Now, I know that's not true." We hugged, and I cried.

Living with Mark's suicide attempt and hospitalization this time was, in an odd way, easier. I knew what to do, what I could handle emotionally, and what was important and unimportant. I called Lisa and asked her to tell the rest of the family—relating the story four or five times would be too much.

I called Robert every day to tell him how his brother was doing. He couldn't understand why anyone would want to kill himself, especially Mark. Sometimes he called him and they talked about the Giants and old friends from school.

Mark's illness took a place in my life where it neither dominated my days nor was banished to a dark basement. It fell somewhere in the middle. It wasn't a nasty, evil secret or the consuming obsession of my life. It was a biological, medical fact of life, and I defied anyone to disapprove of my frankness about it or to impose some insidious guilt by suggesting that it wouldn't have happened if I had been a more attentive mother.

I met the common dinner-party question "Where are your children?" with equal love for both my offspring.

"The older is an engineer living in San Francisco, and the younger is in a hospital in Boston," I stated. If they asked why, I would explain that he was being treated for manic depression. In short, he was ill and in the hospital, and he should get funny cards and potted plants, not whispers and embarrassed silences. I had a moral obligation to treat Mark and his life with the same pride and worth as Robert's engineering accomplishments.

To my constant surprise, I found interest and sympathy. No one recoiled from my declarations, but instead would almost perk up and say, "You know, [my father, daughter, aunt . . . fill in the blank] has the same thing." And I would fall into an intimate conversation with someone who five minutes earlier had been a stranger. This was a new experience for me, opening up myself and my family to people I didn't know. Even more remarkable was that this emotional sharing didn't feel uncomfortable or unnatural. I guess I had changed, and I liked the more-open me.

I changed other ways too. I began to lose the qualities that had earned me the family nickname "Sarge." My judgmental, impatient bossiness softened. I no longer snapped at the slow salesclerk, coldly ignored the panhandling street person, or blasted my horn at the tentative driver. I saw a person behind the limitations. These people could be Mark sometime, someplace. To mistreat them would be to mistreat Mark. Small kindnesses assumed new importance. (However, I did continue to hone my sharp tongue on medical-insurance clerks.)

Mark left Hillview after two months, and entered a halfway house where he lives today. He doesn't have the sunny front room, but his room is clean and spare. For three hours every morning, he and the other residents attend group therapy. In the afternoons, he goes to classes or does volunteer work. He's expected to share the cooking and housekeeping chores. He hates "being part of the mental-health system," but knows he has to earn his way out with responsible living.

He's no longer on Prozac. His hands don't shake anymore, and he takes daily doses of lithium and Trilafon to keep the mania at bay.

The halfway house is horrendously expensive—almost $3,000 a month—so we regularly borrow to pay the bills. But I don't worry much about the money. I'm just glad Mark is safe and getting healthy.

Chris and I took a long-overdue trip to Bangkok for our twenty-fifth wedding anniversary using free tickets from his frequent flyer miles. He wanted to see Thailand again after twenty years. We took long walks along the Chao Phraya River, shared spicy meals, made love, and finished each other's sentences. We didn't talk much about Mark, but when a tall, blond young man passed by, we both conjured him up in Boston. We didn't feel guilty about not bringing him along. He had his own life.

Mark has to find his own way in the world, and he knows that now. Slowly, he is acquiring insight and accepting himself, not according to my ancient expectations or as his old high school friends remember him, but as his self-image develops and grows. "Our experiences are so different," he says after talking to old friends. "I feel so much older." He's shaping his character as it fits him.

Chris and I have stepped back from Mark. We don't call him; he calls us. Every few months and on holidays, he comes home. He regularly sees a social-worker therapist and Dr. Rostov, and he's learning to listen to their advice. He is still determined to go back to school and earn a degree.

I know he's going to make it. He'll have a long and wonderful life. The manic depression will not go away, but he'll learn to control it when it appears again. His life won't be like other people's, but I *know* he will find peace and happiness.

Appendix A:
Studies

These are the institutions, researchers, and projects working under grants as of 1989 from the Alcohol, Drug Abuse and Mental Health Administration. The institutions or the individual researcher may be helpful in locating a doctor who treats manic depression.

California
- University of California at Irvine: Joseph Chong-Sang Wu, "PET Study of Sleep Deprivation in Affective Illness."
- University of California at San Diego: Christian J. Gillin, "Psychobiological Study of Psychiatric Disorders."
- Stanford University, Palo Alto: Roland Ciaranello, "Neurochemistry and Childhood Psychopathology."

Connecticut
- Yale University, New Haven: Malcolm B. Bowers, Jr., "Clinical Science Research Center in Psychiatry."
- Yale University, New Haven: George R. Heninger, "Neurobiological Basis of Major Psychiatric Disorders."

Indiana
- Larue D. Carter Memorial Hospital, Indianapolis: Joyce G. Small, "Lithium and Carbamazepine in the Treatment of Mania."

Florida
- University of Miami, Miami: Janice A. Egeland, "Genetic Studies of Affective Disorders Among Amish."

Iowa
- University of Iowa, Iowa City: Nancy C. Andreasen, "Neurobiology and Phenomenology of Major Psychosis."

- University of Iowa, Iowa City: William Coryell, "Psychobiology of Depression: Clinical Studies."

Maryland

- Johns Hopkins University, Baltimore: Raymond J. DePaulo, Jr., "Genetic Linkage Studies in Bipolar Patients."
- Johns Hopkins University, Baltimore: Robert G. Robinson, "Mood Disorders in Stroke Patients."

Massachusetts

- McLean Hospital, Belmont: Bruce M. Cohen, "Mental Health Research Center for the Study of Psychotic Disorders."
- Boston University, Boston: Steven H. Zeisel, "Assessment of Lithium Treatment/Toxicity."
- Massachusetts General Hospital, Boston: Martin B. Keller, "A Follow-up Study of Children with Affective Disorders."

Michigan

- Wayne State University, Detroit: Natraj Sitaram, "Enhanced Adrenergic Activity in MAOI Treatment Responders."

Minnesota

- University of Minnesota, Minneapolis-Saint Paul: Richard A. Depue, "Studies of Persons at Risk for Depressive Disorders."

New York

- Cornell University Medical Center, New York: James H. Kocsis, "Diagnosis and Treatment of Dysthymic Disorders."
- Cornell University Medical Center, New York: Robert C. Young, "Geriatric Mania."
- New York State Psychiatric Institute, New York: Miron Baron, "Genetic Markers in Affective Disorders."
- New York State Psychiatric Institute, New York: Myrna M. Weissman, "Genetic Studies of Depressive Disorders."
- New York University, New York: Arnold J. Friedhoff, "Mental Health Clinical Research Center for Organic Affective and Schizophrenic Disorders."

North Carolina
- University of North Carolina at Chapel Hill: Arthur J. Prange, Jr., "Hormones in Cause and Treatment of Affective Disorders."

Pennsylvania
- University of Pittsburgh at Pittsburgh: David J. Kupfer, "Clinical Research Center Study of Affective Disorders."
- University of Pennsylvania, Philadelphia: Aaron T. Beck, "Psychopathology of Depression, Anxiety and Suicide."

Texas
- University of Texas Southwestern Medical Center at Dallas: Augustus J. Rush, "Clinical Research Center Study of Neuropsychobiology in Affective Disorders."

Utah
- University of Utah, Salt Lake City: William F. Byerley, "Molecular Genetics of Manic Depression and Schizophrenia."

Vermont
- University of Vermont, Burlington: Robert H. Lenox, "Molecular Mechanisms of Lithium Action in Affective Illness."

APPENDIX B:
SUPPORT GROUPS

This is a list of the state organizations of the National Alliance for the Mentally Ill (NAMI) (1-800-950-NAMI). The individual names are the state president, unless otherwise indicated. The addresses and phone numbers are the organization's, unless the group does not have a state office, in which case it's the president's phone and address.

Alabama
Bob Brown
#5 Jackson's Oak
Daphne, AL 36526
(205) 987-8338

Alaska
Francis Cater
c/o 4050 Lake Otis Parkway
Suite 103
Anchorage, AK 99508
(907) 561-3127

Arizona
Sue Davis
9420 E. Casitas Del Rio Drive
Scottsdale, AZ 85255
(602) 585-4661

Arkansas
Kathleen Peek
Hendrix Hall, Room 233
4313 W. Markham
Little Rock, AR 72205
(501) 661-1548

California
Dan Weisburd
1111 Howe Avenue
Suite 475
Sacramento, CA 95825
(916) 567-0163

Colorado
Larry Zimmerman
1100 Fillmore St.
Denver, CO 80206
(303) 321-3104

Connecticut
Edna Jacobs
62 Alexander St.
Manchester, CT 06040
(203) 643-6697

Delaware
Ron Norris
4th Street Plaza, Suite 12
2500 W. 4th St.
Wilmington, DE 19805
(302) 427-0787

District of Columbia
Cynthia Lewis
422 8th Street, S.E.
Washington, DC 20003
(202) 546-0646stle

Florida
Joyce Friedman
400 S. Dixie Hwy, #14
Lake Worth, FL 33460
(407) 582-1835

Georgia
Willys R. Knight
1256 Briarcliff Rd., N.E.
Suite 412S
Atlanta, GA 30306
(404) 894-8860

Hawaii
Edward Sullam
1109 12th Ave., #5
Honolulu, HI 96816
(808) 737-9069

Illinois
Imelda Smith
1728 S. 6th
Springfield, IL 62703
(312) 297-9966

Indiana
Carol Van Dusen
R.R.1, Box 406-B
Lake Village, IN 46349
(219) 992-3720

Iowa
Warren R. Adams
Box 495
Johnston, IA 50131
(515) 225-8666

Kansas
Cecil Eyestone
P.O. Box 675
Topeka, KS 66601
(913) 233-0755

Kentucky
Carl Reed
707 Executive Park
Louisville, KY 40207
(502) 896-1877

Louisiana
Donald Duncan
2431 S. Acadian Thruway
Suite 420
Baton Rouge, LA 70808
(504) 928-6928

Maine
Mary Lou Curtis
Box 222
Augusta, ME 04332
(207) 622-5767

Maryland
Elsie Roberts
2114 N. Charles St.
Baltimore, MD 21218
(301) 837-0880

Massachusetts
Marilyn Helfenbein
27-43 Wormwood St.
Boston, MA 02210
(617) 439-3933

Michigan
Louis Vescio
592 Foxboro
Saginaw, MI 48603
(313) 355-0010

Minnesota
Jack Brown
1595 Selby Ave.
Suite 103
St. Paul, MN 55104
(612) 645-2948

Mississippi
Ron Renz
215 Edinburgh Ct.
Brandon, MS 32024
(601) 992-1227

Missouri
Howard Henderson
444 Bryan Ave.
Kirkwood, MO 63122
(816) 941-0285

Montana
Helen Sampsel
103 S. Strevell
Miles City, MT 59301
(406) 232-1553

Nebraska
Cyndi Eckhardt
R.R.1, Box 3
Inavale, NE 68952
(402) 746-3256

Nevada
Ann Smith
900 Allen Shephard St.
Las Vegas, NV 89128
(702) 363-4452

New Hampshire
Rona Purdy
c/o 10 Ferry St., Unit 314
Concord, NH 03301
(603) 225-5359

New Jersey
Marilyn Goldstein
114 W. State St., 2nd Fl.
Trenton, NJ 08608
(201) 329-2888

New Mexico
Mable Frary
P.O. Box 9049
Santa Fe, NM 87504
(505) 983-6745

New York
Jerry Klein
260 Washington Ave.
Albany, NY 12210
(518) 462-2000

North Carolina
Mary Eldridge
3716 National Drive, #213
Raleigh, NC 27612
(919) 783-1807

North Dakota
Marjorie Christensen
Box 637
Grandville, ND 58741
(701) 385-4355

Ohio
Bernie Schell
65 S. 4th St, Rm. 305
Columbus, OH 43215
(614) 464-2646

Oklahoma
Wayne Rives
525 N.W. 13th
Oklahoma City, OK 73103
(405) 239-6264

Oregon
Adeline Filer
3000 Market St.
Suite 266
Salem, OR 97301
(503) 270-7774

Pennsylvania
Mary Ellen Rehrman
2149 N. 2nd St.
Harrisburg, PA 17110
(717) 238-1514

Rhode Island
Steve Downey
421 Bellevue Ave, #2B
Newport, RI 02840
(401) 621-4588

South Carolina
Dr. Eugene Wright
P.O. Box 2538
Columbia, SC 29202
(803) 736-1542

South Dakota
Donna Yocom
Box 221
Brookings, SD 57006
(605) 692-5673

Tennessee
Ray Sinor
1900 N. Winston Rd., #511
Knoxville, TN 37919
(615) 877-4109

Texas
Carol Schaper
400 W. 15th St.
Suite 619
Austin, TX 78701
(512) 474-2225

Utah
Joy D. Verde
P.O. Box 58047
Salt Lake City, UT 84158
(801) 584-2023

Vermont
Nancy Lanoue
67 Main St.
Poultney, VT 05764
(802) 453-4719

Virginia
Beverly Fleming
P.O. Box 1903
Richmond, VA 23215
(804) 225-8264

Washington
Bernice Buchheit
10629 S.E. 244th
Kent, WA 98031
(206) 854-1797

West Virginia
Judith Krall
25 Clinton Hills
Triadelphia, WV 26059
(304) 242-8850

Wisconsin
Bob Nugent
1245 E. Washington Ave.
Suite 76A
Madison, WI 53703
(608) 257-5888

Wyoming
Bob Walker
1949E A St.
Casper, WY 82601
(307) 464-5521

APPENDIX C:
STATE ORGANIZATIONS

These are chapters of NAMI that have more than two hundred members and can also be contacted for information and help.

Washington Advocates for the Mentally Ill
Eleanor Owen, Executive Director
802 NW 70th St.
Seattle, WA 98117
(206) 789-7722

AMI of Greater Chicago
Laura Guilfoyle, Executive Director
833 N. Orleans
Chicago, IL 60610
(312) 642-3338

AMI of Orange County (CA)
Lisa Kyriss, Administrative Secretary
17341 Irvine Blvd., #105
Tustin, CA 90504
(714) 544-8488

AMI of Montgomery County (MD)
Mary Kundrat, Executive Director
7300 Whittier Blvd.
Bethesda, MD 21218
(301) 229-7811

AMI of Greater Milwaukee
Sandra Quirk, Executive Director
4011 W. Capitol Dr., #205
Milwaukee, WI 53216
(414) 442-9424

FAMI
381 Park Ave. So.
Suite 620
New York, NY 10016-8806
(212) 684-FAMI

Northeast Ohio Alliance for the Mentally Ill
Gloria Mills, Executive Director
2800 Euclid Ave., Suite 240
Cleveland, OH 44115

AMI of Baltimore
Linda Koban, Executive Director
2114 N. Charles St.
Baltimore, MD 21218
(301) 539-0525

San Diego AMI
Patricia Grimes, Executive Director
450 Olive St.
San Diego, CA 92103
(619) 543-1434

Missouri AMI
131 W. Monroe, Suite 8
St. Louis, MO 63133
(314) 966-4670

AMI of Northern Virginia
2101 Wilson Blvd., #302
Arlington, VA 22201
(703) 525-0686

AMI Dane County (WI)
Julie DeHaven, Administrative Assistant
1245 E. Washington Ave., #173
Madison, WI 53703
(608) 255-1695

AMISA
738 N. 5th Ave., Suite 100
Tucson, AZ 85701

AMI of Memphis
Carolyn Raney, Executive Director
499 Patterson, 3rd Flr.
Memphis, TN 38111
(901) 323-5928

AMI of Greater Kansas City (MO)
3600 Walnut
Kansas City, MO 64111
(816) 753-5150

Louisville AMI
Evelyn True, Secretary
707 Executive Suite
Louisville, KY 40205
(502) 896-1877

AMI of Lane County (OR)
Ginny Krumdieck, Coordinator
59 Coburg Rd., Suite E
Eugene, OR 94701
(503) 343-7688

AMI of Springfield (MO)
1504 N. Robberson
Springfield, MO 65803-2841
(417) 864-7119

NOTES

Chapter 2: What Is Manic Depression?

Page 43: "Some medical professionals consider . . ." An invaluable resource and excellent book is *The Broken Brain, The Biological Revolution in Psychiatry*, by Nancy Andreasen, M.D. (New York: Harper & Row, 1984).

Page 44: "Just as the disease has . . ." Interview with Alexander Vuckovic, M.D., McLean Hospital, Belmont, MA.

Page 44: "Anyone observing Isaac . . ." Nancy C. Andreasen, M.D., and Ira D. Glick, "Bipolar Affective Disorder and Creativity: Implications and Clinical Management," *Comprehensive Psychiatry*, Vol. 29, No. 3 (May/June 1988), pp. 207–17.

Page 45: "Manic depression has often been misdiagnosed . . ." Sources used for general information about the illness and its diagnosis include Anastasios Georgotas and Robert Cancro, eds., *Depression and Mania* (New York: Elsevier Science Publishing, 1988); J. John Mann, ed., *Phenomenology of Depressive Illness, The Depressive Illness Series, Vol. 1* (New York: Human Sciences Press, 1988); Howard H. Goldman, ed., *Review of General Psychiatry* (Los Altos, CA: Lange Medical publications, 1984); Ronald R. Fieve, M.D., *Moodswing* (New York: William Morrow, 1989); Demitri Papolos, M.D., and Janice Papolos, *Overcoming Depression* (New York: Harper & Row, 1987).

Page 46: "Eating habits are sometimes skewed . . ." Researchers have noticed that affective illness, especially depression, occurs in bulimics, and continue to study this connection. See Alan B. Levy, M.D., et al., "How are Depression and Bulimia Related?" *American Journal of Psychiatry*, 146 (1989), 162–69.

Page 47: "Yet even after doctors . . ." Peter A. Bick, M.D., and Marcel Kinsbourne, M.D., "Auditory Hallucinations and Subvocal Speech in Schizophrenic Patients," *American Journal of Psychiatry*, 144 (1987), 222–25.

Page 47: "Hallucinations and delusions appear . . ." James C. Ballenger, M.D., et al., "The 'Atypical' Clinical Picture of Adolescent Mania," *American Journal of Psychiatry*, 139 (1982), 602–5.

Page 48: "One study indicates . . ." Donald W. Black, M.D., et al., "Suicide in Subtypes of Major Affective Disorder," *Archives of General Psychiatry*, 44 (1987), 878–80.

Page 48: "This was a critical issue . . ." This study appeared in Janice A. Egeland, Ph.D., and Abram M. Hostetter, M.D., "Amish Study, I: Affective Disorders Among the Amish, 1976–1980," *American Journal of Psychiatry*, 140 (1983), 56–61; Abram M. Hostetter, M.D., et al., "Amish Study, II: Consensus Diagnoses and Reliability Results," *American Journal of Psychiatry*, 140 (1983), 62–66; Janice A. Egeland, Ph.D., et al., "Amish Study, III: The Impact of Cultural Factors on Diagnosis of Bipolar Illness," *American Journal of Psychiatry*, 140 (1983), 67–71.

Page 49: "If we take into account . . ." See *Depression and Mania*, p. 198.

Page 49: "According to one doctor . . ." See *Phenomenology of Depressive Illness*, p. 98.

Page 49: "Professionals disagree about . . ." In *Depression and Mania*, p. 198, for instance, Dr. Julien Mendlewicz states, "Most studies have reported an appreciable difference between the sexes in the distribution of bipolar illness. The sex ratio generally accepted is two females to one male." Yet in the same textbook, p. 32, Doctors Elizabeth Charney and Myrna Weissman conclude from other data, " . . . the rates for bipolar disorder did not differ widely by sex."

Page 50: "Researchers at Syracuse University . . ." Barry Glassner, Ph.D., and C. V. Haldipur, M.D., "Life Events and Early and Late Onset of Bipolar Disorder," *American Journal of Psychiatry*, 140 (1983), 215–17.

Page 50: "While these conclusions . . ." Thomas A. Wehr, M.D., et al., "Sleep Reduction as a Final Common Pathway in the Genesis of Mania," *American Journal of Psychiatry*, 144 (1987), 201–4.

Page 51: "Doctors Harrison Pope . . ." Harrison G. Pope, M.D., and David L. Katz, M.D., "Affective and Psychotic Symptoms Associated with Anabolic Steroid Use," *American Journal of Psychiatry*, 145 (1988), 487–90.

Page 51: "Recently, doctors at the National . . ." Robert M. Post, M.D., et al., "Cocaine-Induced Behavioral Sensitization and Kindling: Implications for the Emergence of Psychopathology and Seizures," *Annals of New York Academy of Sciences*, 537 (1988), 292–307.

Page 51: "Some experts put the ratio . . ." See *Depression and Mania*, p. 56.

Page 52: "A single episode happens . . ." The *Phenomenology of De-*

pressive Illness provided much of this information on timing and duration of episodes.

Page 52: "Researchers have found that . . ." David J. Miklowitz, Ph.D., et al., "Family Factors and the Course of Bipolar Affective Disorder," *Archives of General Psychiatry*, 45 (1988), 225–29.

Page 52: "As someone gets older . . ." Robert M. Post, et al., "Graphic Representation of the Life Course of Illness in Patients with Affective Disorder," *American Journal of Psychiatry*, 145 (1988), 844–47.

Page 53: "Some medical experts believe that most . . ." This idea is discussed in *Depression and Mania*, p. 59.

Page 53: "Mixed mania strikes . . ." See Steven K. Secunda, M.D., "Diagnosis and Treatment of Mixed Mania," *American Journal of Psychiatry*, 144 (1987), 96–98.

Page 54: "This cycle can be as regular . . ." See Thomas A. Wehr, M.D., et al., "Rapid Cycling Affective Disorder: Contributing Factors and Treatment Responses in 51 Patients," *American Journal of Psychiatry*, 145 (1988), 179–84.

Page 54: "According to researchers, people with . . ." See David J. Kupfer, M.D., et al., "Is Bipolar II a Unique Disorder?" *Comprehensive Psychiatry*, Vol. 29, No. 3 (May/June 1988), pp. 228–36.

Page 55: "Another, less grievous form . . ." A thorough discussion of milder forms of bipolar disorder appears in Hagop S. Akiskal, M.D., "The Milder Spectrum of Bipolar Disorders: Diagnostic, Characterologic and Pharmacologic Aspects," *Psychiatric Annals*, 17:1 (1987), 32–36.

Page 55: "It is a controversial category . . ." The problems in defining and diagnosing schizoaffective are discussed in James J. Levitt, M.D., "The Heterogeneity of Schizoaffective Disorder: Implications for Treatment," *American Journal of Psychiatry*, 145 (1988), 926–35.

Page 57: "For instance, doctors have found . . ." See Sashi Shukla, M.D., "Failure to Detect Organic Factors in Mania," *Journal of Affective Disorders*, 15 (1988), 17–20.

Page 58: "Perhaps most important . . ." Before the advent of *DSM-III*, doctors turned to its predecessor, *DSM-II*, which was much less comprehensive, less clear, and less precise. Using this volume, an individual psychiatrist making a diagnosis of manic depression had to decide which symptoms were more important, how often they had to appear, and how long they lasted. Another psychiatrist diagnosing the same patient could put more emphasis and weight to certain symptoms, and so arrive at a different conclusion.

The medical profession was well aware of the shortcomings in *DSM-II*, and methodically set out to correct the deficiencies. The criteria and standards set forth in *DSM-III* took six years to research and test by fourteen committees of medical professionals. For diagnoses, the book lists individual symptoms, the minimum number of necessary symptoms, and how often and/or how long symptoms must be present.

The *DSM-III* subdivided mental illness into many more categories and used a much more precise vocabulary. Whereas *DSM-II* called its categories "diseases," *DSM-III* applied the term "disorder," thus establishing a demarcation between purely physical diseases and the broader scope of mental illness. In *DSM-II*, manic depression was labeled "manic-depressive psychosis" and in *DSM-III*, the illness is a "bipolar disorder."

Language was further refined in the revised *DSM-III*, as "Affective Disorders" became "Mood Disorders." By changing the grouping to mood disorders, the manual stepped away from jargon and emphasized that the illnesses relate to "prolonged emotion that colors the whole psychic life."

Page 62: "There are dozens of these scales . . ." We include a sampling of them not to encourage amateur diagnosis but to familiarize the unknowing with names and terms they may overhear in hospital corridors or read upside down in a doctor's office. These scales and criteria are just part of the arcane vocabulary of mental illness. They are described in detail in Robert L. Spitzer, M.D., et al., "Research Diagnostic Criteria," *Archives of General Psychiatry*, 35 (1978), 773–82, and Jean Endicott, Ph.D., and Robert L. Spitzer, M.D., "A Diagnostic Interview," *Archives of General Psychiatry*, 35 (1978), 837–44.

The RDC and SADS.   A widely consulted source is the Research Diagnostic Criteria (RDC) and its companion scale, the Schedule for Affective Disorders and Schizophrenia (SADS). The RDC lays out criteria for select psychiatric disorders, specifying what symptoms are included or excluded in a diagnosis. The SADS is a one-to-two-hour interview that gathers descriptive and factual information from a patient and family about an illness, its history and severity, and its course.

There are three variations of the SADS—the regular version, a lifetime version (SADS-L) that examines the disorder's past and present, and a version that measures changes in the disorder (SADS-C). The information from the SADS interview is then compared with criteria in the RDC.

Other scales described here are explained in James L. Hedlund, Ph.D, and Bruce W. Vieweg, M.S., "The Hamilton Rating Scale for Depression: A Comprehensive Review," *Journal of Operational Psychiatry*, Vol. 10, No. 2, 1979; Christine E. Brierley, et al., "The Manchester Nurse Rating Scales for the Daily Simultaneous Assessment of Depressive and Manic Ward Behaviors," *Journal of Affective Disorders*, 15 (1988), 45–54; Steven K. Secunda, et al., "Mania: Diagnosis, State Measurement and Prediction of Treatment Response," *Journal of Affective Disorders*, 8 (1985), 113–21; and Chapter 41 in *Depression and Mania*, "Assessment of Depression and Mania."

The Hamilton Depression Scale. Used extensively and a model in the field, this scale takes the form of a seventeen- to twenty-nine-question patient interview. It measures the severity of the illness *after* diagnosis, and is often used to gauge the effectiveness of certain drugs and treatment programs.

The Beck Depression Inventory. This is given to patients to rate themselves on twenty-one items and offers an immediate picture of how a patient is feeling and responding to treatment. Self-rating scales have the obvious advantage of avoiding the biases of doctors and nurses, but they also tend to offer just a snapshot of a person's condition.

The Present State Examination (PSE). This diagnostic tool consists of thirty-three points relating to behavior and one hundred and seven patient questions. In contrast to the Hamilton Scale and others that focus on depression, the PSE identifies mania as well.

Scales for Nurses. While most criteria and rating scales are used by doctors, some are designed for nursing staff watching ward behavior. They may be used for psychiatric patients with uncertain diagnoses or to track a patient's progress. The Manchester Nurse Rating Scales for Depression and Mania, for instance, lists five positive and ten negative behaviors. While these indicators seem highly subjective (e.g., "laughs or smiles at funny comments or events," and "is disinhibited and antisocial"), the ratings are considered very reliable. Other nursing-staff scales are the Manic State Scale and the Young Mania Scale.

Page 63: "One such interview is the . . ." The Camberwell Interview and others are described in the David J. Miklowitz, "Family Factors and the Course of Bipolar Affective Disorder," *Archives of General Psychiatry*, 45 (1988), 225–31.

Page 63: "Researchers at the National Institute . . ." See Robert M. Post, et al., "Graphic Representation of the Life Course of Illness in Patients with Affective Disorder," *American Journal of Psychiatry*, 145 (1988), 844–48.

Page 64: "While suffering families have been telling . . ." The genetic origins have been examined from a number of angles. Studies of family lineage, twins (both single-egg, identical, and two-egg, fraternal), and adoptions have traced the illness within a family and as it progressed through ancestors and relatives. The study of the Old Order Amish in Lancaster, Pennsylvania, offers even more dramatic evidence of the disorder's movement through individual families. Researchers traced family lineage and were able to identify multigenerational pedigrees that revealed remarkably high incidence of affective disorders. While the Amish as a whole experience mental illness somewhat less than the general population, affective disorders appear to cluster in families.

Researchers discovered, for instance, a couple (father diagnosed as obsessive-compulsive) in the late 1800s who produced 8 children, 6 of whom were psychiatric cases. In the next generation, 8 of the 35 children were "psychiatric cases" (precise definitions weren't given) and in the next generation, 25 of 191 were psychiatric cases. See Kenneth K. Kidd, Ph.D., et al., "Amish Study, IV: Genetic Linkage Study of Pedigrees of Bipolar Probands," *American Journal of Psychiatry*, 141 (1984), 1042–47.

Page 64: "Other researchers think the risk . . ." In thirteen studies that figured the percentage of close relatives of bipolar patients who were affectively ill, the average risk for female relatives was 61 percent and for male relatives, 39 percent. (These studies are reported in *Depression and Mania* and refer to affective patients, a much larger group than only manic-depressives.) When looking at the chances of relatives of bipolar patients being bipolar themselves, the numbers drop to around 5.7 percent. (John Rice, Ph.D., et al., "The Familial Transmission of Bipolar Illness," *Archives of General Psychiatry*, 44 (1987), 441–47.) Generally, the risk is highest for children of bipolar patients and lowest for parents.

Studies of twins comparing monozygotic siblings (one egg) and dizygotic siblings (two eggs) confirm the genetic connection. (*Depression and Mania* offers detailed descriptions of twin and adoption studies.) If one monozygotic twin is manic-depressive, the likelihood that his sibling will also be varies from 50 percent to 93 percent. For dizygotic twins, the likelihood of both being manic-depressive drops to a range from zero to 39 percent.

Adoption studies point to similar conclusions. Researchers comparing rates of manic depression in adopted children find much more illness among the children whose biological parents are affectively ill. The connection between affective illness and blood relatives holds true from the parents' point of view too. Adoptive parents of children with affective disorders showed markedly less psychiatric illness than the children's biological parents. Figures in one study of parents of adopted bipolar children report 12 percent of the adoptive parents with affective illness and 31 percent of the biological parents with similar illness. A striking feature of the genetic connection is that, among major psychiatric disorders, it is strongest in affective illnesses. The likelihood of schizophrenia appearing in families is less than for bipolar and unipolar disorders.

Page 64: "Scientists continue to explore . . ." Investigators have been focusing on the dominant, sex-linked X chromosome and various traits linked to it, such as certain types of color blindness. (Some studies report a higher than normal incidence of color blindness among bipolar patients). The X-chromosome connection suggests that the disease may travel through the maternal side of families. Scientists believe that bipolar illness may be transmitted through both the X chromosome and non-sex-determining chromosomes, and so conclude that the disorder may well have more than one cause.

The best-known of these studies has taken place, again, among the Amish. Researchers in the Amish studies, which tested bipolar families for color blindness and certain blood typing, reported finding what's called a "marker gene" near chromosome 11. Two years after that discovery, the same scientists retraced their steps and concluded that they misread the data—the faulty gene near chromosome 11 may not be connected to manic depression. Despite this setback, researchers remain firm about the genetic origin of manic depression. In reporting on this reversal, the biology editor of *Nature* magazine declared, "They [readers] should have no reason to doubt the existence of genetic predisposition to psychiatric disease." (The original Amish study was by Kenneth K. Kidd, Ph.D., et al., "Amish Study IV: Genetic Linkage Study of Pedigrees of Bipolar Probands," *American Journal of Psychiatry*, 141 (1984), 1042–48. The new findings appeared in *Nature*, Nov. 16, 1989.)

Page 65: "Brain chemistry is another . . ." Theories about the excess or absence of certain chemicals causing mania and depression reach back to ancient times. Excess bile and phlegm were often blamed for melancholia and dark moods. Today, researchers gather evidence about neurotransmitters, chemicals that carry messages through the brain and to the body, and certain hormones of the endocrine system.

Page 65: "Among the brain chemicals . . ." One of the earliest and most widely believed theories, called the "catecholamine hypothesis," holds that depression is caused by low levels of norepinephrine, and mania by high levels of this chemical. There are similar suspicions about serotonin. These chemicals seem to be natural suspects, for they operate in areas of the brain that regulate arousal and alertness.

An elevated level of dopamine, active in three regions of the brain, has already been spotted as a likely contributor to schizophrenia. Parkinson's disease, a neurological disorder causing physical slowing, is probably related to a lowered level of this chemical. And some researchers believe that elevated levels of dopamine also contribute to mania. In human and animal studies, scientists have noticed that drugs known to stimulate dopamine production in the brain, such as amphetamines and cocaine, trigger a hyperactivity similar to mania. The hyperactivity then recedes when the patient or animal receives drugs known to block dopamine production.

The neurotransmitter acetylcholine, involved with motor function, sleep, thinking, pain senses, hormone regulation, and moods, is active throughout the brain. Its levels are affected by many drug treatments, and some researchers theorize that it has a role in the genesis of manic depression. (Invaluable sources in understanding neurotransmitters and brain chemistry are The Broken Brain by Nancy C. Andreasen, and Drugs and the Brain by Solomon H. Snyder (New York: Scientific American Library, 1986).

Chapter 4: Drugs and Other Antidotes
Page 92: "To patients, taking medication . . ." See Ronald Diamond, "Drugs and the Quality of Life: A Patient's Point of View," *Journal of Clinical Psychiatry*, 46 (Sec. 2) (1985), 29–35.

Page 93: "Doctors report that one third to one half . . ." This is particularly true with longtime users of lithium because of its unpleasant side effects, as described in Michael J. Gitlin, et al., "Maintenance Lithium Treatment: Side Effects and Compliance," *Journal of Clinical Psychiatry*, 50 (1989), 127–31.

Page 94: "Yet new drugs for mental illness . . ." Recently, advocates for AIDS patients successfully pressured the FDA to release promising treatment to patients more quickly. This response may percolate down to patients waiting for new mental-illness medication.

Page 94: "The federal Food and Drug . . ." FDA explains its drug program in *From Test Tube to Patient: New Drug Development in the United States* (Rockville, MD: Department of Health and Human Services, 1988). This booklet includes suggestions for how patients can participate in clinical trials.

Page 95: "One study comparing patients . . ." See Alan J. Gelenberg, "Lithium Efficacy and Adverse Effects," *Journal of Clinical Psychiatry*, 49, Suppl. (1988), 8–9.

Page 96: "Cade concluded in his . . ." John F. Cade, "Lithium Salts in the Treatment of Psychotic Excitement," *Medical Journal of Australia*, 2 (1949), 349–52.

Page 96: "Lithium does double duty . . ." A pioneer in lithium research is Mogens Schou, M.D., who has written extensively on it. His article, "Lithium Treatment of Manic-Depressive Illness," *JAMA*, 259 (1988), 1834–36, is a good summary of the topic. Other sources of information are James W. Jefferson, M.D., and John H. Greist, M.D., "Lithium: A Practitioner's Guide," *Hospital Therapy*, 12 (1987), 74–99; H. I. Kaplan and B. J. Sadock, eds., *Comprehensive Textbook of Psychiatry* (Baltimore, MD: Williams & Wilkins, 1989); and James W. Jefferson, M.D., "Lithium: A Therapeutic Magic Wand," *Journal of Clinical Psychiatry*, 50 (1989), 81–86.

Page 97: "The latest research suggests . . ." Karen Wright, "How does lithium counter both mania and depression?" *Scientific American*, Vol. 258 (1988), p. 36.

Page 98: "The side effects of lithium . . ." These are covered in detail in Michael J. Gitlin, M.D., et al., "Maintenance Lithium Treatment: Side Effects and Compliance"; Jane E. Garland, M.D., "Weight Gain with Antidepressants and Lithium," *Journal of Clinical Psychopharmacology*, 8 (1988), 323–29; and Gelenberg, "Lithium Efficacy and Adverse Effects."

Page 99: "Carbamazepine is a relatively . . ." Sources about this alternative to lithium include Vernon M. Neppe, M.D., et al., "Introduction: Fundamentals of Carbamazepine Use in Neuropsychiatry," *Journal of Clinical Psychiatry*, 49, Suppl. (1988), 4–6; William E. Falk, "Carbamazepine (Tegretol) for Manic-Depressive Illness: An Update," *Biological Therapies in Psychiatry*, Vol. 8, No. 6 (1985); Frances R.

Frankenburg, M.D., et al., "Long-Term Response to Carbamazepine: A Retrospective Study," *Journal of Clinical Psychopharmacology*, 8 (1988), 130–32; and James C. Ballenger, M.D., "The Use of Anticonvulsants in Manic-Depressive Illness," *Journal of Clinical Psychiatry*, 49, Suppl. (1988), 21–24.

Page 99: "Doctors find it especially . . ." See James C. Ballenger, M.D., "The Clinical Use of Carbamazepine in Affective Disorders," *Journal of Clinical Psychiatry*, 49, Suppl. (1988), 13–19.

Page 99: "Some doctors also believe that . . ." See Vernon M. Neppe, M.D., "Carbamazepine in Nonresponsive Patients," *Journal of Clinical Psychiatry*, 49, Suppl. (1988), 22–28.

Page 100: "As with other anticonvulsants . . ." Its use for rapid-cycling patients is well-documented in Robert M. Post, M.D., "Introduction: Emerging Perspectives on Valproate in Affective Disorders," *Journal of Clinical Psychiatry*, 50, Suppl. (1989), 3–9; Joseph R. Calabrese, M.D., and Gustavo A. Delucchi, M.D., "Phenomenology of Rapid Cycling Manic Depression and Its Treatment with Valproate," *Journal of Clinical Psychiatry*, 50, Suppl. (1989), 30–34; and Susan L. McElroy, M.D., et al., "Valproate in the Treatment of Rapid-Cycling Bipolar Disorder," *Journal of Clinical Psychopharmacology*, 8 (1988), 275–79.

Page 100: "It may be less effective with depression . . ." See Richard Brown, M.D., "U.S. Experience with Valproate in Manic Depressive Illness: A Multicenter Trial," *Journal of Clinical Psychiatry*, 50, Suppl. (1989), 13–16.

Page 100: "This class of drugs . . ." An invaluable source of information on approved drugs and drugs under study is Jean K. Bouricius, "Psychoactive Drugs and Their Effects on Mentally Ill Persons" (National Alliance for the Mentally Ill: Arlington, VA, 1989).

Page 101: "Nevertheless, they are widely . . ." A good overview is John M. Kane, M.D., "The Role of Neuroleptics in Manic-Depressive Illness," *Journal of Clinical Psychiatry*, 49, Suppl. (1988), 12–13.

Page 101: "When neuroleptics are used for mania . . ." This application is described in Seth Cohen, M.D., et al., "Pharmacological Management of Manic Psychosis in an Unlocked Setting," *Journal of Clinical Psychopharmacology*, 7 (1987), 261–64.

Page 101: "Antipsychotics are powerful chemicals . . ." See John M. Kane, M.D., "Antipsychotic Drug Side Effects: Their Relationship to Dose," *Journal of Clinical Psychiatry*, 45 (1985), 16–21.

Page 103: "This is a relatively new drug . . ." Some of its properties are described in James Claghorn, M.D., et al., "The Risks and Benefits of Clozapine versus Chlorpromazine," *Journal of Clinical Psychopharmacology*, 7 (1987), 377–84.

Page 103: "They are also used in . . ." See William R. Dubin, M.D., "Rapid Tranquilization: Antipsychotics or Benzodiazepines?" *Journal of Clinical Psychiatry*, 49, Suppl. (1988), 5–11.

Page 103: "Their big attraction . . ." See Guy Chouinard, M.D., "The Use of Benzodiazepines in the Treatment of Manic-Depressive Illness," *Journal of Clinical Psychiatry*, 49, Suppl. (1988), 15–19.

Page 104: "Researchers theorize there . . ." see George Gardos, M.D., "Clinical Forms of Severe Tardive Dyskinesia," *American Journal of Psychiatry*, 144 (1987), 895–902.

Page 105: "Antipsychotic drugs are the main . . ." The mystery of the cause of TD is described in Ross J. Baldessarini, M.D., "Clinical and Epidemiologic Aspects of Tardive Dyskinesia," *Journal of Clinical Psychiatry*, 46 (1985), 8–13.

Page 105: "One study reveals that . . ." See William M. Glazer, M.D., and Hal Morgenstern, Ph.D., "Predictors of Occurrence, Severity, and Course of Tardive Dyskinesia in an Outpatient Population," *Journal of Clinical Psychopharmacology*, 8 (1988), 10S–16S.

Page 105: "Some doctors suspect smoking . . ." The smoking connection is raised in *Psychoactive Drugs and Their Effects on Mentally Ill Persons* (National Alliance for the Mentally Ill, Arlington: VA, 1989).

Page 106: "Researchers say that experimenters . . ." See Ross J. Baldessarini, M.D., "Current Status of Antidepressants: Clinical Pharmacology and Therapy," *Journal of Clinical Psychiatry*, 50 (1989), 117–26.

Page 107: "This flip-flop from depression . . ." The "switching" controversy is aired in Thomas A. Wehr, M.D., and Frederick K. Goodwin, M.D., "Do Antidepressants Cause Mania?" *Psychopharmacology Bulletin*, 23 (1987), 61–63; Thomas A. Wehr, M.D., and Frederick K. Goodwin, M.D., "Can Antidepressants Cause Mania and Worsen the Course of Affective Illness?" *American Journal of Psychiatry*, 144 (1987), 1403–11; Jules Angst, M.D., "Switch from Depression to Mania, or from Mania to Depression: Role of Psychotropic Drugs," *Psychopharmacology Bulletin*, 23 (1987), 66; and Thomas A. Wehr, M.D., "Rapid Cycling Affective Disorder: Contributing Factors and Treatment Responses in 51 Patients," *American Journal of Psychiatry*, 145 (1988), 179–85.

Page 107: "On the other side, a group . . ." See David J. Kupfer,

M.D., et al., "Possible Role of Antidepressants in Precipitating Mania and Hypomania in Recurrent Depression," *American Journal of Psychiatry*, 145 (1988), 804–8.

Page 108: "Some researchers say patients . . ." See the chapter "Monamine Oxidase Inhibitors" in *Depression and Mania*.

Page 108: "Yet sometimes patients don't . . ." See Barry H. Guze, M.D., et al., "Refractory Depression Treated with High Doses of a Monamine Oxidase Inhibitor," *Journal of Clinical Psychiatry*, 48 (1987), 31–32.

Page 109: "Doctors have identified the kinds . . ." See Solomon C. Goldberg, Ph.D., et al., "Who Benefits from Tricyclic Antidepressants: A Survey," *Journal of Clinical Psychiatry*, 49 (1988), 224–28.

Page 109: "Often doctors start treatment . . ." Understanding side effects is discussed in Mark H. Pollack, M.D., and Jerrold F. Rosenbaum, M.D., "Management of Antidepressant-Induced Side Effects: A Practical Guide for the Clinician," *Journal of Clinical Psychiatry*, 48 (1987), 3–8.

Page 110: "But even when these . . ." See the chapter "Tricyclic Antidepressants" in *Depression and Mania*.

Page 110: "Researchers continue to tinker . . ." See J. Mendels, M.D., "Clinical Experience with Serotonin Reuptake Inhibiting Antidepressants," *Journal of Clinical Psychiatry*, 48, Suppl. (1987), 26–30.

Page 112: "Although ECT has been controversial . . ." See L. G. Kiloh, "The Trials of ECT," *Psychiatric Developments*, 2 (1987), 205–18.

Page 112: "ECT was devised in the . . ." See Max Fink, M.D., "Meduna and the Origins of Convulsive Therapy," *American Journal of Psychiatry*, 141 (1984), 1034–41.

Page 112: "But studies pitting ECT . . ." See Arthur Rifkin, M.D., "ECT Versus Tricyclic Antidepressants in Depression: A Review of the Evidence," *Journal of Clinical Psychiatry*, 49 (1988), 3–7 and Joyce G. Small, M.D., et al., "Electroconvulsive Treatment Compared With Lithium in the Management of Manic States," *Archives of General Psychiatry*, 45 (1988), 727–32.

Page 112: "A survey of hospital patients . ." See James W. Thompson, M.D., and Jack D. Blaine, M.D., "Use of ECT in the United States in 1975 and 1980," *American Journal of Psychiatry*, 144 (1987), 557–62.

Page 113: "Studies conclude that sometimes . . ." See Donald W. Black, M.D., et al., "Treatment of Mania: A Naturalistic Study of Electroconvulsive Therapy Versus Lithium in 438 Patients," *Journal of Clinical Psychiatry*, 48 (1987), 132–39.

Page 113: "Like many medical procedures . . ." Barry Alan Kramer, M.D., "Practice Patterns of Electroconvulsive Therapy: A California Perspective (1984)," *Convulsive Therapy*, 2 (1986), 239–44.

Page 114: "Thus, researchers are always learning . . ." For example, see Harold A. Sackeim, Ph.D., "Effects of Electrode Placement on the Efficacy of Titrated, Low-Dose ECT," *American Journal of Psychiatry*, 144 (1987), 1449–55.

Page 114: "As many as 60 percent . . ." See Mary Jean McKelvy, M.A., "Substance Abuse and Mental Illness, Double Trouble," *Journal of Psychosocial Nursing and Mental Health Services*, 25 (1987), 20–25.

Page 115: "For the manic or psychotic . . ." See Louis H. Reich, M.D., et al., "Excessive Alcohol Use in Manic-Depressive Illness," *American Journal of Psychiatry*, 131 (1974), 82–86.

Page 115: "As one doctor puts it . . ." See Edward J. Khantzian, M.D., "The Self-Medication Hypothesis of Addictive Disorders: Focus on Heroin and Cocaine Dependence," *American Journal of Psychiatry*, 142 (1985), 1259–64.

Page 115: "In one study, 70 . . ." See "Sleep Patterns Scrutinized as Depression Therapy," *JAMA*, Feb. 19, 1988.

Page 115: "Although rarely used and . . ." See Donald R. Ross, M.D., "The Psychiatric Uses of Cold Wet Sheet Packs," *American Journal of Psychiatry*, 145 (1988), 242–45.

Chapter 6: Finding Professional Help

Page 142: "Even after early episodes . . ." Two experts helped explain this issue to us: Mauricio Tohen, M.D., clinical director, Psychosis Program, McLean Hospital, and Joseph Lipinski, M.D., director of Mental Health Research Center, McLean Hospital.

Page 143: "Dr. Robert Benson . . ." Robert Benson, M.D., "The Forgotten Treatment Modality in Bipolar Illness: Psychotherapy." *Diseases of the Nervous System*, 36 (1975), 634–37.

Page 143: "It's a documented fact . . ." These studies are in Deborah F. Holden, Ph.D., and Richard R. J. Lewine, Ph.D., "How Families Evaluate Mental Health Resources, and the Effects of Illness," *Schizophrenia Bulletin*, 8 (1982), 626–33, and Kayla F. Bernheim, Ph.D., and Tim Switalski, "Mental Health Staff and Patient's Relatives: How They View Each Other," *Hospital and Community Psychiatry*, 39 (1988), 63–68.

Page 147: "Some psychoanalysts are M.D.'s . . ." A psychoanalyst is a special kind of therapist, but not to be confused with psychotherapist. Psychoanalysts may be doctors who have completed a four-year residency in psychiatry, then enrolled for years of training at a psychoanalytic institute. Not all psychoanalysts are doctors or have this training. Anyone can call himself a "psychoanalyst." The term is not regulated by law, as is "psychiatrist." Some psychoanalysts are more experienced and more schooled than others, especially those trained under the auspices of the American Psychoanalytic Association (APA), its state affiliates and training institutions. Most psychoanalysts trained by the APA are doctors who have completed residency in psychiatry. Some are Ph.D.'s in psychology. The APA training entails classes in psychoanalytic theory and technique, submitting to personal analysis, and conducting extensive analysis of three patients under the supervision of an experienced analyst. At the end of this education, which requires six to ten years, a psychoanalyst receives certification from the APA.

Page 147: "While some of these people . . ." For information about the various professions, we contacted the relevant organizations: American Board of Medical Specialties (1 Rotary Center, Suite 805, Evanston, IL, 60201), The American Board of Psychiatry and Neurology, Inc. (500 Lake Cook Road, Suite 335, Deerfield, IL 60015), American Board of Professional Psychology, Inc. (2100 East Broadway, Suite 313, Columbia, MO, 65201), and National Association of Social Workers (7981 Eastern Avenue, Silver Spring, MD 20910).

Page 149: "Declares a special article . . ." Toksoz B. Karasu, M.D., "Psychotherapy and Pharmacolotherapy: Toward an Integrative Model," *American Journal of Psychiatry*, 139 (1982), 1102–11.

Page 152: "A report in the *American Journal* . . ." Bernard D. Beitman, M.D., "The Movement Toward Integrating the Psychotherapies: An Overview," *American Journal of Psychiatry*, 146 (1989), 138–47.

Page 152: "Researchers estimate that one third . . ." See Barry E. Wolfe and Marvin R. Goldfried, "Research on Psychotherapy Integration: Recommendations and Conclusions from an NIMH Workshop," *Journal of Consulting and Clinical Psychology*, 56 (1988), 448–51.

Page 153: "A special article in *The American* . . ." Beitman article, "The Movement Toward Integrating . . ." 146 (1989), 138–47.

Page 153: "Some experts go so far . . ." Irene Elkin, Ph.D., et al., "Conceptual and Methodological Issues in Comparative Studies of Psychotherapy and Pharmacolotherapy, I: Active Ingredients and Mechanisms of Change, *American Journal of Psychiatry*, 145 (1988), 909–17.

Page 153: "The therapies we describe here . . ." *Depression and Mania* offers more detailed descriptions of the principles and techniques of cognitive, behavioral, and interpersonal therapies. They're also discussed in Toksoz B. Karasu, M.D., "Psychotherapies: An Overview," *American Journal of Psychiatry*, 134 (1977), 851–62.

Page 158: "Some doctors think group therapy . . ." The benefits of group therapy are described in Fred R. Volkmar, M.D., et al., "Group Therapy in the Management of Manic-Depressive Illness," *American Journal of Psychotherapy*, 35 (1981), 226–34, Lawson Wulsin, M.D., et al., "Group Therapy in Manic-Depressive Illness," *American Journal of Psychotherapy*, 42 (1988), 263–70, and "Marc Galanter, M.D., "Zealous Self-Help Groups as Adjuncts to Psychiatric Treatment: A Study of Recovery, Inc.," *American Journal of Psychiatry*, 145 (1988), 1248–53.

Page 159: "The 'duty to protect' precedent . . ." See Robert Weinstock, M.D., "Confidentiality and the New Duty to Protect: The Therapist's Dilemma," *Hospital and Community Psychiatry*, 39 (1988), 607–9.

Chapter 8: Hospitals to Halfway Houses and Beyond
Page 185: " 'Stigma has become . . .' " *McLean Review*, Belmont, MA, 1989.

Page 186: "The film *Frances* . . ." In psychosurgery, also called a lobotomy or leucotomy, the frontal lobe of the cerebrum is cut into or across to control certain behavior. In the 1950s, doctors in state hospitals used this technique frequently. Yet while it calmed agitation, it also caused severe personality problems. It's no longer used in psychiatry.

Psychiatric-hospital history is described by Nancy Andreasen, M.D., *The Broken Brain, The Biological Revolution in Psychiatry* (New York: Perennial Library, 1984).

Page 186: "The history of mental-health care . . ." H. H. Goldman, *Review of General Psychiatry* (Los Altos, CA: Lange Medical Publications, 1984).

Page 186: "In 1908, Clifford Beers . . ." Clifford A. Beers, *A Mind that Found Itself* (London: Longmans Green, 1908).

Page 187: "The new agency's mission . . ." Information from the National Institute of Mental Health, Public Inquiries Branch, Room 15C-05, 5600 Fishers Lane, Rockville, MD 20857.

Page 187: "By 1980, the number of mentally ill . . ." Raymond M. Glasscote, et al., *The Uses of Psychiatry in Smaller General Hospitals*

(Joint Information Service of the American Psychiatric Association and the National Mental Health Association, Washington, D.C., 1983).

Page 188: "Untangling these problems usually . . ." *McLean Hospital Neuropsychiatry Unit Information for Patients and Families* (Belmont, MA, 1987).

Page 188: "Most patients, unless they have extraordinary . . ." Trevor R. Hadley, Ph.D., "Accreditation, Certification, and the Quality of Care in State Hospitals," *Hospital and Community Psychiatry*, 39 (1988), 739–42.

Page 189: "Public-funding sources such as . . ." Walt Bogdanich, "Prized by Hospitals, Accreditation Hides Perils Patients Face," *Wall Street Journal*, Oct. 12, 1988.

Page 189: "Using a pass-or-fail . . ." Jack Zusman, M.D., "Quality Assurance in Mental Health Care," *Hospital and Community Psychiatry*, 39 (1988), 1286–90.

Page 189: "Over the past twenty years . . ." Raymond M. Glasscote, et al., *The Uses of Psychiatry in Smaller General Hospitals.* (Joint Information Service of the American Psychiatric Association and the National Mental Health Association, Washington, D.C., 1983).

Page 190: "A recent study suggests . . ." Philpp E. Bornstein, M.D., "The Uses of Restraints on a General Psychiatric Unit," *Journal of Clinical Psychiatry*, 46 (1985), 175–78.

Page 190: "Yet other experts cite . . ." Interview with Alexander Vuckovic, M.D., McLean Hospital.

Page 190: "Researchers have discovered that . . ." Seth Cohen, M.D., et al., "Hospitalization Effect in Acute Mania," *General Hospital Psychiatry*, 10 (1988), 138–41.

Page 191: "Forensic hospitals are for . . ." Interview with Dr. Robert Phillips, director, Whiting Forensic Institute, Middletown, CT.

Page 192: "For many with mental illness, the emergency room . . ." Interviews with Kathleen D. Thayer, R.N., M.S.C.S., psychiatric nurse clinician, Charlotte Hungerford Hospital, Torrington, CT, and Lynn Baglila, R.N., emergency-room staff nurse, New Milford Hospital, New Milford, CT.

Page 193: "Some professionals feel that . . ." Interview with Drs. Benjamin Liptzin and Lloyd Sederer, McLean Hospital, Belmont, MA.

Page 193: "The issue of patient rights becomes . . ." Paul S. Applebaum, M.D., "The Right to Refuse Treatment With Antipsychotic Medications: Retrospect and Prospect," *American Journal of Psychiatry*, 145 (1988), 413–19.

Page 194: "In many states, patients . . ." Although the courts have differed considerably in their decisions concerning patients who refuse medication, the patient-rights movement has produced a healthy side benefit. By refusing, and thus initiating a review of treatment, patients have prompted doctors to reevaluate their prescriptions and sometimes improve a treatment protocol.

Page 194: "A study of patients who refused medication . . ." Paul S. Applebaum, M.D., "The Right to Refuse Treatment With Antipsychotic Medications: Retrospect and Prospect." *American Journal of Psychiatry,* 145 (1988), 413–19.

Page 194: "What follows are the formal . . ." This list of patient rights is given to all involuntary patients pursuant to Washington State law. It was distributed by Sacred Heart Hospital, Spokane, WA.

Page 196: "Closely linked to a patient's civil rights . . ." *McLean Hospital Neuropsychiatry Unit Information for Patients and Families.* McLean materials are used as a model because they describe a level of care and treatment considered among the best in the country.

Page 196: "According to the National Center . . ." *Washington Times,* Aug. 1, 1989.

Page 197: " 'The problem,' states the director . . ." William Anthony, director, Boston University Center for Psychiatric Rehabilitation, reported by Mark Feinberg in "Being Normal," *Boston Globe,* Nov. 20, 1988.

Page 197: "An important difference is how . . ." Michael R. Madow, M.D., "Issues in the Diagnosis and Treatment of Adolescents in a General Hospital Inpatient Unit," *General Hospital Psychiatry,* 10 (1988), 122–28.

Page 197: "Conditions are changing . . ." Advocacy groups are now tackling the issue of empty weekends, time when patients stay in a facility (and pay) even though daily programs are offered only Monday through Friday. Most patients' insurance coverage allows a limited number of hospital days a year (for example, sixty), and to have over 25 percent of this time spent on blank, weekend days is a waste of resources and valuable treatment time.

Page 197: "One noteworthy sign of progress . . ." Mark Feinberg, "Being Normal," *Boston Globe,* Nov. 20, 1988, and Karen V. Unger, "Rehabilitation Through Education: A University-based Continuing Education Program for Young Adults with Psychiatric Disabilities on a University Campus," *Psychosocial Rehabilitation Journal,* 10 (1987), 37–49.

Page 198: "Health-care costs are regulated . . ." Private hospitals are not only available to those who can pay their fees. Arrangements for lower pay schedules can be made with a hospital's patient-account office, and anyone wanting treatment should talk with them.

Page 198: "Patients and families faced . . ." James P. Koch, J.D., *Health Care Insurance and Psychiatric Illness* (DRADA Educational/ Information Committee: Baltimore, MD, 1989).

Page 198: "Here's a comparison . . ." "Ischemic" refers to either localized tissue damage from a loss of oxygen due to a disruption in arterial blood flow or to coronary-artery disease in general. This chart appeared in *The New York Times*, Feb. 9, 1989.

Page 199: "Mentally ill patients may qualify . . ." *Families and Professionals: Partners in Recovery*. A Curriculum Concerning the Family's Role and Perspective in the Treatment and Care of Individuals With Severe Psychiatric Illness, Connecticut Alliance for the Mentally Ill, 1989.

Page 199: "The other Social Security program . . ." *U.S. Department of Health and Human Services*, Social Security Administration, Washington, D.C.

Page 200: "Wills, and trusts, have to be . . ." Theresa M. Varnet, "Future Financial Planning," *Exceptional Parent*, Nov./Dec. 1988. On the same subject, Ms. Varnet recommends an article by Darcy Chamberlain, *Illinois Law Review*, July 1987, and an article by Carol Mooney, "Discretionary Trusts: An Estate Plan to Supplement Public Assistance for Disabled Persons," *Arizona Law Review*, 25 (1983), 939.

Page 201: "The question 'Where next?' . . ." Sources for information on residence treatment include Sacred Heart Hospital, Spokane, WA; Hartford Hospital Transitional Living Facility, Hartford, CT; the Maple Avenue Apartment Program, Hartford, CT; Wild Acres Inns, Inc., Woburn, MA.

Page 202: "The National Alliance for the Mentally Ill . . ." Ann Malaspina, "A Powerful Alliance," *Boston Globe*, May 21, 1989, Erica E. Goode, "When Mental Illness Hits Home," *U.S. News & World Report*, April 24, 1989, and National Alliance for the Mentally Ill, 2102 Wilson Boulevard, Arlington, VA 22201. (703-524-7600).

Chapter 10: Twists and Turns
Page 229: "While less than 1 . . . " It is impossible to make an absolute correlation between suicide and manic depression, so figures are in ranges. This range came from *Depression and Mania*; Jan Fawcett, M.D.,

et al., "Clinical Predictors of Suicide in Patients with Major Affective Disorders: A Controlled Prospective Study," *American Journal of Psychiatry*, 144 (1987), 35–40; and Donald W. Black, M.D., et al., "Effect of Psychosis on Suicide Risk in 1,593 Patients with Unipolar and Bipolar Affective Disorders," *American Journal of Psychiatry*, 145 (1988), 849–52.

Page 229: "In one study . . . " Peter R. Roy-Byrne, M.D., et al., "Suicide and the Course of Illness in Major Affective Disorder," *Journal of Affective Disorders*, 15 (1988), 1–8.

Page 230: "This connection points to . . . " The family connection in manic depression has been the subject of much research and reported in John Rice, Ph.D., et al., "The Familial Transmission of Bipolar Illness," *Archives of General Psychiatry*, 44 (1987), 441–47; David J. Miklowitz, Ph.D., et al., "Family Factors and the Course of Bipolar Affective Disorder," *Archives of General Psychiatry*, 45 (1988), 225–31.

Page 230: "Again, the Old Order . . . " The Amish study dealing with suicide is Janice A. Egeland, Ph.D., et al., "Suicide and Family Loading for Affective Disorders," *JAMA*, 254 (1985), 915–18.

Page 231: "One study compared . . . " Alec Roy, M.D., "Family History of Suicide," *Archives of General Psychiatry*, 40 (1983), 971–74.

Page 231: "Other studies comparing identical . . . " Ming T. Tsuang, M.D., "Risk of Suicide in the Relatives of Schizophrenics, Manics, Depressives and Controls," *Journal of Clinical Psychiatry*, 44 (1983), 396–400.

Page 231: "Researchers have columns . . . " Aaron T. Beck, M.D., and Robert A. Steer, "Clinical Predictors of Eventual Suicide: a Five- to Ten-Year Prospective Study of Suicide Attempters," *Journal of Affective Disorders*, 17 (1989), 203–9.

Page 231: "This presuicide depression . . . " This bleakness is described in detail in *Depression and Mania*, p. 70.

Page 232: "The patient with . . . " See Donald Black, M.D., et al., "Effect of Psychosis on Suicide Risk."

Page 232: "Patients from broken . . . " See Jiri Modestin, M.D., and Walter Kopp, "Study on Suicide in Depressed Inpatients," *Journal of Affective Disorders*, 15 (1988), 157–62.

Page 232: "The lives of people . . . " See Jan Fawcett, M.D., "Clinical Predictors of Suicide . . ."

Page 232: "There is the 'risk-taker' . . . " These two types are described in *Depression and Mania*, p. 72.

Page 233: "All these rise and . . . " Studies on the effects of circadian rhythms, including sleeping habits, are reported in Eunice Corfman, *Science Reports: Depression, Manic Depressive Illness, and Biological Rhythms* (Bethesda, MD: National Institute of Mental Health), 1982, and *Depression and Mania*, p. 312.

Page 234: "Researchers have discovered . . . " See *Depression and Mania*, p. 106.

Page 234: "A newspaper story . . . " SADs has been researched and written about at length by Dr. Norman Rosenthal, Clinical Psychobiology Branch, National Institutes of Health. His findings have appeared in Norman Rosenthal, M.D., et al., "Seasonal Affective Disorder," *Archives of General Psychiatry*, 41 (1984), 72–80; Thomas A. Wehr, M.D., and Norman E. Rosenthal, M.D., "Seasonality and Affective Illness," *American Journal of Psychiatry*, 146 (1989), 829–39. The newspaper story about this research was in *The Washington Post*, June 12, 1981.

Page 235: "Doctors say that . . . " These seasonal influences are discussed by P. A. Carney, et al., "Bipolar Patients Taking Lithium Have Increased Dark Adaptation Threshold Compared with Controls," *Pharmacopsychiatry*, 21 (1988), 117–20.

Page 235: "These psychiatrists attribute . . . " Wehr and Rosenthal, "Seasonality and Affective Illness," raise the issue of psychiatrists' attitudes.

Page 235: "In the nineteenth century . . . " Reports about past and present "mad artists" are in Nancy C. Andreasen, M.D., and Ira D. Glick, "Bipolar Affective Disorder and Creativity: Implications and Clinical Management," *Comprehensive Psychiatry*, Vol. 29, No. 3, (1988), pp. 207–17, and Nancy C. Andreasen, M.D., "Creativity and Psychiatric Illness," *Psychiatric Annals*, 8:3 (1978), 113–19.

Page 236: "A survey of more recent . . . " Kay R. Jamison, Ph.D., "Mood Disorders and Patterns of Creativity in British Writers and Artists," *Psychiatry*, 52 (1989), 125–34.

Page 236: "Scientists first studied . . . " The first study is thought to be C. Lombroso, *The Man of Genius* (London: Walter Scott, 1891).

Page 236: "While doctors find less . . . " Nancy C. Andreasen, M.D., "Creativity and Mental Illness: Prevalence Rates in Writers and Their First-Degree Relatives," *American Journal of Psychiatry*, 144 (1987), 1288–92.

Page 236: "These traits are documented . . . " Hypergraphia is mentioned in *Review of General Psychiatry*, Howard H. Goldman, Ph.D. (Los Altos, CA: Lange Medical Publications, 1984).

Page 236: "The affective illness/creativity junction. . . " Andreasen has written extensively on this subject. She reports on this study in "Creativity and Mental Illness."

Page 237: "That probe of fifteen . . . " Nancy C. Andreasen, M.D., and Arthur Canter, Ph.D., "The Creative Writer: Psychiatric Symptoms and Family History," *Comprehensive Psychiatry*, 15 (1974), 123–31.

Page 237: "She discovered that 38 . . . " Kay R. Jamison, Ph.D., "Mood Disorders and Patterns of Creativity in British Writers and Artists."

Page 237: "The intense creativity . . . " Kay R. Jamison, Ph.D., et al., "Clouds and Silver Linings: Positive Experiences Associated with Primary Affective Disorders," *American Journal of Psychiatry*, 137 (1980), 198–202.

Page 238: "Unlike previous research . . . " Ruth Richards, et al., "Creativity in Manic-Depressives, Cyclothymes, Their Normal Relatives, and Control Subjects," *Journal of Abnormal Psychology*, 97 (1988), 281–88.

Page 238: "She concluded, 'Families . . . ' " Nancy C. Andreasen, M.D., "Creativity and Mental Illness: Prevalence Rates in Writers and Their First-Degree Relatives."

Page 239: "Researchers have detected it . . . " Hagop S. Akiskal, M.D., et al., "Affective Disorders in Referred Children and Younger Siblings of Manic-Depressives," *Archives of General Psychiatry* 42 (1985), 996–1003.

Page 239: "Recent reports estimate . . . " Michael Strober, Ph.D., et al., "A Family Study of Bipolar I Disorder in Adolescence," *Journal of Affective Disorders*, 15 (1988), 255–68.

Page 239: "Thus researchers are devoting . . . " William J. Chambers, M.D., et al., "The Assessment of Affective Disorders in Children and Adolescents by Semistructured Interview," *Archives of General Psychiatry*, 42 (1985), 696–702.

Page 240: "In younger children, the mania . . . " Symptoms and age of onset are discussed in detail in Hagop S. Akiskal, M.D., "Affective Disorders in Referred Children and Younger Siblings of Manic-Depressives."

Page 240: "In testing adolescents . . . " These questions from the Diagnostic Interview for Children and Adolescents, Parent and Child Versions (Herjanic and Reich, 1982) appeared in Gabrielle A. Carlson, M.D., and Javad H. Kashani, "Manic Symptoms in a Non-Referred Adolescent Population," *Journal of Affective Disorders*, 15 (1988), 219–26.

Page 241: "In a study of more than four hundred . . . " Oscar G. Bukstein, M.D., et al., "Comorbidity of Substance Abuse and Other Psychiatric Disorders in Adolescents," *American Journal of Psychiatry*, 146 (1989), 1131–41.

Page 242: "They also recommend psychotherapy . . . " J. John Mann, ed., *Phenomenology of Depressive Illness, The Depressive Illness Series, Vol. 1* (New York: Human Sciences Press, 1988).

Page 242: "And just as teenagers . . . " *Depression and Mania*, p. 592.

Page 243: "Studies indicate that 90 percent . . . " Ramzy Yassa, M.D., et al., "Prevalence of Bipolar Disorder in a Psychogeriatric Population," *Journal of Affective Disorders*, 14 (1988), 197–201.

Page 243: "One study of sixty-seven . . . " This study and others were reported in *Depression and Mania*, p. 597.

Page 243: "In a study of 217 . . . " Ramzy Yassa, M.D. "Prevalence of Bipolar Disorder. . . "

Page 243: "Mania in older people . . . " *Depression and Mania*, p. 597.

Page 244: "They raise similar theories . . . " *Depression and Mania*, p. 598.

Page 245: "We interviewed them . . . " This group is a great resource and support organization: The Depression and Related Affective Disorders Association (DRADA), Meyer 4–181, 600 N. Wolfe Street, Baltimore, MD 21205.

INDEX

Page numbers beginning with **257** refer to appendixes and notes.

A

Academy of Certified Social Workers (ACSW), 152
acetylcholine, 65, 278
acne, 98
adolescents:
  drug abuse among, 197
  manic depression in, 44, 48, 49, 229, 239, 240–242
  as mental patients, 196–198, 199
affective disorders:
  in Amish community, 48–49
  as chronic condition, 215
  creativity and, 236–237
  diagnosis of, 240, 242
  emotional resilience and, 65
  family history and, 57, 62, 64
  "high risk" group for, 237
  manic depression as, 46, 48–49
  suicide rate for, 229, 230, 231
  types of, 53–57
agoraphobia, 45
agranulocytosis, 116
akathisia, 102, 103, 110, 116
akinesia, 116
Akineton, 102
Al-Anon, 192
Alcohol, Drug Abuse and Mental Health Administration, 147, 257

Alcoholics Anonymous (AA), 192
alcoholism:
  cyclothymia and, 55
  depression and, 241, 248
  in dual-diagnosis patients, 114, 160, 193
  manic depression and, 40–41, 48, 63, 142, 160, 230, 241, 246, 249
  self-medication and, 114, 115
  stigma of, 185
  suicide and, 230, 232
Alison (manic depressive), 246–247
allergic reactions, 100
"all or nothing" thoughts, 155
alogia, 116
alprazolam, 103
Alzheimer's disease, 242
amantadine, 102
amenorrhea, 116
American Board of Medical Specialties (ABMS), 148–149
American Board of Professional Psychology, 151
American Journal of Psychiatry, 111, 146, 149, 152, 153
American Psychoanalytic Association (APA), 284
Amish community:
  affective disorders in, 48–49
  manic depression in, 48–49, 276, 277
  suicide rate in, 230–231
amitriptyline, 110
amoxapine, 109–110
amphetamines, 57, 108, 114

Anafranil, 110
analytic therapy, 150
Anderson, Dr., 89, 126–127, 129, 130–132, 138
Andreasen, Nancy, 65, 236–237, 238
angioedema, 116
anhedonia, 116, 117
anhidrosis, 116
anorgasmia, 116
antianxiety drugs, 92, 102, 103–104, 193, 242
anticholinergic side effects, 109, 116
anticonvulsants, 99–101
  as drug family, 92
  lithium vs., 99
  side effects of, 100
  types of, 99–101
antidepressants, 106–111
  for children, 242
  as drug family, 9
  effectiveness of, 106–107, 187
  lithium vs., 106
  manic episodes triggered by, 107
  market for, 106
  as monoamine oxidase inhibitors (MAOIs), 107–108, 109, 110, 216–217
  prescription of, 55
  rapid cycling aggravated by, 54
  research on, 11
  second-generation, 107, 110–111
  side effects of, 57, 108, 109, 110, 111
  tricyclic (TCAs), 107, 108–110
antipsychotics, 101–106
  for children, 242
  as drug family, 92
  effectiveness of, 101
  lithium vs., 101
  side effects of, 101–102, 242
  TD (tardive dyskinesia) as side effect of, 101, 103, 104–106
  types of, 102–104
anxiety, 45–46, 108, 110, 111, 239, 250
  drugs used for, 92, 102, 103–104, 193, 242
apartments, supervised, 201
aphasia, 116
arbitrary inferences, 155
Aristotle, 235

arrhythmia, 116
Artane, 102
Asendin, 109–110
assumptions, false, 154
asylums, insane, 186
ataxia, 116
Ativan, 104
attention-deficit disorder (ADD), 239, 242
attorneys, 194
Aventyl, 109, 110
Axel (Mark's friend), 168, 169, 171, 174, 175

B

Balzac, Honoré de, 238
barbiturates, 103, 106, 113
Beck Depression Inventory, 275
Beers, Clifford, 186
behavior:
  abnormal, 156
  alteration of, 47–48, 156–157
  dangerous, 190
  disorders of, 47
  learned, 156
  monitoring of, 143
  obsessive-compulsive, 111, 232
  self-destructive, 46
behavioral disinhibition, 99–100
behavioral therapy, 150, 152, 156–157
Benadryl, 102
Benson, Robert, 143
benzodiazepines, 103–104
benztropine, 102
Berlioz, Hector, 235
Berryman, John, 236
biofeedback, 150
biperiden, 102
bipolar disorders:
  depressive and manic episodes of, 50
  diagnosis of, 245
  mild forms of, 49
  onset of, 243
  primary, 44
  psychotherapy for, 143
  sleeping patterns of, 233–234
  type I, 54, 56
  type II, 54, 55, 56, 234
  types of, 53–57
  see also manic depression

Blake, William, 235
blepharospasm, 104
blood diseases, 57
blood pressure, 100, 107, 108, 109
blood tests, 57, 100
"blues," 240
"board certified" doctors, 148, 149
"board eligible" doctors, 148
body language, 72
bradycardia, 116
bradykinesia, 116
brain:
    chemistry of, 65, 97, 243–244,
        278
    injuries to, 116, 188, 242
    organic disorders of, 243
    seizures of, 112, 113
    surgery for, 91, 96, 195–196
breathing, rapid, 109
Broken Brain, The (Andreasen), 65
bronchodilators, 57
bulimia, 111
bupropion, 111
business investments, unsound, 59
buying sprees, 59

C

Cade, John, 91, 95–96, 98
caffeine pills, 32
Calan, 100–101
calcium channel blockers, 100–101
Camberwell Family Interview, 63
carbamazepine, 99–100, 103, 246
carbohydrates, 234
catatonia, 59, 116, 246
catecholamine hypothesis, 278
Center for Psychiatric Rehabilitation,
    197–198
"cheese reaction," 107–108
Cheever, John, 237
children:
    abuse of, 159
    adopted, 277
    antidepressants for, 242
    antipsychotics for, 242
    anxiety in, 242
    delusions in, 242
    depression in, 242
    hallucinations in, 242
    lithium prescribed for, 242

    manic depression in, 239–241, 242,
        277
    psychiatrists for, 149
    schizophrenia in, 242
    therapy for, 242
chlordiazepoxide, 103
chlorpromazine, 178, 179, 183, 214,
    215
chorea, 117
Chris (Mark's father):
    analytical personality of, 25
    Mark's illness as viewed by, 25, 30,
        33, 34–35, 80–82, 85, 137–138,
        139, 163, 176, 213, 226, 253
    Mark's refusal to talk to, 20, 23
    Mark's relationship with, 28, 33–34,
        36, 77, 121, 129, 136–137, 224,
        253–254, 255–256
    Vietnam experience of, 29, 71–72,
        179
circadian rhythms, 232–234
clomiprimine, 110
clonazepam, 104
clorazepate, 104
clozapine, 101, 103, 105
Clozaril, 101, 103, 105
cocaine, 28, 51, 57, 114, 185, 241
Cogentin, 102
cognitive therapy, 150, 153–155, 157
Coleridge, Samuel Taylor, 235
community hospital, 187, 189–190
Community Mental Health Centers Act,
    187
concentration, diminished, 60, 98, 244,
    246, 252
conditioning, behavioral, 156
conduct, disorders of, 197
constipation, 102, 109, 116
consultation-liaison psychiatrists, 148
corticosteroids, 57
Cousin Bette (Balzac), 238
Covington Lodge, 207–209, 211
crack, 18, 51
cramps, stomach, 98, 110, 241
creativity:
    depression and, 237, 238
    madness and, 44, 229, 235–239
    moods and, 236
    schizophrenia and, 236, 237
criminals, habitual, 46
cyclothymia, 55–56, 238

D

death, obsession with, 60–61
decongestants, 108
delusions, 47–48
  in children, 242
  mood congruent, 56–57, 59, 61
  mood incongruent, 56, 59, 61
  as symptom, 243
  see also hallucinations
dementia, 187
Depakene, 100
Depakote, 100
depression:
  alcoholism and, 241, 248
  alternation of mania and, 45, 50, 52–
    53, 54, 107, 115, 244
  as aspect of manic depression, 44,
    48–49
  childhood origins of, 157
  in children, 242
  "classic," 43, 109
  creativity and, 237, 238
  drug abuse and, 241
  DSM-III-R criteria for, 60–61
  in elderly, 242, 243
  electroconvulsive therapy (ECT) for,
    112–114
  inactivity and, 248–249
  interpersonal therapy (IPT) for, 155
  as learned behavior, 156
  listlessness of, 156
  Mark's episodes of, 252
  in men vs. women, 49, 55
  moderate, 111
  organic basis of, 57, 61, 278
  physical exercise as antidote to,
    246
  postpartum, 233
  premenstrual, 233
  psychotherapy for, 142
  psychotic, 48, 61, 101, 105
  remission of, 61
  sleeping patterns affected by, 233
  suicide caused by, 48, 221, 229,
    231–232
  "summer," 234
  thinking patterns of, 154, 155, 157
  unipolar, 45, 50, 54–55, 229, 231–
    232
  "winter," 234

Depression and Mania (Georgotas and
    Cancro, eds.), 154
Depressive and Related Affective Disor-
    ders Association, 159, 245
dermatitis, 100
desipramine, 109, 110
Desyrel, 111, 117
diagnosis:
  of affective disorders, 240, 242
  of bipolar disorders, 245
  dual, 114, 160, 193, 241
  hospital procedures for, 187–188
  lithium as aid to, 97, 246
  of manic depression, 44–45, 53, 57–
    64, 73, 97, 239–241, 242, 246,
    248
  scales for, 61–62, 274–275
diagnostic imaging, 187
Diagnostic Interview for Adolescents
    and Children, 240–241
Diamond, Ronald, 93
Diane (Mark's mother):
  anger of, 21
  as businesswoman, 87, 88, 121, 161
  concessions to Mark's behavior made
    by, 120–121
  control needed by, 68, 124
  deception avoided by, 128, 254–255
  denial or "magical thinking" by, 69,
    79, 84–89, 123, 139, 165, 167,
    209, 253
  emotions shared by, 254–255
  friends' advice to, 68–69, 84–86, 128
  grief expressed by, 34, 38, 79, 86,
    170, 177
  guilt felt by, 71–72, 82, 89, 121–122,
    137, 165, 254
  I Ching used by, 86, 87, 88, 130, 163
  information sought by, 21, 72–73
  insomnia of, 36, 72
  manic depression as viewed by, 42,
    68–69, 254–255
  Mark's arrest and reaction of, 19–20
  Mark's doctors as viewed by, 41–42,
    72–75, 89, 130–132
  Mark's relationship with, 23–25, 32,
    36, 68–70, 75, 173, 175, 210–
    211, 226, 255–256
  marriage of, 26–27, 255
  as mother, 71–72, 82, 89, 121–122,
    137

religious convictions of, 87, 220
sentimental streak of, 34
textbook consulted by, 68, 86
therapy considered by, 86, 131
diazepam, 103, 104
dietary deficiencies, 187
diphenhydramine, 102
diplopia, 117
discipline problems, 239
Diseases of the Nervous System, 143
distractibility, 58
divalproex sodium, 100
divorce, 243
dizziness, 100, 102, 109
dopamine, 51, 65, 278
doxepin, 110
dreams, 233–234
drowsiness, 100, 102, 103, 116
drug abuse:
  among adolescents, 197
  cyclothymia and, 55
  depression and, 241
  in dual-diagnosis patients, 114, 160,
    193
  mania and, 241
  manic depression and, 46, 48, 51,
    57, 142, 160, 230, 241–242
  Mark suspected of, 18–19, 20, 25,
    28, 30, 32–33, 36–37, 41, 67–
    68, 74, 128
  self-medication and, 114–115, 241
  suicide and, 230, 232
drugs:
  absorption of, 93
  addiction to prescription, 103
  blood levels of, 97, 150
  clinical trials for, 94–95
  discontinuation of, 52, 92, 244
  experimental, 94–95
  families of, 92
  interactions between, 95, 99, 101,
    103
  lag time for, 97, 109
  market for, 94–95, 106
  names of, 95
  physiological reactions to, 93, 158
  prescription of, 93
  in psychotherapy, 143, 160
  safety profile for, 193
  side effects of, 92, 95, 116–117, 143,
    144, 160, 246

for suicide attempts, 109, 111, 192
symptoms controlled by, 92, 93
synergistic effect of, 99
see also specific drugs
drug therapy, 91–117
  alternatives to, 111–116
  clinical predictors for, 101
  dangerous behavior treated by, 190
  effectiveness of, 91–93
  group support for, 158
  "holidays" from, 105–106
  hormone regulation and, 278
  for manic depression, 65, 91–117,
    146
  for Mark, 72, 73, 75, 81, 129, 130,
    175–179, 181, 183, 205, 211,
    214, 215, 219, 220, 221, 222,
    225, 227
  metabolism and, 93
  misconceptions about, 186
  modern era of, 91
  in outpatient programs, 190
  as prescribed by licensed doctors,
    147
  psychotherapy vs., 141, 149–150
  refusal of, 92–93, 194, 195
  relapses prevented by, 142
  as reminder of mental illness, 142
  "safety profile" for, 93
  for schizophrenia, 101
  self-medication vs., 114–115, 241
DSM-III-R (Diagnostic and Statistical
    Manual of Mental Disorders), 56,
    273–274
  manic depression as defined by, 57–
    61
"duty to protect" precedent, 159
dysarthria, 117
dysphagia, 117
dysphoria, 117
dystonia, 117
dysuria, 117

E

eating patterns, 46, 123, 125, 129, 130
eclectic therapy, 150, 152, 153, 157
"ecstasy," 242
EEGs (electroencephalograms), 57, 113
Egeland, Janice, 230–231
Elavil, 110

Eldepryl, 108
elderly:
  depression in, 242, 243
  hormonal changes in, 244
  lithium prescribed for, 243
  mania in, 242, 243
  manic depression in, 52, 229, 242–
    244
  neuroleptics for, 243
electroconvulsive therapy (ECT), 59,
    91, 92, 111–114, 150, 186, 195
emergency rooms, 192–193
emotions:
  as affected by manic depression, 142–
    143, 215
  learning of, 156
  resilience of, 65
encephalitis, 243
endocrine lab tests, 188
Enlightenment, 186
epilepsy, 57, 99, 112, 243
estrogen, 233
euthymia, 117
Evan (Mark's grandfather), 26, 40–41
exercise, physical, 246
extrapyramidal, 117
eye movements, involuntary, 104

F

family:
  affective disorders in, 57, 62, 64
  emotional atmosphere of, 63–64, 65,
    144
  health insurance as concern of, 144
  history of mental illness in, 48–49,
    57, 62, 64, 191, 230–231, 276,
    277
  hospitals and cooperation of, 191,
    192
  incidence of suicide in, 230–231
  manic depression in history of, 62–
    64, 238, 276–277
  mental illness and involvement of, 9,
    226
  therapy for, 143–147, 158, 160
Family History Research Diagnostic Cri-
    teria, 62
fatigue, 60, 109
fever, 243
fever therapy, 91

FICA, 199
Fieve, Ronald, 21
"flight of ideas," 46, 58, 238
flu, 243
fluoxetine, 111, 248, 252, 255
fluphenazine, 102, 105
fluvoxamine, 111
Food and Drug Administration (FDA),
    94–95, 96
Foothills Hospital, 39–42
forensic hospitals, 191
Frances, 186
Frank (Mark's grandfather), 27, 32, 34,
    36–37, 39
fraternal twins, 231, 276–277
Fremont Hospital, 36–39
Freud, Sigmund, 186

G

genius, madness and, 44, 229, 235–239
geriatric psychiatrists, 148–149
goal-directed activity, 59
Goethe, Johann Wolfgang von, 235
grandiosity, 47, 58, 100, 157, 238
grief, abnormal, 155
group homes, 181–184, 201–202, 205–
    206
group therapy, 157–159, 191, 192,
    201–202, 218, 220, 255
guilt, 60

H

Halcion, 104
Haldol, 102, 105, 221, 246
halfway houses, 158, 188, 198, 201–
    202, 252
hallucinations, 47–48
  auditory, 47
  in children, 242
  command, 48
  as early warning sign, 239
  mood congruent, 56–57, 59, 61
  mood incongruent, 56, 59, 61
  see also delusions
hallucinogens, 18, 241, 242
haloperidol, 102, 105, 221, 246
Hamilton Depression Scale, 275
Hansen's disease, 185
Harp, Dr., 174, 176–177, 179, 205–
    206

Harvard Medical School, 185
head, twisting of, 104
headaches, 100, 241
head trauma, 57
Health Care Financing Administration
    (HCFA), 189
hearings, judicial, 194
heartbeat, irregular, 102, 103, 116, 117
heart disease, 100, 109, 111, 112, 198–
    199
Helen (Mark's aunt), 40, 174–175
Hemingway, Ernest, 44, 236
heroin, 32, 114
heterocyclic antidepressants, see tricyclic
    antidepressants (TCAs)
Hillview Hospital, 206–207, 209, 211–
    225, 253, 255
Hinckley, John, 191
Holy Cross Hospital, 174–184, 212,
    214
homeless, mental patients as, 186
Hopkins, Gerard Manley, 235
hormones, 115
    circadian rhythms affected by, 233
    in elderly, 244
    imbalance in, 57, 65, 278
hospitals, mental, 185–203
    accreditation of, 145, 189
    admissions to, 212
    community, 187, 189–190
    confidentiality of, 175–176
    "contract" between patients and, 191
    costs of, 198–201
    diagnostic procedures in, 187–188
    effectiveness of, 9
    emergency room of, 192–193
    family's cooperation with, 191, 192
    forensic, 191
    health care in, 185–192, 195
    income of, 198
    inpatient care of, 188, 200
    insurance for, 198–201
    length of stay in, 9, 201
    locked wards of, 39, 144, 174, 179–
        180, 182, 191
    Mark's experiences in, 36–42, 67–75,
        174–184, 211–225
    medical record-keeping by, 189
    monitoring of, 189
    outpatient programs of, 188, 190
    reform of, 186–187

release from, 144, 201–203
research or teaching, 145, 188
staff of, 189, 194
state, 188–189, 206
stigma of, 185–186, 188–189
treatment programs in, 187–188, 192
"humors," 235
hyperactivity, 44, 46, 48–49, 101, 156,
    249
hypergraphia, 47, 236
hypernatremia, 117
hyperphagia, 117
hypersomnia, 60, 108, 117
hypertension, 100, 107, 108, 109
hypomania, 54, 237–238, 240
hyponatremia, 117
hypothyroidism, 98

I

I Ching, 86, 87, 88, 130, 163
"ideas of reference," 47
identical twins, 231, 276–277
imipramine, 110
impotence, 102
Inderal, 102
index episode, 93
inpatient care, 188, 200
insanity, see madness
insomnia, 50, 60, 101, 110, 115, 241,
    249
    terminal, 233
Institute for Living, 206–207
insurance, health:
    family's concern about, 144
    for hospitals, 198–201
    Mark's coverage under, 40, 166, 175,
        182, 206, 212–213, 216, 218–
        219, 255
interpersonal therapy (IPT), 155–156
Iowa Writers' Workshop, 236–237, 238
iproniazid, 107
Irving, John, 237
ischemic heart disease, 198–199
isocarboxazid, 108

J

Jamison, Kay, 237
Joint Commission on Accreditation of
    Healthcare Organizations
    (JCAHO), 189

Joyce, James, 236
judgment, impairment of, 59

K

Katz, David, 51
Keats, John, 44
kidney damage, 97
"kindling theory," 51
King, Bob, 19, 24, 74, 78, 84, 86, 88
Klein, Dr., 74, 75, 81, 82, 84, 85
Klonopin, 104
Kraeplin, Emil, 186

L

lab tests, 188
Lee, Dr., 41–42, 67, 70, 72–75
leprosy, 185
lethargy, 108, 109, 208, 227
Librium, 103
Lifetime Creativity Scale, 238
light therapies:
    "natural spectrum," 116
    research on, 11
listlessness, 116
lithium, 95–99
    anticonvulsants vs., 99
    antidepressants vs., 106
    antipsychotics vs., 101
    blood levels of, 97
    for children, 242
    classification of, 93
    diagnosis aided by, 97, 246
    diet and, 97–98
    discontinuation of, 52, 92, 101
    discovery of, 91, 95–96, 98
    effectiveness of, 96–97, 99, 187, 242
    for elderly patients, 243
    electroconvulsive therapy (ECT) vs.,
        113
    hand tremors caused by, 98, 100,
        181
    maintenance levels of, 158, 246, 249,
        250
    Mark's treatment with, 72, 73, 75,
        81, 129, 130, 175, 176, 177,
        178, 181, 183, 205, 211, 215,
        255
    overdoses of, 97–98
    prescription of, 42, 55, 141, 245
    psychotherapeutic support for, 143

relapses reduced by, 95
responsiveness to, 57
side effects of, 92, 98–99, 100, 181,
    246
U.S. approval for, 96
weight gain from, 98, 246
Lithium Information Center, 98–99
liver damage, 100
logorrhea, 117
lorazepam, 104
Lowell, Robert, 236, 237
Loxapine, 102
loxitane, 102
LSD, 18, 241
Ludiomil, 110
lunacy, 22, 186

M

McLean Hospital, 185
madness:
    creativity and, 44, 229, 235–239
    as term, 22, 43
magnetic-resonance scans, 57, 188
magnification, 155
Manchester Nurse Rating Scales for De-
        pression and Mania, 275
mania:
    acute, 100
    alternation of depression and, 45, 50,
        52–53, 54, 107, 115, 244
    antidepressants and, 107
    as aspect of manic depression, 44,
        49–50
    automatic thoughts in, 154–155
    as behavioral problem, 156
    childhood origins of, 157
    destructive, 246–247
    drug abuse and, 241
    DSM-III-R criteria for, 58–60
    duration of, 50
    in elderly, 242, 243
    electroconvulsive therapy (ECT) for,
        113, 114
    hyperactivity as symptom of, 44, 46,
        48–49, 101, 156, 249
    hypo-, 54, 237–238, 240
    illness as cause of, 243
    interpersonal therapy (IPT) for, 155
    Mark's episodes of, 176, 225, 227
    in men vs. women, 243

mixed, 53
myths about, 229
organic basis of, 57
psychotherapy for, 142
psychotic, 59
remission of, 59–60
sleeping patterns affected by, 50, 233
stress and, 249–250
suicide caused by, 232
manic depression:
  in adolescents, 44, 48, 49, 229, 239,
    240–242
  in adopted children, 277
  as affective disorder, 46, 48–49
  aging and, 52, 242
  alcoholism and, 40–41, 48, 63, 142,
    160, 230, 241, 246, 249
  in Amish community, 48–49, 276, 277
  as amorphous disease, 45, 53–57
  baseline personality as distinct from,
    44, 46
  behavior altered by, 47–48
  "bipolar I," 54, 56
  "bipolar II," 54, 55, 56, 234
  causes of, 64–65
  in children, 239–241, 242, 277
  as chronic illness, 52, 165–166, 215,
    225
  chronological chart of, 63–64
  circadian rhythms of, 232–234
  classic form of, 54
  depression as aspect of, 44, 48–49
  diagnosis of, 44–45, 53, 57–64, 73,
    97, 239–241, 242, 246, 248
  diagnostic scales for, 61–62, 274–275
  dreaming affected by, 233–234
  drug abuse and, 46, 48, 51, 57, 142,
    160, 230, 241–242
  drug therapy for, 65, 91–117, 146
  DSM-III-R criteria for, 57–61
  dual-diagnosis, 160, 241
  early warning signs of, 239
  eating patterns affected by, 46
  in elderly, 52, 229, 242–244
  emotional impact of, 142–143, 215
  episodes of depression vs. mania in,
    45, 50, 52–53, 54, 107, 115,
    244
  family history and, 62–64, 238, 276–
    277
  "flight of ideas" in, 46, 58, 238

genetic origins of, 64, 249, 276–277
grandiosity in, 47, 58, 100, 157, 238
as heterogenous disorder, 64
as "Hydra-headed," 43–44, 49
latency period of, 52–53
level of functioning for, 244, 249
as life-threatening, 93
mania as aspect of, 44, 49–50
median interval between cycles of, 52
in men vs. women, 49, 64
mild form of, 55–56, 238
as mood disorder, 42, 45–46
nature of, 43–65
observation of, 44
onset of, 49–51, 52, 142, 239–244
organic basis of, 57, 64–65, 81, 145,
  146
personal relationships destroyed by,
  239
prognosis for, 160
progression of, 51–52
psychological origin of, 146
rapid cycling in, 54, 99, 100, 107
recovery from, 160, 243, 244–250
referrals for, 145–147, 173, 257–259
remission of, 52, 59–60, 61
research on, 45, 257–259
schizophrenia vs., 45, 49, 56, 57, 59,
  61, 73, 97, 105, 229, 242, 246,
  249
seasonal patterns of, 51, 116, 229,
  234–235
segment of population prone to, 49
sexual activity affected by, 46, 59
single episodes of, 51–52
sleeping patterns affected by, 46, 50,
  58, 232–234
stages of, 244
state organizations for, 267–269
stress and, 50, 51, 62, 243
suicide rate for, 63, 68, 93, 106,
  229–232, 241, 245
"switching" in, 107
symptoms of, 43, 45–49, 57–61,
  146, 244
as term, 43–44
therapy for, 81, 142–143, 145, 150,
  151
triggers for, 50–51
in twins, 276–277
see also depression; mania

manic-depressive individuals:
  cooperation of, 73
  day-to-day lives of, 158, 244–250
  emotional atmosphere at home for,
    63–64, 65, 144
  lack of insight by, 62
  physical appearance of, 47
  profiles of successful, 244–250
  seclusion of, 190–191, 192
  self-discipline needed by, 202
  self-image of, 239
  siblings of, 144
  support groups for, 143, 159, 202–
    203, 261–265, 267–269
  work habits of, 245, 247, 248–249
  see also Mark
Manic State Scale, 275
Manson, Charles, 191
maprotiline, 110
marijuana, 241
Mark:
  academic performance of, 24, 30, 73,
    86, 162, 165, 170–171, 208,
    251, 256
  angels as delusions of, 25–26, 70,
    78–79, 164, 217–218, 219, 222,
    223, 226, 227
  in Arizona, 130, 133, 134, 138–139,
    161, 162–163, 165, 166
  arrest of, 17–20, 39, 41
  assessment of, 213, 215, 217–218
  baseline personality of, 20, 76–78,
    220, 255
  "black moods" of, 133
  childhood of, 29, 71–72, 75–76, 121,
    168, 222
  Christmas celebration for, 121–123
  clothing worn by, 24, 39, 208, 210–
    211, 214
  in Colorado, 17–22, 76–78
  commitments of, 37–42, 172–184,
    211–225, 253–254
  concentration difficult for, 252
  cooperation of, 72
  court appearance of, 19, 24, 74, 84,
    85
  crafts as interest of, 178, 180, 183,
    205, 221–223, 226
  denial by, 138–139
  depression of, 252
  diagnosis of, 41–42, 208, 213

  doctors consulted by, 41–42, 72–75,
    81, 82, 84, 85, 89, 130–132,
    162
  drawings by, 127, 180
  drinking in secret by, 252
  drug addiction suspected of, 18–19,
    20, 25, 28, 30, 32–33, 36–37,
    41, 67–68, 74, 128
  drug therapy for, 72, 73, 75, 81, 129,
    130, 175–179, 181, 183, 205,
    211, 214, 215, 219, 220, 221,
    222, 225, 227
  drug trials of, 222
  eating habits of, 123, 125, 129, 130
  eye contact avoided by, 180
  as family matter, 28, 33, 80–82, 128
  family photographs of interest to,
    124
  in group home, 181–184, 205–206
  group therapy for, 218, 220, 255
  handwriting of, 164, 222
  health insurance for, 40, 166, 175,
    182, 206, 212–213, 216, 218–
    219, 255
  high-pitched voice of, 161, 162
  at Hillview Hospital, 211–225
  hospitalizations of, 36–42, 67–75,
    174–184, 211–225
  in Idaho, 167–184
  initial manic episode of, 17–20
  job held by, 251–252
  legal proceeding for transfer of, 181–
    182, 183–184
  lethargy of, 208, 227
  lies told by, 84, 85, 119
  "lightning rod" constructed by, 129–
    130
  lithium taken by, 72, 73, 75, 81,
    129, 130, 175, 176, 177, 178,
    181, 183, 205, 211, 215, 255
  mania of, 176, 225, 227
  medical history of, 40, 74–75, 215,
    217–218
  mental illness in family history of, 31,
    40–41, 174–175
  as mental patient, 41, 67–68, 73–75
  money needed by, 78, 84
  monologues of, 24, 25, 126
  music as interest of, 162, 163–165,
    173, 180–181, 205
  New York trip of, 124–126

"normal" behavior of, 130, 131–134, 138–139, 220–221, 228
peer relationships of, 217, 218, 223–225
personal recollections of, 21, 25–26, 30, 35–36, 70–71, 83–84, 123–124, 127, 134, 163–165, 170–171, 175, 178, 218, 227
physical appearance of, 24, 25, 39, 76, 119, 172, 179, 208, 222
probationary period of, 120–121
psychotic thinking of, 215, 225
reactions of relatives to, 24–25, 27–30
religious fanaticism of, 18, 30, 219–220, 227
remission period of, 179–184, 219–228
residence treatment house considered for, 207–209, 211, 225, 226, 252, 255
satanic fantasies of, 123–124, 127, 129, 130, 134, 217–218, 219
"secret messages" received by, 78–79
sedation of, 39, 67
self-image of, 252, 255–256
silences of, 125–126
smoking by, 24, 36, 181
spinal pain of, 163, 169, 170, 171
suicide attempts of, 134–138, 218, 253–254
suicide considered by, 221, 224, 252
as taboo subject, 23, 82, 128–129, 162, 166
tape recording by, 163–164
Thanksgiving visit of, 23–42
therapy for, 81, 86, 131, 138, 213, 215, 252
Thorazine prescribed for, 178, 179, 183, 214, 215
treatment as viewed by, 209, 213, 218, 219, 252
tremors of, 181, 252, 255
Trilafon prescribed for, 255
uncontrolled behavior of, 19–20, 24, 28, 31, 34, 81, 171–174
vandalism by, 17–19
violence of, 17–20, 28, 33–34, 173
voices heard by, 18, 20, 33–34, 36, 217–219, 227
weight loss of, 172, 179

Marplan, 108
Marshall, Paul, 30, 32
Massachusetts General Hospital, 185
MDMA ("ecstasy"), 242
Medicaid, 189, 200
Medical Journal of Australia, 96
Medicare, 103, 189
medication:
    preventive, 9
    self-, 114–115, 241
    side effects of, 63
    see also drugs; drug therapy
meditation, 250
Meduna, Ladislas, 112
melancholia, 43, 109, 112, 278
    involutional, 249
Mellaril, 102
Melville, Herman, 235
memory, loss of, 98, 113, 246, 247, 250
menstruation, 116, 233
mental illness:
    ambiguousness of, 81
    biological vs. psychological basis of, 149–150
    drug therapy as reminder of, 142
    in family history, 48–49, 57, 62, 64, 191, 230–231, 276, 277
    family involvement in, 9, 226
    information about, 9–10
    medical costs compared with costs of, 198–199
    as medical problem, 186
    onset of, 197
    organic illness vs., 187
    popular misconceptions about, 10, 166–167
    research funding for, 11
    stigma of, 9, 142, 185, 247, 250
    see also specific mental illnesses
mesoridazine, 102
metabolism:
    disorders of, 57
    drug therapy and, 93
metal intoxications, 57
midnazolam, 104
Mind that Found Itself, A (Beers), 186
Moban, 102
molindone, 102
monoamine oxidase inhibitors (MAOIs), 107–108, 109, 110, 216–217

moods:
    changes in, 242
    congruent, 56–57, 59, 61
    creativity and, 236
    disorders of, 42, 45–46
    incongruent, 56, 59, 61
    learning of, 156
    popular misconceptions about, 42
    stabilization of, 11
Moodswings (Fieve), 21
morphine, 114
mouth, dryness of, 102, 109, 116
multiple sclerosis, 243
muscular dystrophy, 166
Museum of Modern Art, 125
music, fascination with, 47, 162, 163–
    165, 173, 180–181, 205, 236
myasthenia, 117

N

naprotiline, 110
Narcotics Anonymous, 192
Nardil, 108
National Alliance for the Mentally Ill
    (NAMI), 159, 202–203, 261,
    267
National Association of Social Workers,
    152
National Board of Medical Examiners,
    148
National Center for Health Statistics,
    198
National Depressive and Manic Depres-
    sive Association (NDMDA), 159,
    203
National Institute of Mental Health
    (NIMH):
    as advocacy group, 202
    educational programs of, 10
    research by, 51, 63, 187
National Institutes of Health, 94, 234
National Mental Health Act, 187
nausea, 92, 100, 102, 110, 241
Navane, 102
negatives, discounting of, 155
neuroleptic malignant syndrome, 102
neuroleptics, 55, 92, 101, 187
    for elderly patients, 243
    see also antipsychotics
neurologic lab tests, 188

neurosis, 239, 248
neurosyphilis, 243
neurotransmitters, 51, 65, 97, 107, 108,
    110, 278
Newton, Isaac, 44
niacin deficiency, 187
Nietzsche, Friedrich, 44, 236
Nijinsky, Waslaw, 236
norepinephrine (noradrenaline), 51, 65,
    107, 278
Norpramin, 109, 110
nortriptyline, 109, 110
November, suicide rate in, 231
nurses, psychiatric, 158, 275

O

obsessive-compulsive behavior, 111,
    232
O'Connor, Flannery, 237
outpatient programs, 188, 190
oxazepam, 104

P

painters, 237
Pamelor, 109, 110
panic disorder, 45, 108
paranoia, 47, 56, 160
paresthesia, 117
Parkinson's disease, 101–102, 117,
    278
Parnate, 108
patient-rights movement, 193–194
patients, mental:
    activities of, 192
    adolescent, 196–198, 199
    advocacy groups for, 202–203
    clothes worn by, 195
    commitment of, 193, 194–195
    in community-living situations, 201–
        202
    cooperation of, 73, 191
    dangerous, 159, 190–191
    denial by, 10
    as "disabled workers," 199
    "downward drift" of, 49
    "dual-diagnosis," 114, 160, 193, 241
    evaluation of, 192
    family histories of, 191
    financial resources of, 195
    homeless as, 186

involuntary vs. voluntary admission
of, 193
legal representation for, 194–195
letter-writing by, 195
Mark as example of, 41, 67–68, 73–
75
medical records of, 189
observation of, 188
percentage of, in hospitals, 187
personal belongings of, 195
with physical disabilities, 201
physical restraint of, 190, 192, 221
privacy for, 75, 196
privileges of, 191
professional consultation by, 196
rights of, 193–196
Safety Issue for, 193
seclusion of, 190–191, 192
telephoning by, 195
treatment needed by, 193–194
treatment refused by, 194
visitors for, 195
withdrawal of, 10
see also manic-depressive individuals
Paul (manic-depressive), 248–249
PCP, 18, 242
pellagra, 187
perphenazine, 221, 255
personality:
adult disorders of, 242
baseline, 20, 44, 46, 76–78, 220, 255
disorders of, 46, 55, 197, 242
of psychotherapists, 153
personalizing, 155
petechia, 117
phenelzine, 108
phobias, 45, 108
phototoxicity, 117
Phyllis (Diane's friend), 68–69, 84–86,
165–167
Physicians' Desk Reference, 179
placebos, 94
platelet counts, 100
Plath, Sylvia, 236
"play" interviews, 240
Poe, Edgar Allan, 235
polydipsia, 117
polyuria, 117
Pope, Harrison, 51
positive predictions, 155
postpartum depression, 233

prefrontal leucotomy, 91, 96
pregnancy, 111, 112
premenstrual depression, 233
Present State Examination (PSE), 275
"pressured speech," 46, 58, 100
priapism, 117
Prolixin, 102, 105
prolonged-sleep treatment, 91
propranolol, 102
protriptyline, 110
Prozac, 111, 248, 252, 255
psychiatric units, 190–192
psychiatrists, 147–150
psychiatry, 186–188
psychoanalysis, 152, 157
psychoanalysts, 147, 284
psychodynamic therapy, 153
psychologists, 151
psychomotor agitation, 59, 60
psychopharmacologists, 147, 149, 214,
247
psychopharmacology, 96, 149–150
psychosis:
in depression, 48, 61, 101, 105
episodes of, 9
as label, 22
in mania, 59
nonaffective, 231
in thinking, 187, 215, 225, 242
psycho-surgery, 91, 96, 195–196
psychotherapists:
accessibility of, 146
accreditation of, 145, 148–149, 151,
152
background of, 145–146
clinical experience of, 145, 151
current research known by, 145–146
as generic term, 151, 284
interviews with, 146–147, 150–151
personalities of, 153
types of, 147–152
psychotherapy, 141–160
analytic, 150
behavioral, 150, 152, 156–157
for bipolar disorders, 143
childhood experiences explored in,
157
for children, 242
cognitive, 150, 153–155, 157
confidentiality of, 144, 153, 159–160,
167

psychotherapy (cont.)
   for depression, 142
   diagnosis in, 143, 160
   different methods of, 152–153
   drug therapy vs., 141, 149–150
   eclectic, 150, 152, 153, 157
   ethics of, 159, 160, 176
   family's involvement with, 143–147,
      158, 160
   focus on present time in, 153, 156,
      157, 225
   group, 157–159, 191, 192, 201–202,
      218, 220, 255
   individual, 192
   information about, 143–145, 159–160
   interpersonal (IPT), 155–156
   legal issues in, 159, 176
   for mania, 142
   for manic depression, 81, 142–143,
      145, 150, 151
   Mark's experiences in, 81, 86, 131,
      138, 213, 215, 252
   medical information from, 144
   misconceptions about, 143–144
   necessity for, 141–143
   patient's behavior monitored by, 143
   patient-therapist relationship in, 144,
      153, 159–160, 167
   practical, 153, 157–158, 225
   psychodynamic, 153
   reality, 225
   referrals for, 145–147, 173
   reflective, 156
   rehabilitation, 157–159
   short-term, 153, 155
   "somatic," 150
   supportive, 157–159
   survey of techniques in, 152
   symptoms alleviated by, 150
   "talking," 81, 150–159
   treatment plan in, 143, 144, 146,
      150, 153, 160
pulse, rapid, 116

Q

"quality assurance," 189

R

rapid cycling, 54, 99, 100, 107
rashes, skin, 100

reality therapy, 225
rehabilitation therapy, 157–159
REMs (rapid eye movements), 233
Research Diagnostic Criteria (RDC), 274
residential treatment centers, 201, 206–
      209, 211, 225, 226, 252, 255
restlessness, 104, 110, 116
retardation, mental, 239
Richards, Ruth, 238
Robert (Mark's brother), 27–28
   Mark's illness as viewed by, 30, 32,
      177–178, 227, 254
   Mark's relationship with, 177–178,
      224, 225, 227–228
Roethke, Theodore, 236
roles, social, 155
Rostov, Dr., 213, 214–216, 220, 225,
      226, 252, 253, 256
Roth, Philip, 237
Roy (manic-depressive), 245–246
Ruth (manic-depressive), 249–250

S

Safety Issue, 193
"safety profile," 93
salivation, excessive, 103
Sarton, May, 5n, 86
Schedule for Affective Disorders and
      Schizophrenia (SADS), 274
schizoaffective disorder, 44, 56–57
schizophrenia:
   catatonic, 59, 116, 246
   in children, 242
   costs of, 199
   creativity and, 236, 237
   drug therapy for, 101
   electroconvulsive therapy (ECT) for,
      112
   as hereditary disease, 112
   manic depression vs., 45, 49, 56, 57,
      59, 61, 73, 97, 105, 229, 242,
      246, 249
   organic basis of, 278
   prevalence of, 11
school, fear of, 239
Schumann, Robert, 235
sculptors, 237
seasonal affective disorders (SADs),
      234–235
sedatives, 103, 108

seizures, brain, 112, 113
selective abstractions, 155
selegiline, 108
self-images, negative, 154
Serax, 104
Serentil, 102
serotonin, 65, 107, 110
sexual problems, 46, 59, 102, 109
Shakespeare, William, 235
shock therapy, 59, 91, 92, 111–114,
    150, 186, 195
Sinequan, 110
skin problems, 98, 100, 116, 117
sleep deprivation, 115, 150
sleeping patterns, 46, 50, 58, 232–234
sleeping pills, 103
Social Security, 187, 199–200
Social Security Disability Insurance
    (SSDI), 187, 199, 200
Social Security Supplemental Income
    (SSI), 187, 199–200
social workers, 152, 158, 181, 192, 256
sodium levels, 117
sodium valproate, 100
somatic antidepressant treatment, 59
"somatic" therapy, 150
speech:
    excess, 117
    loss of, 116
    "poverty" of, 116
    "pressured," 46, 58, 100
    slurred, 100
    subvocal, 47
    unclear, 117
speed, 241
Starlight Express, 80, 82
Stelazine, 102
steroids, anabolic, 51, 242
straitjackets, 186
stress:
    in interpersonal relationships, 155
    mania triggered by, 249–250
    manic depression triggered by, 50,
        51, 62, 243
    suicide and, 230, 231
strokes, 57, 107
Styron, William, 236
subvocal speech, 47
suicide:
    affective disorders and, 229, 230, 231
    alcoholism and, 230, 232

in Amish community, 230–231
average age for, 230–231
depression as cause of, 48, 221, 229,
    231–232
drug abuse and, 230, 232
drugs for prevention of, 109, 111,
    192
electroconvulsive therapy (ECT) for,
    112–113, 114
emergency care for, 192
family history of, 230–231
genetic connection for, 230–231
ideation in, 60–61
mania as cause of, 232
manic depression and, 63, 68, 93,
    106, 229–232, 241, 245
Mark's experiences with, 134–138,
    218, 221, 224, 252, 253–
    254
in men vs. women, 230–231
nonviolent vs. violent, 231
by "obsessionals," 232
preoccupation with, 232
proneness to, 54, 144, 191, 193,
    229–231, 232
by "risk-takers," 232
scientific research on, 229–231
seasonal patterns for, 231, 232, 234–
    235
stress as factor in, 230, 231
in twins, 231
sun, sensitivity to, 100, 102
support groups, 143, 159, 202–203,
    261–265, 267–269
supportive therapy, 157–159
Supreme Court, U.S., 194
surgery, brain, 91, 96, 195–196
Surmontil, 110
sweating, excess, 109
"switching," 107
Symmetrel, 102
synergistic effect, 99
syphilis, 57, 187, 243
systemic lupus erythematosus, 57

T

tachycardia, 117
"talking" therapy, 81, 150–159
Tarasoff decision, 159
tardive akathisia, 104, 110

tardive dyskinesia (TD), 101, 103, 104–106, 110, 151
tardive dystonia, 104
Tegretol, 99–100, 103, 246
temperature, body, 115
teratogen, 117
testosterone, 233
therapy, *see* drug therapy; psychotherapy
thinking:
  automatic, 154–155
  disorders of, 47
  impaired, 60, 98, 246
  negative, 154, 155, 157
  psychotic, 187, 215, 225, 242
thioridazine, 102
thiothixene, 102
thirst, 92, 98
Thorazine, 178, 179, 183, 214, 215
three-quarter-way houses, 188, 201
thyroid-function tests, 57
tinnitus, 117
Tofranil, 110
Tolstoy, Leo, 44
tomography, computerized, 57, 188
tomography, positron-emission, 188
tranquilizers, 92
  major, 101
  minor, 101, 103, 115
transitional-living quarters, 201
Tranxene, 104
tranylcypromine, 108
trazodone, 111, 117
tremors, 98, 100, 104, 109, 181, 252, 255
triazolam, 104
tricyclic antidepressants (TCAs), 107, 108–110
trifluoperazone, 102
trihexyphenidyl, 102
Trilafon, 221, 255
trimipramine, 110
trusts, 200
tumors, 57, 243
twins, 231, 276–277

U

uric acid, 95
urination, problems with, 98, 109, 116, 117
urine tests, 57, 247

V

Valium, 103, 104
valproate, 100
valproic acid, 100
Van Gogh, Vincent, 44, 180
verapamil, 100–101
Versed, 104
vision:
  blurred, 92, 100, 102, 109, 116
  double, 117
Vivactil, 110
vomiting, 110
Vonnegut, Kurt, Jr., 237
Vuckovic, Alexander, 9–11

W

weight:
  gain of, 98, 102, 109, 246
  loss of, 110, 172, 179
Wellbutrin, 111
Western Psychiatric Institute, 107
wet-sheet packs, 115
white blood-cell count, 100, 103, 116
wills, 200
Wolf, Hugo, 235
Wordsworth, William, 235
worthlessness, feelings of, 60
writing, excessive, 47, 236

X

Xanax, 103
X-chromosome, 277

Y

Young Mania Scale, 275